JAMES MASON

For Anthony and Howard

DIANA DE ROSSO

JAMES MASON

A PERSONAL BIOGRAPHY

LENNARD PUBLISHING
1989

Lennard Publishing
a division of Lennard Books Ltd
Musterlin House, Jordan Hill Road, Oxford OX2 8DP

British Library Cataloguing in Publication Data
Rosso, Diana de
James Mason: a personal biography.
1. Cinema films. Acting. Mason, James,
1909–1984 – Biographies
I. Title
791.43′028′0924

ISBN 1 85 291 033 X

First published 1989
© Diana de Rosso 1989

Designed by Geoff Green

Cover design by Pocknell and Co.

Phototypeset in Linotron Sabon by Goodfellow & Egan Ltd, Cambridge

Reproduced, printed and bound in Great Britain by
Butler and Tanner Limited, Frome

CONTENTS

PERSONAL ACKNOWLEDGEMENTS

I WOULD like to offer my grateful and sincere thanks to the many contributors to this biography listed below. I fear that I may have inadvertently failed to include some names and I can only beg forebearance, and ask that they accept my deepest apologies for any omissions.

To Clarissa, James's widow, I pay a special tribute as she, in the midst of a very stressful and painful time in her life, afforded me the opportunity of seeing many personal papers and pictures which added greatly to my understanding of James's last years.

I am also very indebted to my researcher Sandy Collison without whose enthusiasm and hardwork the compilation of this book might well have been a far more onerous task. Finally, but in no way least, I wish to thank Roderick Brown of Lennard Publishing, and his colleagues, for their constant support and kindly advice.

Harry Andrews; Ben Arbeid; Claire Bloom; Val Birall (née Mason); Richard Broke; Max Bygraves; Alan Bridges; Peter Brook; Kevin Brownlow; Ken Bright; Peter Beales; Phyllis Calvert; Cyril Cusack. Elspeth Cochrane; Peter Coke; Jack Cardiff; Ted Cox; Ken Evans; Robert and Carmen Flemyng; Ivan Foxwell; Susan George; Sir John Gielgud; Sir Alec Guinness; Paul Grunder; David Gray; Patricia Hayes; Rosamund John; Deborah Kerr; Margaret Lockwood; George and Elvi Hale Murcell; Clarissa Mason; Rex and Halo Mason; Tany Moiseiwitsch; Barry Norman; Peter Noble; Dilys Powell; Roy Pickard; Kaye (Webb) and Katie Searle; Victor Spinetti and Leonard Sachs; and The Huddersfield Daily Examiner; The British Film Institute and John Kobal.

Diana de Rosso

PROLOGUE

JAMES Mason was my brother-in-law and I knew him from 1936, when he was just 27 and on the threshold of his career as a great film actor, until the end of his life. He died in 1984 at the age of 75.

When I was invited to write about his life I felt that, even if I didn't have the literary experience usually required for such a task, I did possess one specific attribute which might outweigh this lack of practice in the craft. My advantage was that I knew James before he became a star, before he was courted, packaged and finally exported to Hollywood.

I am not going to examine James's career in great depth – there are other professional biographers whose job that is, and his own book goes into great details which I don't need to reproduce here. But I will try to give my own personal portrait of the man who, I believe, remained an enigma to many who worked with him and was, in truth, diffident and shy and like many actors found it easier to play a part rather than cope with a private life invaded by gossip columnists, scandalmongers and so on. He was a man of many complexities and few faults. His dry humour and bashful self-depreciative uncertainty left him at odds with his talents. He could accept his shortcomings but was unable to fully believe in his capacity as an actor. He was of a meticulously tidy mind, a craftsman with a critical faculty which at times led him into conflict with his advisers and those who regarded him as a money machine to be exploited. There is no doubt in my mind that James, as an actor, was often undervalued as an artist and this to some degree undermined his own confidence in his ability – particularly when he undertook certain roles simply for the necessary money and for which, understandably, he received little praise.

Yet he was possessed of a determined, even stubborn nature and once he was committed to a line of action few people could wield sufficient influence over him to make him change his mind. But one such person was, of course, his first wife – my half-sister Pamela Ostrer.

James's early career as an actor gave him a love of the theatre and of the actors and actresses who reaped negligible financial rewards but felt themselves rich in payment of their souls – performers who revered the written word and honoured the playwrights and authors long gone from the world. Although the theatre remained a kind of bogey for him, James hankered after recognition in this sphere and the numerous disappointments he suffered in this area of his career was a source of hidden pain. He was prepared to accept the cuts and thrusts of the critics, he was willing to concede that by becoming a star of the cinema he had formed a brilliant technique not easily adapted for the living stage, but nevertheless his failure to achieve the success he sought in the theatre caused him much hurt. He set himself the highest standards and whatever fell below that mark was deemed failure in his own eyes. Perhaps the acclaim as a consummate reader of English poetry that he enjoyed later on went some way towards healing that bitter disappointment.

In the pages that follow I will hope to show a man vulnerable and sensitive, kindly and thoughtful, misunderstood and sometimes misrepresented, disliked by some but who, over a long and distinguished career, made many long and lasting friendships. A man remembered with love and affection by those who were privileged to say "I knew James Mason".

Diana de Rosso

THE EARLY YEARS

JAMES Neville Mason was born in Huddersfield, Yorkshire, on 15 May 1909, the third and youngest son of John Mason and his wife Mabel, nee Hattersley Gaunt. His father, Yorkshire born and bred, was a textile merchant who lived and died in Huddersfield at Croft House, the home to which he and his wife moved at the time of their marriage.

In his autobiography *Before I Forget*, James's account of his home life and his first schooldays conjures up a happy and well-balanced childhood, with holidays at the seaside and all the traditional customs of the day carefully observed. His was a solid, respectable, middle-class Edwardian background – one of good manners, of etiquette and politeness, with a set way of doing things, prosperous, with properly defined boundaries of behaviour and expectation. Croft House was large and rambling and terribly cold in the winter. Parts of it were very old, built in the sixteenth or seventeenth centuries, but the main parts of the house were Victorian. There was a wonderful large garden with a tennis court and plenty of room for cricket in the holidays. James and his two elder brothers grew up in comfortable security, in a household ruled by his mother and run by a maid, cook, governess and gardener.

Their father was of necessity absent from much of the boys' daily life in their childhood as his work kept him away from home for long hours. If he was unable to participate in their growing up as much as he would have wished "Muv" made up for it by teaching them to play tennis and cricket, organising coaching, overseeing, influencing and often joining in with their activities. James was only five when the First World War broke out and the boys played endless games of "soldiers" together. "Muv" encouraged their patriotic fervour and made beautiful miniature uniforms for them to wear. They loved "dressing up" and it lent drama and conviction to their fantasies. She was a highly moral woman herself and she insisted that her sons were brought up with a sharply defined sense of right and wrong. They each had to keep a "Good Deed Book" in which they were required to write an account of some act of helpfulness or generosity they had performed – every day. Needless to say it was hard for them to keep up to her exacting standards.

James had a weakness which got him into trouble on many occasions when he should have been on his best behaviour, for even as a small boy he was a terrible giggler. His brother Rex recalled an incident when the family were visiting their great-uncle for tea in the public lounge of the Crown Hotel in Harrogate. The old man was very deaf and would shout his remarks, however personal, unaware that they might reach the ears of those for whom they were not intended. He yelled, confidentially, "See the old lady over there" (pointing) "she's wearing a wig y'know". It was too much for James who collapsed in uncontrollable hysterics and while his parents were overcome with embarrassment his brothers enjoyed their discomfort – kicking James under the table to increase his mirth until they were forced to make an exit.

From his preparatory school at Windermere in the Lake District James followed his brothers, Rex and Colin, to public school at Marlborough where, according to himself, he shone neither academically nor at the obligatory team sports. Whether or not this was true, he obviously maintained a sufficiently high standard to allow him to progress to Cambridge University in 1928. His original intention, of which his parents thoroughly approved, was to read Classics with a view to entering the Indian Civil Service. But by the end of his second term at Peterhouse he had formed the opinion that the role of "Pukka Sahib" would not suit him so, with the blessing of his tutor, he transferred his studies to the School of Architecture. He had already demonstrated a talent for drawing, and perhaps he chose to study architecture because it appealed to his rather aesthetic temperament. He maintained a love of architecture all his life, but I don't think he really hankered after a career in that profession.

Alongside his ability as a draughtsman he had a facility for caricature which allowed his puckish sense of humour full rein. Family, friends and foes alike, found themselves faced with unflattering and very recognisable sketches of themselves. His cartoon portraits of human beings were never very kind, unlike his drawings of animals which were always much softer and more affectionate. James didn't exempt himself from his talent for mockery. He caricatured his own features with a brutal pen and I must put on record here that nobody could ever accuse him of self-conceit.

He was, when I first met him, still shy and diffident, quite unaware of his capacity to turn heads and radiate attraction to both sexes. He was still very inexperienced and naive in his understanding of women, but I felt there was a steely determination underlying his diffidence. He was prepared to live on a shoestring, in digs of varying squalor, go hungry, walk miles for an interview and accept the most meagre of salaries in his quest to achieve his right to work in the theatre.

This interest in acting had been fired during his second year at Cambridge by his contact with the new Festival Theatre Company, which was a revelation. The director of the season, Tyrone Guthrie, a man of unique talent, was to become a life-long friend and advisor. To the consternation of his parents, who had been satisfied that their son would progress through university to a respectable profession, when James had graduated he took the momentous decision to opt for a career "on the boards".

It must be remembered that even in the 1930s the stage was there to be enjoyed – but not embraced – by Society. There were still many prejudices against having an actor in the family. It offered no status, no regular income and was regarded as a dubious and possibly immoral way of life. The code of behaviour in those days was still bound by a rigid, not to say snobbish, attitude to the arts. There was enjoyment to be had from watching the performers, painters, singers, dancers and actors, but it was not considered desirable by those who came from the solid middle-class background to which James and his family belonged, to become involved.

I think James's decision to seek a career in the theatre was viewed with greater apprehension by his mother than his father, but subsequent events caused a rift between him and the whole family which took a while to heal.

James told me that from 1932 onwards, he took whatever parts he was offered in the theatre. His first real opportunity came when he joined the Jeavon Brandon Thomas company for a summer season of repertory at several of the most popular resort theatres and it was during this season that he became very friendly with Patricia Hayes and Leonard Sachs. Pat was playing the ingenue roles and the two young men the "utility juveniles". Both Pat and Leonard sometimes wondered why James had opted for an acting career as, even allowing for his dark romantic looks, he seemed by nature unsuited to the stage. He had very little experience and Leonard had to teach him to do his make-up properly. He was a hard worker but showed little sign at this stage of any natural talent and his innate shyness and hesitant manner could be irritating to those of a more outgoing personality.

Nevertheless, they spent many happy times together – like the Three Musketeers, one for all and all for one, and being young and on the threshold of life they enjoyed each others' company and had a lot of fun together. The lack of money didn't bother them and they would share their cheap cigarettes at the tail end of the week – ten for the princely sum of fourpence!

James guarded his privacy and independence fiercely, preferring not to share digs with anyone, but he attached himself to Pat and Leonard and always searched out their company in preference to any other.

Then James joined the Hull Repertory Company, which led to a job with Henry Cass's Company at Croydon and a transfer with the play *Gallows Glorious* to the Shaftesbury Theatre in the West End of London. It was here that he met Tyrone Guthrie again. Guthrie invited him to audition for his new company at the Old Vic, led by Charles Laughton, and now, for the first time, James could have real experience of classical drama and Shakespeare. Tanya Moiseiwitsch, who was working at the Old vic at the time as a student in scenic design, remembers that James made a great impression on her. He was wonderful looking, and vocally there was something very special. He seemed to be devoted to what he was doing because he was one of the few who would stay on after rehearsals had finished to work on his own bits. He was eager to work over-time and then of course there was the performance at night. There was quite a pronounced sense of hierarchy in the company and any actor who bothered to say "good morning" to the students made them feel quite honoured. James was one of the few who did, perhaps because he wasn't so very far from his own student days, and his big friendly smile had a devastating effect on the students. The part in which James had his biggest success in this season was 'Yasha' in *The Cherry Orchard*. Even now it is remembered by fellow actors like Sir Alec Guinness and Sir John Gielgud as outstanding. When I asked both these distinguished actors if they would like to contribute their memories of James to this book they both mentioned this performance together with 'Claudio' in *Measure for Measure*.

In the Spring of 1934 he found himself in the West End again. He had two small parts (suitor to the Queen and Bothwell's valet) in *Queen of Scots*. The play was a fountain of talent – directed by John Gielgud, it featured Laurence Olivier as Bothwell and Gwen ffrangcon-Davies as the Queen. There were two young actresses in the cast playing ladies-in-waiting with time on their hands (and, who knows, love in their hearts?) who whiled away the time they were off-stage preparing a good tea for James and Olivier to enjoy between performances. James would have relished the free tea, for he was very poor at the time, and no doubt Olivier would have entertained them well for he was a splendid raconteur.

After *Queen of Scots* James went to Dublin to join the famous Gate Theatre Company, where Orson Welles had worked the previous season. Here he worked under the famous Hilton Edwards/Michael Macliammoir regime and was elevated at last to leading parts. Amongst a number of challenging roles, he played the swaggering restoration fop Heartfree in Vanbrugh's *The Provok'd Wife*, and the part he was later to make his own in the film of Shakespeare's *Julius Caesar*, Brutus. The actor Cyril Cusack, who was co-incidentally to appear with James in both the first and the penultimate films he made, remembers seeing his Brutus at the Gate and that it was "a very attractive performance with a special, unique quality – hard to describe but I would apply the word "purity" – a true performance and one certainly to be remembered'. The Christmas show that year was the Victorian melodrama *The Drunkard* in which James found a taste for the comedy lying so close to the surface of such plays and which he would indulge years later in Hollywood.

The atmosphere of freedom and excitement at the Gate Theatre released some of his inhibitions and helped him enjoy life. Dublin's was an informal and classless society, relaxed and open, a city where amusing conversation is the greatest pastime. It was here I think that

James began to mature both as an actor and as a person. In Ireland there was not the same prejudice against actors, and they were, in fact, rather revered. He loved Ireland and he relished the inconsequential gossip and sharp wit so characteristic of the Irish.

He was a listener, not a participator, and the flow of bandinage amused and appealed to him.

At this point I must pay tribute to one person to whom I know that James owed a lot – his landlady in Dublin. She was a fey, delightful lady called Maisie Brock and if kindness is a virtue Maisie was without equal. A tiny, thin creature who wore an assortment of hats worthy of the most flamboyant actress, she was noted for the various colours of her hair and her Fu Manchu fingernails. Her son Cecil, who was at the time a struggling young actor, told her of the shy and charming young Yorkshireman who had arrived at the Gate Theatre, and Maisie took him into her home and her heart because, as she said, "The dear of him, he needed food and comfort!" And this she provided for the equivalent of ten shillings a week, feeding him up as only the Irish can, with massive breakfasts and plates of sandwiches to be consumed late at night after the performance. Until her death I don't think Maisie ever missed a film in which James appeared.

Some years later I, too, had reason to bless her sweet and generous nature. James charged her to act as my guardian angel when I made my operatic debut as Gilda and Lucia di Lammermoor in Dublin in the early part of the Second World War. She became my friend and companion, and treated me with the same loving-kindness for which James had been so grateful. Unlike James, who started his apprenticeship in the theatre at the bottom, I was offered the chance to start my own career at the top. I had no experience whatsoever but I grabbed the opportunity with delight and, perhaps due to my total ignorance, survived! But that's another story.

Just before the Dublin season ended James returned to London in pursuit of a half-promised job in a Theatre Club presentation of a play about Queen Victoria in which he expected to be cast as Prince Albert. In the event it was a misguided move as the part went to another actor. The night before he left Ireland James went to see the famous Abbey Theatre Company performing in their own Dublin theatre and, to her surprise and delight, bumped into Tanya Moiseiwitsch whom he had last seen as a lowly scenery painter at the Old Vic. He not only recognised her and stopped for a conversation but he wrote a letter to her the very next day from the boat taking him back to England. It was the kind of spontaneously friendly gesture that became typical of him throughout his working life and a manifestation of the genuine interest he had in other people.

Back in England James met the man who was to change the course of his career and to alter his life irrevocably. Albert Parker was an American film director working in England for Twentieth Century Fox. In the early days of the silent movies he had been very successful, notably with the Douglas Fairbanks film *The Black Pirate* – and he employed Rudolph Valentino in his first important part. He spotted James at a theatrical party given by Diana Churchill, literally "across a crowded room", engineered an introduction and without preamble said to him "Have you ever been in movies?" Discounting his one and only film job (a brief appearance in 1934 in a Douglas Fairbanks epic called *The Return of Don Juan* from which he was hastily and humiliatingly released) James replied "No".

There and then Al Parker offered him a screen test at the Fox British Film Studio, at Wembley in North London. So in 1935 James Mason, hardworking and aspiring young actor in the British theatre, signed his first film contract and began work for Al Parker on a low-budget "quota-quickie" movie called *Late Extra*. His fellow performers were Alastair Sim, Cyril Cusack, Michael Wilding and Donald Wolfit. The leading lady was Virginia Cherrill, who had recently played opposite Charlie Chaplin in *City Lights*. This modest debut led to another job – a part in a low-budget film called *Twice Branded* and, that finished, he then started work on his third film, again no masterpiece, called *Troubled Waters*. The title was both apt and prophetic because the cameraman was a very handsome young fellow named Roy Kellino – married to my sister Pamela.

THE MAKING OF A STAR

I FIRST remember meeting James in the kitchen at the Kellinos' flat, where he was waiting to help carry to the table a somewhat frugal meal consisting of grilled herrings and a salad, which we were all to share for lunch. I had no idea who he was but, knowing Pam, I presumed he was just another admirer, one of a passing collection who came and went at odd intervals. Although she had not long been married to Roy Kellino she was not averse to a flirtation, particularly if the suitor seemed to be thoroughly smitten.

Pam was an arresting beauty, vivacious, amusing – and used to having her own way. Roy was no match for her strong will and nor, apparently, was James, notwithstanding the emphatic disapproval shown by his mother. Understandably "Muv", as he called her, was shocked and upset at the thought of her youngest son falling into the clutches of an actress already married to someone else, and James did little to reassure her when he tried to confound the issue by implying that he was courting not Pam but her younger sister, Sheila, who was unmarried. I've never forgotten his shamefaced, albeit laughing, confession of his deception which hoodwinked nobody, and which earned him a slap in the face from the outraged Mrs Mason. He always laughed when he was at fault – it was his way of turning away wrath.

James had first seen Pam on the set of *Troubled Waters*. Filming had over-run late into the evening and Pam had turned up at the studio to complain and take Roy home. Even then she was a force to be reckoned with, though barely nineteen, and she looked wonderful. Black hair, dark eyes, ivory skin and a beautiful little oval face with delicate features and full red lips. A clear, sweet voice. Small bones, slim body and beautiful legs, about 5′5″ – really quite stunning – and an unusual beauty for the time. A mysterious quality – more like Merle Oberon than the conventional English Rose. Unconventional for the time – like James. James was attracted and intrigued and soon found an opportunity to invite the Kellinos to a party. Now he was well and truly smitten, and he remarked to a friend of his that he had found the girl he intended to marry. "Not possible, old boy", said the friend, "She's married already – to the cameraman you're working with." James's reply was short and to the point, "Too bad – I'll get rid of him." The fact is that one must believe this to be true – James could show a singlemindedness bordering on ruthlessness when his mind was made up and set. He wanted Pam and that was it.

Not surprisingly, his mother never accepted that it was James who pursued Pam. She always believed that Pam was the adventuress who captured James. Pam found him very attractive, and she was always highly susceptible to good-looking men, but she didn't pursue him at this stage. It was a short while later, maybe a matter of weeks, that she got an offer to appear in a play. She was never noted for her acting ability and she was absolutely delighted – she thought this could be stardom, somebody had spotted her. She was more than pleased to discover that James was the star of the play (an intimate little musical presented on just two successive Sundays at the Arts Theatre by his old friend Leonard Sachs) but she didn't connect this with her own opportunity. However, after a few rehearsals she asked the producer why he had chosen her for the part and he said, rather baldly "Well, I didn't, as it happens, but Mr Mason refused to do the play unless you were offered it." Pam was certainly not an unwilling victim, but James was the instigator of the affair.

The anger that his mother showed at his behaviour didn't shake his determination in any way. Although he was so aware of his family ties and his background (and the duty he felt towards his father in particular who he knew had made sacrifices to give him his excellent education), these things didn't actually weigh the balance against his determination to woo Pam and win her. This was very odd in someone whom all his friends described as such a shy and uncon-fident person.

The antipathy that was apparent from the outset between Mrs Mason and Pam was rooted in the contrasting social spheres they inhabited, and it was aggravated by Pam's indifference towards the values of James's parents. It was not just a generation gap – it was a matter of up bringing, of attitudes. Pam considered the Masons' views narrow, and she under-valued the solidity of their traditions, having no sympathy with what she termed "their pompous and hypocritical outlook". Not surprisingly "Muv" found little that was commendable in Pam, and it would have taken a miracle to have the two women come to terms with James as a common factor.

Over and above the clash of temperament, the chasm that developed between them led to a breach that was more hurtful to James than he first recognised. A man in love is not ideally situated to sort out the incompatibilities of his family and the object of his desire, and it proved to be no contest. Pam won, hands down, and James remained estranged from his family for a considerable time. While the coolness continued, he allowed himself to be weaned further and further from his roots.

It was never a complete break because he maintained a steady contact by letter, particularly with his father for whom he had a very deep affection, but because of the ill-feeling between Pam and his mother the close-knit family ties suffered considerably. From 1938 until 1953 I don't believe James visited his Yorkshire home at all, but there is no doubt that something of his heart remained firmly planted in Huddersfield.

A further complication was that James genuinely liked Pam's husband. He and Roy were both besotted by the film industry. They used to spend hours building little model cardboard sets together, talking over camera angles, lighting subtleties and the complexities of direction and production. They had a very deep friendship – and at the centre of it, the spider in the web, was Pam. So Roy was to be relegated to the background and discarded, as a husband if not as a friend, and the manner in which James set about usurping Roy's position was intriguing – if dubious.

Quietly, consistently, daily he appeared at the Kellino home though from time to time Roy would rebel and order James to get the hell out of his house. Always, with good grace, James would retreat to his own flat until a day or so had elapsed, and he felt free to return to Dorset House.

At this time my mother had a flat nearby, just opposite Madame Tussaud's, and she visited Pam and Roy quite frequently. On the many occasions that James accompanied her back to her home he never once excused himself or indicated that he was sorry to be causing the break-up of Pam's marriage. He seemed devoid of any sense of guilt or wrongdoing and, a point my mother found quite extraordinary considering James's background and upbringing, to be without any feeling for fair play. His behaviour was simply not "cricket".

It has to be said that Roy was weak in allowing this invasion of his home, and Pam must also carry some guilt for having encouraged the attentions of so obvious an admirer. Was she in love with James? Or was she in love with love – basking in their adulation and the image of herself as a beautiful young woman desired and courted by two men, both talented, attractive and, if not famous, at least beckoned by fame. The answer, I believe, lies somewhere in the middle.

In order to understand this unusual situation, one has to know a little of the background to Pam herself. The product of a broken home, she was the eldest child of Isidore Ostrer and Helene Spear-Morgan. She represented everything that was perfect to her father, who adored and spoiled her hopelessly. He was the son of penniless Jewish immigrants from Eastern Europe and when he married Helene he was extremely poor. Helene's widowed mother was horrified at the match because she had been engaged to the son of a very wealthy and prestigious old Scottish family whom, even as the banns were being called in Paisley Abbey, she abandoned for Isidore. They were married in 1914 and Pam was born in 1916. Isidore made a precarious living by, amongst other dubious activities, playing dominoes for money on the train between Southend and London. At first they lived in a house in Southend which they rented for £1 per week.

Isidore had told Helene that she need never be bothered with his family, but in fact all his brothers came to live with them in the house. His parents spoke hardly any English and they were so poor that as the boys grew up they sometimes had to share one or two shirts amongst the five of them (the shirtless ones staying indoors) and their biggest treat was a cheap bag of broken Nice biscuits which the grocer would save for them. The only money Isidore and Helene had when they married was £100 which she had saved from her earnings as a dancing teacher and, to his fury, she squandered £5 of it on buying herself an Aberdeen Scottish terrier.

Into this volatile and impecunious household two more children were born after Pam. Her sister Sheila arrived eighteen months later,

in 1918, and their brother Vivian in 1919. It was fortunate that by
1920 their father had begun to make his fortune as a businessman
but less so that the marriage was breaking up. Their new-found
affluence allowed Helene and her mother to take a holiday in France.
There she met and fell in love with a young Italian count, who was to
be my father. I was born in 1921. Meanwhile the marriage between
my mother and Isidore deteriorated, and the divorce proceedings
were ugly and bitter. In those days it was accepted that it was the
duty of a "gentleman", whatever the circumstances, to protect the
good name of his wife. But Isidore did nothing of the kind: my
mother was named the guilty party and a long and vicious legal battle
resulted in my mother being pilloried quite unnecessarily. Fortunately the muck-raking did not cloud her future, nor my childhood, but
I firmly believe that it had a profound psychological effect on Pam.

I lived with our mother, mainly in Menton, and Pam and Sheila
and Vivian remained in England with Isidore. However, they were
often sent to visit us in France – possibly when their father needed
some respite or privacy – and from time to time Isidore too would
appear on the Côte, staying at the best hotel, importing his Rolls
Royce complete with chauffeur, and trying to monopolise my
mother, despite his former treatment of her, and to the fury and
jealousy of my own father. By now a very wealthy man Isidore
conceived that his one wish was to re-marry Mama, a rather
unsettling ambition for all concerned.

Pam's brief sojourns in Menton over the years as she grew up
ceased once she embarked on her acting career. Either through
indulgence or laziness her father had somehow allowed her to avoid
proper schooling and gave her total freedom to do whatever she
chose. When she decided that she wanted to have a place of her own
it probably suited him very well to give her a flat in New Cavendish
Street, in London, to share with her younger sister Sheila. The girls
were just sixteen and fourteen respectively when they had to take full
responsibility for themselves in their own home, but it was a
convenient solution for their father, who was contemplating a second
marriage to a lady of doubtful reputation who was most certainly *not*
an acceptable choice to his children.

Pam was still only sixteen when she met Roy Kellino. Unchaper-
oned, and indeed left to their own devices, romance became intense,
and they were soon married. They moved into the flat in Dorset

House in the area of London's Marylebone Road, while Sheila took a smaller apartment on her own next door. Both girls had allowances from their father, but little guidance or protection and our mother, loving and caring as she was, had no jurisdiction over any decisions taken on behalf of the Ostrer children.

It was thus an unexpected heritage of intensity and unconventionality that James encountered when he made his appearance in the Kellinos' life. Roy had little faith in Pam's ability as an actress, but I feel certain that she would have been far more successful if she had then applied herself to her career with the zeal she has since shown in her various professional activities. However, as their relationship developed, she took on the role of *Mere Poule* to both Roy and James and put all her energy into nursing their careers, and playing the part of agent/manager when negotiations over fees and billings had to be dealt with. For the men it was an ideal situation as they were able to stand back from vulgar bartering whilst Pam gave battle on their behalf. And she proved a veritable tigress, particularly as James's career advanced from "promising" to established stardom.

It must be said that Pam was on occasions a poor diplomat, and she would appear to be offhand and dismissive with people who came from a milieu different from her own. It made her seem self-centred, egotistical, selfish and opinionated – traits inherited from her father who, although mild in manner, considered himself virtually omnipotent in every field of knowledge. Always denying that he was critical of others he would nevertheless dismiss any view that did not coincide with his, and Pam showed the same failing. She was completely indifferent to anyone outside her chosen circle and could be seen to alienate the goodwill shown to her (and James) by rebuffing, without grace, overtures of friendship. If I seem critical of Pam's character it is because I feel she did herself a disservice, causing friction where it could have been avoided and making enemies instead of friends, but one must remember that she was very young, very lovely and in some ways, very vulnerable.

Roy, an extremely good-looking, warm-hearted and sunny-natured man, was happy to be dominated. He was not particularly ambitious, easily manipulated and quite content to allow Pam to direct his life. But it was surprising to see how easily James accepted the same kind of domination.

Intellectually James was Pam's superior, a thoughtful, well-educated and intelligent man, seven years her senior. One can only suppose that he was bewitched and mesmerised by so alien a creature, whose attitude to life was centred upon the things and the people to whom she could relate, and the Devil take those who opposed her. In her defence there is little doubt that she worked hard to promote the careers of both men. She not only cared about them, she was prepared to be considered a tough bitch while Roy and James sat back charmingly and let her take control of the business side of their professional lives. Over the years James allowed Pam to take on and argue with agents, quarrel over money, and generally earn herself a rather undeserved reputation. It was years later, near the time of their divorce in 1964, that James remarked to me rather plaintively that he had always assumed that Pam had enjoyed the cut and thrust of negotiation, to which I replied, caustically I fear, that he could have asked her if the role of number one Bitch held any allure for her.

Following *Troubled Waters* James appeared in several more films – *Prison Breaker, Blind Man's Buff* (1936), *The Secret of Stamboul, The Mill On the Floss, Fire Over England, The High Command, Catch as Catch Can* and *Return of the Scarlet Pimpernel* (1937), but not content to follow his career in the cinema alone, he also managed to appear in a variety of plays – with Pamela Kellino as his leading lady. Nigel Balchin wrote a play for them called *Miserable Sinners*, rather an uncomfortably apt title. They played at the Arts Theatre, the Rotunda in Dublin and at the Q Theatre just outside London. They even wrote a couple of plays together.

In 1937, James appeared without Pam in Robert Sherwood's play *The Road to Rome*. It went on at the Embassy Theatre, Swiss Cottage, and later transferred to the Savoy Theatre where James's name went up in lights in the West End for the first time. I remember that James particularly admired Ena Burrill, the actress who played the Roman leader's wife. She not only looked beautiful but had a voice which caressed the ear. I suggested to James that she had a snake-like quality but he advised me that not everybody had my penchant for reptiles (I was about sixteen) and that they might not consider such praise a compliment.

His next appearance in the West End was in *Bonnet Over The Windmill* by Dodie Smith. This proved to be a success (though, like most of the plays in which James appeared, it failed to run longer than three months) and introduced James to another young actor, Peter Coke, who was just starting out on his theatrical career and who would become a good friend.

By an odd coincidence my mother and I already knew Peter Coke from Menton where, after leaving school at Stowe, he was being groomed for the Consular Service. In his spare time he played the juvenile leads in an Amateur Dramatic Group formed by the British contingent resident there. It was from his experience with the Menton Players that he decided to desert the Consular Service for a career in the theatre. Like James, his family opposed and disapproved of a theatrical career for him, and this common experience forged a bond between them, but in Peter's case, he found support from his grandmother and he went to the Royal Academy of Dramatic Art where he won the Irene Vanburgh award. War service put a temporary stop to his promising career, but later he was to make his name as the hero of the popular BBC Radio *Paul Temple* programmes and find success as a playwright, most famously with *Breath of Spring* with Athene Seyler which was a box office hit and had a phenomenally long run.

PETER COKE

I first met James Mason when Dodie Smith engaged me to be in her play *Bonnet over the Windmill* – James was to be the star and she was so determined to have me and Ann Firth appear that she paid us both a retaining fee so that we took no other work! This came as a marvellous surprise, so we used part of the money to insure ourselves against "breakages" and went off to ski in Wengen with several other members of the cast including James, who with Pamela and Roy Kellino, stayed in a de Luxe Hotel, whilst we ordinary mortals settled happily in lesser pensions! I had met Pam before her marriage to Roy when she visited her mother in Menton, but we saw little of her or James in Switzerland as, because of contracts James was not allowed to ski, only indulge in a little very sedate skating.

Despite James and wonderful sets, *Bonnet over the Windmill* didn't have the success of Dodie's other plays, but I got to know James pretty well during the run and we played squash quite frequently. A marvellous game and we were both pretty keen on winning! I suppose we had a special bond as we both had disappointed our parents by having opted out of our original chosen professions. Architecture in James's case and the Consular Service in mine – hardly rebels, but in those days the stage was considered rather risque to say the least. Even stardom was regarded a trifle askance!

James Laver's play about Byron and Shelley was the only other occasion that I trod the boards with James, who as Byron looked quite magnificent, as though he had stepped out of a National Gallery portrait – again unfortunately, it was not a success but there was one scene when a very beautiful girl with bare breasts (probably the first time every seen in a straight play) came in and sat directly before James. I always imagined Pam sitting every night in a front stall, pearl-handled revolver at the ready if he dared do anything but give her the most cursory glance!

James was strikingly good looking but never seemed aware of the power of his looks. I never saw any vanity in him though I do remember being surprised when he gave me a lift to the film studios one early morning. He had obviously had his hair waved and was wearing a massive clip to maintain his coiffure. But I would guess that this was due to instructions from the make-up department. On another of those before-dawn drives he gave me some advice which surprised me but gave me an insight on how to succeed in the film world (not that I ever did). "Always undercut your salary if it means you'll get the part by so doing." Years later I learned that he would negotiate his fees if there was a specific part he was determined to play.

James and Peter were good foils for each other, the former dark and mysterious, the latter with red-gold hair, blue eyes and a fair complexion. Total opposites in looks and character, yet their friendship blossomed and flourished over many years. James was an intensely loyal person and the fact that he could hold different views or have a differing sense of values never clouded his liking or caring for his friends, and Peter was the same. When James and the Kellinos were casting their film *I Met a Murderer* he invited Peter to take part. Peter accepted at once, delighted to be given the chance to work on the film and at the same time to broaden the friendship begun in the theatre. I will show how this bond survived later differences and opposing views.

Christmas 1937 saw Pam, Roy and James on holiday together at

Wengen in Switzerland. It was here that James and Pam wrote the first draft of the script for the film, then called *Deadwater*, which was to become *I Met a Murderer*. Mama and I joined them, and on one occasion I earned a dressing-down from Pam for risking James's neck and taking him on my two-man toboggan down the run from Kleine Scheidegg. Not a word was said about *my* neck, I may add! As a spirited teenager I felt that risks were to be enjoyed and, when Pam pointed out that film stars had clauses in their contracts forbidding such childish pranks, I thought even less of actors than I had before.

Nevertheless James was allowed to skate, from time to time, a careful and sedate session with Esma Cannon as his partner. Esma was a tiny little woman, an utterly enchanting, brilliant comedienne, and like the rest of us was cat-mad. She and Grace, her darling of a mother, lived together in Radnor Mews and I remember many happy hours spent with them on my visits to London. Fortunately for all concerned James suffered no mishaps on the ice under her gay tutelage. Roy, meanwhile, his eye ever-appreciative of a pretty woman, indulged in other sports without risking life or limb, while Pam watched with horror the drunken antics of British undergraduates who congregated at the Palace Hotel Bar after their strenuous workouts on the slopes. Pam abhorred sport, and the early mornings it required were anathema to her. Tea dances in ski boots she found merely tiresome. While the rest of us enjoyed our annual visits to Wengen, it was not Pam's scene at all. James, though, always retained his liking for sport in general, for swimming, tennis and, to a lesser degree, my passion for riding. Riding was the be-all and end-all of my life as a child and until 1939, when the war pushed me into a very different world and career.

Mama had a house at Kingsgate, on the Kent coast, where we spent our summer holidays each year. I remember the garden as she had a passion for lilac and laburnum trees and the hedges around our home were always a lovely sight. Our old gardener, Mr Bennett, had seen action in the First World War, serving in the Buffs, and he liked nothing better than regaling my younger brother and me with bloodthirsty stories of the trenches. Being young and without the sensitivity of later years, we lapped it up.

For a while Pam, Roy and James took a house and garden next door to ours. James caused quite a stir amongst the local ladies when they observed him tearing down to the sea on his bike. Of course, the oddity of the menage caused a lot of gossip and Mama was always being interrogated as to "WHO is Pam married to?" I must admit to finding Roy more to my liking than James at this stage. Why? Because he showed greater interest in my horses, to whom, according to Mama, I gave everything "but pearl necklaces". An exaggeration, but as I was the only member of my family to be horse-mad, I tried to make allowances for the others' lack of enthusiasm. Roy wasn't a very good rider, rather insecure in the saddle, but he was a willing pupil and I was forever telling him to keep his toes up, straighten his back, keep his hands down, lengthen his reins and so on – I had the nagging tongue of the fanatic. James, being the quieter person, more remote and reserved, tended to make me aware that I was still a teenager and he a mature older man. A man in his late twenties seemed aged to me, and although Roy was no younger, he seemed so to me, being more boyish and sunnier in temperament.

Such a confusing household attracted an intrigued audience, and when Pam visited us, she took great delight in making sudden dramatic entrances into our drawing room when Mama was entertaining friends – with both Roy and James in tow. Scandalised eyebrows would be raised, much to Pam's amusement. Beautiful as she was, Mama would often have to criticise her for her lack of manners, usurping the conversation and always excluding those who were not part of the film world – which meant the bulk of our friends. We were sport, animal and garden lovers, and the main topics of interest in our house were cricket, tennis, cats, horses, dog-shows and gardens. Mama loved the theatre and music-hall, but the cinema held no more interest for her than anything else, and the rest of the family were neither fascinated nor impressed. But the Mason/Kellino conversations were centred on films, scripts, billings, directors and so on, and we had little in common but our family ties.

It was in this summer of 1938 that I noticed Roy casting admiring glances towards a very sweet girl who had done the continuity work on *I Met A Murderer*. Jo was not a traditional beauty but she was attractive and had a kind and gentle personality. She, too, enjoyed riding but like Roy was not very experienced or, to my mind, very safe in the saddle. My animals were not easy rides, but Roy had set his heart on riding one of my greys and the more I refused the more insistent he became and one day James, acting as peacemaker, took me on one side and suggested I give in and end the interminable arguments. "But James", I said, "Onyx will pull his arms out. She has to be ridden on a loose rein and allowed to settle in her own time. As soon as she gives a buck Roy will panic and grab at her head and then she'll throw him".

His reply was revealing. "If he falls on the grass he's not likely to hurt himself, is he? But it will finish the bickering. He thinks you are just being awkward, you feel he's being foolish – put it to the test."

This was typical of James – such sense, so very logical. I listened and agreed it was the best way. Onyx duly obliged by putting Roy on the floor having first nearly torn his arms from their sockets. That should have been that, but then Roy insisted that he should try my brother's mount and take him down to the beach. I warned him that the pony might want to roll in the sea, which he loved, but again I saw disbelief written on Roy's face. "Anyway, you're too big and heavy for the animal," I quickly said – to no avail.   "In that case," Roy replied, "let Jo ride him." Trying to explain that we took the horses into the sea water every day for the benefit to their legs made no difference, and once again James, with his drole humour, suggested to me that a wetting in the summer would do no one any harm. So once more we put it to the test and once more my warnings proved right, only this time it was poor little Jo who got dumped in the briny. My popularity hit a new low with Roy, and his romantic advances got little response from a very wet and unamused girl. James and I had a good giggle over it and, if he told Pam, I've no doubt she enjoyed the joke quite as much as we did. They would both have been amused by the sabotaging of Roy's amorous intentions.

Pam and her sister Sheila both rode, but it never really appealed to them and my poor mother definitely preferred the aroma of Chanel No. 5 to the horsey smell that I always brought into the house from the stables. James never seemed to notice my general dishevellment and, as I got to know him better, I was more than pleasantly surprised to find that he was not only handsome but very human.

I sometimes wondered why James had chosen to become an actor – a very exposed life, as I saw it. He was quiet and reserved and often ill at ease in company and, for all his good looks, he wasn't a "sexy" man. It took me a long time to realise that by playing a part, becoming someone else, one can shed many if not all the inhibitions that are apparent in one's real life. Whether James found relief from his shyness in this way and at this stage of his career I cannot say, but certainly he showed a marked capacity to impose his personality on his films. That he was shy and reserved endeared him to me, and a close bond was forged between us when I discovered his love of animals and gave him his first cat. Top Boy was a pure black, amber-eyed Siamese. He was bred from my queen, Anna, and the sire, Dasco of Petalong (given to me by Pam), both of whom had pedigrees of pure purple breeding, so how one little misfit came about nobody knows – but Siamese he was in shape and voice. He had a lovely temperament, and James fell for him. I don't believe James had ever had a cat of his own before, although there were dogs in his parents' home. Pam adored cats and they seemed to have an affinity with her; they all came to her. Indeed, she had a catlike beauty about her; sensuous, small-boned, she moved beautifully. James recognised this in feline animals, and was fascinated by their individual qualities. He became a cat-lover. Pam nowadays entertains racoons by the score. They enter her living room at night and enjoy cookies and chocolate, they know her and show no fear, so much so that she had one fellow who would scramble onto the piano to help himself with goodies if Pam was too slow in doling out the midnight feast!

One incident which stands out in my mind was when James risked his neck without being called an idiot by Pam. Top Boy somehow got out of James's flat in Marylebone High Street and onto the roof of the building leaving James and Fisher, his valet-cum-chauffeur, to scramble amongst the chimney pots on the rooftops of London, slipping and sliding without thought for their own safety so as to rescue the by then frightened and squalling little cat. Luckily he was recovered without mishap and I noted, rather sourly, that Pam refrained from castigating James for infringing the danger clauses written into his contracts. In Switzerland I had got an earful for being thoughtless and James had got a wigging for being an ass – but then no cat's life had been at risk in that episode.

What many people never recognised in James was his capacity to tease. With his serious expression and hesitant manner he would fox the objects of his teasing, leaving them rattled and angry. But James would have been upset to think he might have inadvertently hurt anyone's feelings. Malice and spite simply did not exist for him. He could be testy and impatient, but never unkind. People misread his character and misunderstood his wry sense of humour. In Hollywood, later on, I heard him described as "that son-of-a-bitch" and I could only feel anger and contempt for those who judged him by their own behaviour.

James was not greedy but, as his reputation grew, he recognised his own worth. He had standards, and no one was more willing to admit than he that some of his films fell way below his own requirements. As early as 1937-38 James earned a name for being his own man and a critic of the hierarchy of the British Film Industry. It did little to endear him to the powerful men then in charge of it.

I found it interesting that, although James was becoming better and better known, more and more sought after, he never changed as a person. If he felt more secure it didn't show, he was still tongue-tied, slow to express himself, wry and dry-witted. He never gave the impression that he enjoyed his good looks, in fact I'd go so far as to say I don't think he ever considered himself handsome. What he knew, as his career progressed, was that he was a very good, hardworking professional, and that gave him pleasure and a sense of achievement.

In March 1938 (before our holiday in Kent), Pam, Roy and James had embarked on a project of their own. It seemed natural for them to work together, which they did to great effect. The film *I Met A Murderer* was a thriller written by James and Pam. The three of them invested their combined savings of £4,500 in the venture, but it was a tiny budget for a full-length movie. The film was to be shot entirely on location (studio costs were out of the question) and they found a suitable farm in Buckinghamshire not far from Marlow. The next priority was a headquarters and accommodation for the unit, and they rented a furnished house in Cookham Dean. The resident maid Violet Taylor and her cat were part of the deal – worth mentioning because this was a relationship which was to last, and Violet eventually went to America to look after Pam and James in New York and Hollywood.

This arrangement meant that Roy, Pam and James were living and working together day and night, as they believed the film was going to be the key to their success and all their hopes and dreams were tied up in it. They invested every ounce of their talents and energies in the enterprise that, they were sure, would put them on the map as independent film-makers. And it was a truly independent production, wholly funded by themselves, with James and Pam taking the main parts in the screenplay that they had written themselves and Roy working as both the director and the senior cameraman. The young Ossie Morris, later to become one of the very best cameramen himself, was his assistant. It was a brave gamble and, when the shoestring would not stretch far enough, they begged and scrounged help from friends and colleagues. Roy borrowed equipment from his contacts at the studios, friends who were actors (including Peter Coke) gave their services free in the smaller parts and Pam and James looked to their other contacts and relatives for support.

But extraordinary as it may seem Pam's father, who was now head of Gaumont British and associated with the very successful Gainsborough Films, not only failed to offer any financial backing but, along with his brothers who were all involved with his companies in varying degrees, turned his back on the entire project. This was very hurtful to Pam as it seemed her own relatives, who were in the best position to help, preferred to see their venture sink without trace.

Whatever the reason, jealousy or perhaps dislike of James, the Ostrers' attitude confounded everyone. But it was a pettiness that was to be seen on many occasions in the future, even though James was to become the biggest asset of their industry.

Had it not been for the coming war there is no doubt that *I Met a Murderer* would have enhanced the careers of all three very considerably. Pam gave a good account of herself both dramatically and as a writer; Roy, a cameraman of immense talent, showed himself a more than competent director, and James fulfilled all the promise he had shown in his earlier work; and the bond that existed between him and the Kellinos gave a great intensity to the quality of the film. The friendship between James and Roy was born of mutual respect of each other's talents. Roy always said that James was a cameraman's dream, that his face had no bad angles whatsoever, and of all the photographers that flocked to the Mason profile, none ever surpassed the magnificent stills taken of James by Roy.

James's looks were special. He was no matinee idol in the style of Tyrone Power, Robert Taylor or Leslie Howard, who were so popular at the time. James represented a kind of challenge because he didn't fit into a mould. He was dangerous and therefore very attractive, and the combination of his dark looks and sensual voice had a devastating effect on his female audiences. To quote a thirteen-year-old fan, confiding her love for him to her friends in the school lavatories: "I wouldn't mind what James Mason did to me as long as he talked all the time." Women adored him, and the qualities that made him so irresistible to them marked him out as one of that rare breed of actors who survived and flourished in a welter of films, some brilliant, some moderate and some plain awful. James was always his own harshest critic, always honest to the point of self-denigration. He sometimes undertook unsuitable roles about which he had an instinctive wariness because of the need to earn the big money on offer and on many occasions, when panned by the critics, his response would be, "How right they are – it was pretty bloody awful!" followed by hearty, if hollow, laughter.

The greatest bit of bad luck to hit *I Met A Murderer* was that the week it was due for general release coincided with the declaration of war in the early part of September, 1939. It had received excellent reviews at its first showing at the Marble Arch Pavilion in June, but Hitler's invasion of Poland caused such panic that all the London cinemas were closed down for a period of weeks. During this time the film itself was "kidnapped" by the distributors and subsequently lost until 1947 when, very fortuitously, it was found in New York and resuscitated at a time when Pam and James's finances were at a very low ebb.

The end of 1939 marked the end of the Kellinos' marriage. Because they all feared that adverse publicity might affect the fortunes of *I Met A Murderer* they conspired to keep the break between Pam and Roy secret. They had agreed that any open gossip and scandal should be avoided until the moment presented itself when the marital changeover would not damage the success of the film. The lease of James's old flat in Marylebone High Street had run its course and he had to make a move, so it seemed a logical solution for James to step into Roy's shoes and Roy, in a civilised manner, to withdraw to James's new flat in up-market Bickenhall Mansions. To disguise the fact that James had moved into Dorset House with Pam and that Roy had been shifted out to live at James's nearby address, an intercom was installed so that any calls for either man could be taken immediately by the flicking of a switch, thereby refuting any whispered suggestions that Pam and Roy had parted.

Sadly, the final split left Roy feeling resentful and ill-used, but his natural good nature did not allow him to act or speak against either Pam or James. Only in regard to the divorce proceedings did he exact a small revenge. He refused Pam's blandishment to "act the gentleman" and allow her to be the innocent party and he named James as co-respondent. In that year James was thirty and Pam still only twenty-three.

Both mothers were offended by the situation, for different reasons. "Muv" was disgusted that her son should have been embroiled by some woman in what was, clearly, an unusual situation. Perhaps because he was the youngest and the only one to go to university (the others were sent abroad to learn languages to fit them for their future professions – Rex in the textile industry and Colin a teacher) I always had the feeling that he was the one on whom she centred her own ambitions. Before her marriage she had hoped for a career of her own and, extraordinarily for a woman at the turn of the century, actually gone to London to study and begin work as a artist. But family responsibilities brought her back to Yorkshire when her mother died, and she had to care for her father and her brothers, and when she married any hope of fulfilment as a painter became an impossibility. So with his fine education and artistic talents James had seemed set to do her credit as a civil servant or an architect. His going into the theatre destroyed any chance of that and then to find him involved – God help everybody! – with a married woman whose own background was extraordinary enough, and whose husband came from a circus family with no background or breeding at all . . . it must have been dreadfully hard for her to take.

Our mother was, by the standards of the day, a very immoral lady. She had divorced one husband, taken up with my father, had numerous lovers and a vast family of children whose paternity was very doubtful. In fact I was so doubtful about the various men trotting around the house that I called them all Papa, because it was so much simpler. But my mother, to whom adultery was of little consequence, found it extraordinary that a man of James's type and background could set out deliberately to take away someone else's wife. He was always friendly and charming to all of us in the family, but he never alluded to the situation and seemed to expect everybody to accept it as being natural and normal. But it wasn't.

I suppose in those days that James's reputation might have suffered by his being branded a homebreaker, but in reality the only harm done was to his relations with his own family. The rift between them deepened, and the estrangement was completed when James chose a line of conduct that further shocked and hurt his parents. When war had been declared he decided to register as a conscientious objector and go before a tribunal to state his reasons.

It would be understandable if his family, and his mother in particular, chose to believe that it was Pam's influence and prompting that had so decided him. It was, without doubt, easier for them to apportion the blame for what seemed to them his shameful and unpatriotic conduct on the evil woman who had entrapped him, rather than accept James's own conclusion that war was an illogical and futile affair which settled nothing and left no winners. My own view is that, had the Nazis invaded this blessed island, he would have found his logical detachment untenable. Pam, because of her Jewish father, would have been an endangered species and James would then have reacted as did his brothers (both of whom joined up at once) and most of his friends. Peter Coke, whom I briefly mentioned before, joined the Cazalet Brigade (which consisted of many actors) and I do remember Pam castigating him for having rushed into uniform so promptly. "You could have waited for your call-up and then you might have been put on a reserved list to entertain the troops," she said. That was her attitude. Perfectly legitimate and reasonable at the start of hostilities, particularly as the period of the "phoney war" seemed to bear out her views. England seemed a safe bastion against Hitler and his hordes at the time. But the picture was to change very rapidly and those, like Peter, who had donned their uniform with honour were to be vindicated by events.

James, whatever his reasons, continued to conduct himself as he had set out to do. He faced a Tribunal and was allowed finally to remain a non-combatant. Both Noel Coward and Michael Redgrave to my knowledge tried hard to change his mind, using their arguments in the most chivalrous and persuasive manner and with the kindliest of intents. They were genuinely anxious that James should not harm what already had the promise of a very fine career, and they probably did feel that if they could make him see that his course of action was likely to injure his future they could at the same time utilise this very exciting, masculine and heroic-looking man who would appeal to a very different group of people than themselves, in the films intended to promote a general patriotism. James was a matinee idol of the moment and he had enormous potential for influence – a good instrument for propaganda. They certainly felt he was doing himself and his career a great deal of harm by making his views public in this way.

But James, whilst accepting that they advised him for the best of reasons, remained determined to follow his chosen path. I am sure that, had he been forced to face a prison sentence for his convictions, he would have taken the punishment with fortitude. His decision must have been made the more difficult to take and keep by the knowledge that both his brothers were in uniform and served with distinction throughout the war. The family could never understand or accept James's apparent dereliction of duty, but nothing at that time could sway his belief that he was right. I don't know if he had regrets later in his life, but one thing is certain – James's growing reputation suffered no setbacks whatsoever, and he was able to consolidate his rise to stardom in the now famous films such as *Thunder Rock*, *The Man in Grey*, *Fanny by Gaslight* and *The Wicked Lady*.

It is interesting that James today in 1988 has great appeal among the young film goers, the 18 or 19 year olds – His face, his voice, even in old age, fascinates and when I've questioned what characteristic is most admired, inevitably the reply mentions mystery or menace. That indefinable brooding dangerous look that was so much part of his charisma.

Ann Todd, I believe, observed this specific quality when playing opposite James in *The Seventh Veil*, one of the first films that allowed the hero to be cruel. It was usual for male stars to be good looking honest and kind, enabling the heroine to anticipate a safe and secure life as the final reel of the film united them – Not so *The Seventh Veil*, yet it was a smash hit. Did the male audience see Ann Todd as a victim and wish they had the power to enthral similarly? Have women always thrilled to the brutish kind of man James purported to be? Was the film's success due perhaps to the lack of love scenes? That in itself was unusual and unpredictable. The sexual attraction between the protaganists was as well scored as was the music but there were no kisses, no touching, was this interesting? I have unfortunately been unable to ask Ann Todd for her personal opinion and to have her sum up her feelings for James as an artist but I know he held her in high esteem and affection both as an actress and a friend.

In the early part of the war Pam and James moved out of London to a small house with large grounds in Beaconsfield. Roy remained in London. He was deemed unfit for active service because he suffered from an incipient ulcer but, as one of the leading cameramen of the day, he was sent to sea to record manoeuvres on board the aircraft carrier HMS Ark Royal. Throughout the war he kept in close touch with Pam and James and their friendship, amazingly, endured. Mama and I were living in London at this time, and Roy virtually adopted us. He chose me to act as his companion when he was lonely, or one of his amours had failed, and we visited quite a number of night clubs together where I have to say he cast his eyes over various, generally unsuitable, ladies. Eventually he met Sue, the attractive blonde who became his second wife, and for a few years our paths divided and we only met again in California, after the war, when he was staying with Pam and James after his second marriage had failed to work out.

During the war we saw less of James and Pam, my work took me abroad and our preoccupations were very different. But one evening stands out in my memory. Pam and James had been dining at the Savoy and they had offered Malcolm Sargent a lift back to the Albert Hall Mansions where he lived. I loved this dapper conductor, "Flash Harry" as he was called, both by his friends and detractors. I can only say, speaking as a singer, he wielded an enormous vitality which communicated itself to performers, particularly in choral works. On this particular night there was an air raid so they all stopped off at my house in Trevor Place to remain with us until the all clear, when Pam and James would resume their drive home to the country having delivered Sargent at his door en route.

Our animal collection had grown rather considerably during the blitz. Several stray dogs and kittens had been adopted and I was heartily embarrassed when the elegant Dr Sargent picked up my newest acquisition, an adorable white poodle bitch named Toti dal Monte after a prima donna I revered. Imagine my chagrin when, replaced on the floor, after much fussing, Toti spent the longest "penny" I have ever seen. It was a veritable torrent, puddling at the conductor's feet. "She's overcome by the occasion," said James, breaking the ghastly silence, and the tension evaporated. Everyone laughed as Mama and I rushed to collect newspaper and mop up the rapidly spreading pool, Pam and James moved their feet, in danger of a soaking, out of harm's way, and drinks were passed.

But this was not the end. My black poodle, Mouche as he had been called by his breeder, decided to make a beast of himself and demand attention from Malcolm Sargent who, fortunately, was an animal lover. Pam tried her best to distract the little brute and so did James, but to no avail, so I tried, with asperity, to restore a little order to the proceedings. But in the heat of the moment I forgot the fact that I had re-named Mouche and called him Malcolm! Yes, indeed, after his namesake and why? Because the dog was a showman and, not to put too fine a point on it, a show-off. One sharp rebuke of "Malcolm, get down! Behave yourself!" worked like a charm, but I felt my face turning red and heard with horror a giggle escape from James. I prayed he would not be overcome by the uncontrollable laughter which was his weakness, for I would have felt humiliated and, far worse, I feared the standing invitation I had just received to attend rehearsals at the Albert Hall would be withdrawn then and there.

I need not have worried. Pam must have kicked James into silence and Sargent himself turned to me with a dazzling smile. "You named him after me – how delightful – I am flattered". Ye gods, it never crossed his mind that I might have named my dog after someone closer to me, a brother, a lover or a relative, neither did it occur to him that I might have used his name for anything other than the most flattering of reasons.

I may add that James too had a habit of naming animals after their human counterparts and we agreed that the humans were rarely as delightful as their namesakes.

In the country Pam and James made a determined, if not very successful, effort to grow vegetables and keep hens, the kind of war effort they could both relate to and enjoy. Cats, of course, abounded. Pam continued to write scripts and novels and became rather more in demand as an author than an actress. And Pam was becoming well known for her formidable guardianship of James's professional interests.

Their marriage ceremony was pure comedy. On February 12th, 1941, at Amersham Registry Office, Pam and James became man and wife. Mama and I were to be witnesses but, at the last moment, we discovered that I was underage and therefore could not be counted as a legal signatory to the wedding certificate, so their great friend Carmen Flemyng was hastily recruited and she recalls the occasion. Carmen had been staying in the house for a few weeks to recuperate from a recent operation, and Pam and James were looking after her. Still convalescent, she knew her friends were to be married that morning, so she decided to keep out of their way until they returned.

CARMEN FLEMYNG

James burst into my room asking if I had a hat? No, I hadn't. Why did he ask?

"Pam and I are getting married and you must be a witness as Diana is too young".

As I hurriedly got dressed and borrowed a hat from Pam she explained that her mother and her sister were to have been witnesses but they had not realised that Diana was under age. The wedding ceremony was very funny, not that the Registrar approved! James got the giggles and nearly collapsed with laughter and only Pam by sharply rebuking him stayed off disaster. He managed, shakily it must be admitted, to say the necessary words, and kiss the bride, after which we returned home to enjoy a little celebration.

James, absent-minded as usual, had failed to realise that he would have to repeat the following words as requested by the Registrar:

"I take thee, Pamela Helen Ghislingham, to be my lawful wedded . . ." "Who?!" James was dumbfounded. "You mean Pamela Helen Kellino." "No, I do not," replied the small man clutching the papers pertaining to the divorce close to his chest. "It says here Ghislingham – orse Kellino."

"Orse?!" We saw that James had begun to laugh. "Orse? Does that mean otherwise?" The registrar was stern and unsmiling. "But everyone calls her by the name of Kellino – won't that do?" The laughter was more pronounced and we witnesses knew what to expect. The official facing James looked nettled by this argumentative male chuckling with mirth on this solemn occasion, and he tried once again to proceed. But by this time James had lost control. It was a weakness that stayed with him for years. If truly amused he would start to chuckle, making little sound, until his mirth was uncontrollable and he would laugh until tears flowed from his eyes.

It may have been caused initially by nervousness and his early shyness in the days when he found it difficult to express himself, but James had a very strong sense of the ridiculous and certain situations left him unable to contain his laughter – even in the solemnity of his own wedding ceremony. The furious and shocked face of the Registrar did little to halt the outburst and it was only a timely sharp rebuke from Pam that enabled him to regain his control and oblige with the legal requirement of using Roy Kellino's family name. I must confess that I had never heard the name before and the severity of the official's manner seemed a trifle unnecessary at the time, though since then I've learned how strictly the documentation of Births, Marriages and Deaths is controlled. Of course, anyone hearing Pam snap reprimands at James during their wedding would have considered him unlucky indeed to be marrying so shrewish a woman, but I should add that James had become quite used to the odd harsh word. We all laughed in a more relaxed way afterwards, toasting the happy couple back at their house.

By 1941 he had already acquired quite a reputation for speaking his mind, without fear or favour, and I've no doubt it made him unpopular in certain circles. I admired him for this open way of criticising what he saw as faults and flaws in this new profession; he took so seriously. I felt he was entitled to make his opinions known whatever the consequences and, oddly enough, it did not have any adverse effect upon his career. Whether it endeared him to the film industry in general is a moot point.

Everyone in our family, if they had anything to say, had to leap in and make themselves heard. Pam was always a brilliant conversationalist, witty and very, very funny. Our mother, her Welsh/Irish humour always to the fore, was equally silver-tongued and amusing. James on the other hand, was slow to express himself, hesitant and vague, so it was not unusual for him to be told to either "hurry up" or "shut up" but he never showed any resentment at being verbally walked-over. If anything, he encouraged it by not insisting on having his say. It struck me quite often that James let the tittle-tattle wash over him, only half listening, while thinking his own thoughts. He was never a natural comic and his quiet manner was the perfect foil for Pam's scintillating repartee. I believe he greatly enjoyed the stream of noise and chatter that poured constantly around his ears.

While he was making *The Wicked Lady* I asked James if he enjoyed working with Margaret Lockwood and whether or not he liked her. He seemed nonplussed at my question and took his time before replying. "I think we get on quite well," he said. I waited. What was to follow? Nothing! He obviously had not considered the matter before.

"You don't like the director, I know that, Pam told me."

Again he looked bemused. "No, I don't. He's incompetent." A little laugh escaped. "I guess Pam told you I thumped him, well, slapped him is nearer the truth. Anyway, the whole thing is rubbish." Maybe so, but it was box office! The film was a fantastic success, it broke records and consolidated James's position as a popular film star/matinee idol without a doubt.

Margaret Lockwood and Phyllis Calvert have contrasting recollections of this time.

MARGARET LOCKWOOD

Having taken a year off in which to have my baby, I duly returned to Gainsborough Studios to make a film called *Alibi*. I remember it for two reasons, one being the poorness of the plot, the second for being my introduction to James Mason as my co-star.

I think the whole film was probably an experience we would both prefer to forget! In those days we artists were given little choice as to our roles and virtually no opportunity to say no even if we regarded our parts in the scripts as being unworthy vehicles – we just had to do our best whatever the material. When Maurice Ostrer gave me *The Man in Grey* to read I was struck by the fact that there were four equally good parts, two female and two male, but I was shocked to find that I was to be cast as the villainess, Hesther, whilst the heroine's part of Clarissa was to be played by Phyllis Calvert. Never having considered myself as an "evil" female, I must confess the prospect was none too pleasing, nor did I rejoice at the idea of once again playing opposite James who remained dour and uncommunicative throughout the filming.

Off the set he was generally to be found with his head stuck in a book, not a bundle of fun to anyone. Not so Jimmy [Stewart] Granger, who was cast in his first starring role. He, unlike James, was gay and friendly with a spontaneous infectious wit which kept us all in stitches – I may add that his language was fruity to say the least, which got him into trouble from time to time. Not that he cared, he captured all our hearts and made the film a pleasure to work on.

James made a great hit as the cruel and heartless Marquis of Rohan, he looked wonderful and was extremely effective in his part, so much so that with such a successful film we were once again cast opposite each other in *The Wicked Lady*. The first day on the set I remember only too vividly! James did nothing but complain, first the script was a load of rubbish, secondly the director little better or possibly even worse than the story. Hardly conducive to good relationships! Nevertheless, James and I played well together, notwithstanding that we had little in common and little rapport.

I found him grumpy and withdrawn but the public adored the film which became the biggest money-spinner of the year. In defence of James's views I must say that the critics heartily endorsed his cry of "Rubbish!" and maybe the brutal reception the film received from the press contributed to its success. People flocked in their thousands to see it, and from there on James and I were regarded as a team, quite mistakenly. In fact, apart from the aforementioned films we never again worked together, he went to Hollywood and I continued in my career here in England.

PHYLLIS CALVERT

I first worked with James Mason, Margaret Lockwood and Stewart Granger on *The Man in Grey* under a director called Leslie Arliss. James and I amongst others certainly agreed that he was so difficult that we swore never to work with him again! However James did and whilst filming *The Wicked Lady* he made the headlines – not "Man bites dog" but "Star hits director".

When I read that James had landed a blow on our least favourite film maker, I rushed round to learn the full story. I confess to feeling a gleeful delight at James's reply. In his typical understated fashion he told me that Arliss had so annoyed him that he found his fist flailing the air and not knowing what to do with it, found himself throwing a punch which connected squarely.

In his usual restrained manner he failed to say what Arliss had done to so annoy him and I didn't press the point. It could have been an argument over James being a conscientious objector, but there was no further mention made of the matter.

I accepted James's decision not to serve in the armed forces, he believed he was doing right and that was enough for me. I imagine it must have been a difficult time for him, both at the studios and elsewhere, it certainly couldn't have been an easy option. I always loved working with James, he was not only a complete professional but a generous co-star – perhaps what I adored most was his attitude to his work – "Give me one good scene and I'm happy to do the part."

That was his view, unlike many other artists at that time who first counted the number of pages in which they appeared before considering whether or not to play the offered role. Since those days I've borrowed James's axiom and when offered parts which have not been considered by others to be important enough for me, I've thought of James's words and told whoever was casting or producing, "Well James Mason would have played a part like this, so that's good enough for me – I'll do it." To sum up, James was, in my view, not only a fine actor, but also a jolly nice man.

The phenomenal success of films such as *The Man in Grey, The Wicked Lady* and others made in the war period linked James's career with the most popular leading actors of the day, Margaret Lockwood, Phyllis Calvert, Patricia Roc, Anne Todd, Stewart Granger and Michael Rennie, to name but a few. His status was by 1947 fully confirmed as being the leading star of the British Film Industry. In December 1944 The Motion Picture Herald's annual poll of box-office returns declared him "Britain's No. 1 money-making film star". In April 1946 he was voted the favourite film actor of half a million British film-goers, and in June 1946 he was presented with the first National Film Award, at the Dorchester Hotel, as the best film actor of the six war years – his name chosen by public ballot. In January 1947, for the fourth year in succession, he was nominated as the biggest box-office draw among British film stars in British films. He was chosen by cinema exhibitors in a pool conducted by the Motion Picture Herald, and *Odd Man Out* in which he starred, was one of the nine films which took the most money at the box-office that year.

In a separate poll, covering international stars, James scored a further triumph by being placed second, the first place being taken by America's Bing Crosby. It's worth remembering that at this time when television scarcely existed for most people, the cinema was the most popular and accessible form of entertainment and it was quite common to go at least once, if not twice, each week. By now James's fan mail was enormous. Five thousand five hundred admirers wrote to him every week (at a time when Winston Churchill's mail from strangers amounted to approximately 650 per week). About 2,500 of the letters were from British fans, about 2,000 from America and 1,000 from the rest of the world, and most of them came from "bobby-soxers" – his teenage fans. Since *The Seventh Veil* the fan mail had increased until it was an avalanche that needed a full-time secretary and eight part-time assistants to deal with it.

James's own personal opinion as to his value and success was hard to fathom. The critical faculty that was ever-present made him doubtful of any lavish praise and he gave the closest possible scrutiny to every detail of his performances, irrespective of box office success. The interviews with his friends and colleagues which are part of the story of James's climb to the top may reveal more of the man as an actor than I am able to do, and here I must acknowledge my deep gratitude to those who have been so willing to discuss the films in which they took part and were so important in helping to promote James's career. Some fellow-performers, producers, directors, agents and others clashed with James at this stage of his career and I know he viewed certain people with a jaundiced eye. Nevertheless he always frankly discussed and made known his complaints, and was honest enough to admit that it was sometimes purely a lack of compatibility and understanding on his part.

PETER NOBLE

Peter Noble, the film writer, published a marvellous book in 1946, called *Profiles and Personalities*, which contained the following portrait of James: "In the British cinema one male star dominates the scene. He is ex-architect James Mason, voted by both cinemagoers and exhibitors Britain's leading box-office personality. This position of eminence has been reached by Mason after ten years of good, solid work in British film studios. His has not been a spectacular rise to fame; rather has it been his consistently excellent work over a number of years in films both first-rate and mediocre.

For an actor, Mason has more than usual sincerity, and also enormous determination. It is the latter which has made him as many enemies as friends and caused him to reject as many roles as he accepts. it was in fact this quality which made him become an actor in the first place. At the age of 22 he began a career as an architect, designing model houses, town halls and sometimes theatres. But the desire to act in the latter rather than design them and the scarcity of opportunity in such employment caused James to answer an advertisement in *The Stage* for a small part player and assistant stage manager. He got the job and started the hard way, touring with a small fit-up company in a florid epic entitled *Rasputin, The Rascal Monk*. His apprenticeship in the theatre culminated three years later in 1934 when he appeared at Dublin's Gate Theatre where he distinguished himself with several fine performances. He was reaching stature as an actor and the fact that he had received no academic stage training revealed itself not at all. Mason appeared an ideal screen type and in 1935 he was offered, and accepted, his first film part in a modest effort called *Late Extra* directed by the man who discovered him, Al Parker.

Though film after film followed in rapid succession during the next few years, he can remember the names of few of them. Perhaps this is just as well, for the "Quota Quickies", infamous result of the Cinematograph Act of 1927, were not noted for their taste or quality. (However James wishes to deny the rumour that he starred in so many "B" pictures that he began to get fan-mail from hornets!). He didn't particularly like being in these rushed and shoddy productions, but they were at least a training ground and served a certain purpose.

In the past six years Mason has risen to occupy an enviable position. Combining a handsome profile with more than usual histrionic ability he has become the most sought-after star in the home industry. But it has been his undoubted flair for period acting which has rocketed him to recent fame. The name "James Mason" on a cinema marquee has caused the queues to lengthen and the shillings to clink merrily at the box-office from the time when his sensual Rohan in *The Man in Grey*, his lecherous aristocrat in *Fanny By Gaslight* and his brutal but amorous highwayman in *The Wicked Lady* have made Masonic villainy pay heroic dividends. Since he first sneered at Margaret Lockwood and drew her to him in a passionate embrace in the highly-coloured film version of Lady Eleanor Smith's even more highly-coloured novel, Mason has never looked back. His particular brand of likeable wickedness has endeared him to millions.

The young Yorkshireman does not fit in very well with the crowd of first-nighters, Savoy diner-outers, sycophants and favour-curriers, or with any of the other well-known types which seem to infest the film world. He is intelligent and outspoken. During a period of general Press adulation for British films Mason has oft-times launched into print with a broadside against British products and producers. This has, understandably, not endeared him to a number of people in British studios, one technical body going so far as to try to ban his pictures!

The well-known Mason determination has shown itself in a variety of ways: his occasional outbursts on the set at what he considers to be inadequate direction, his protestations at having to mouth unrealistic dialogue, these and other incidents of a similar sort are taken to indicate that he has become "star-conscious". This is not so. He is completely sincere in his beliefs that our films will only register an all-round improvement when those of our leading film actors and actresses who care about these things will reject bad scripts, oppose certain technical indifferences and take a real interest in the production. "We can make the best films in the world" says Mason, "but the wartime revival will only continue in the post-war years if constructive criticism is able to get a hearing.

For some time now he has been in the enviable position of being able to reject Hollywood overtures. Recently Mason returned the script of a famous novel to the American company concerned with the comment "As the script does not contain a good part for me I am declining your offer with thanks". Such actions have had the normal repercussions. "Mason is difficult and unmanageable" say his opponents, but there are many who praise him for having ideals and sincerity and for being unafraid to express his opinions as an artist.

Those who know him intimately will affirm that Mason in private life is very unlike the usual idea of a film star. He is bookish, intense, moody – although he *can* be gay and charming. In the restful, whitewashed rooms of his farmhouse are walls lined with books, record albums, drawings and etchings. Britain's favourite villain loves cats, reads a lot, draws well and is a jazz fan. He is gifted in many directions. He writes well, expertly and with a pretty sense of humour, his stories and articles have appeared in many magazines and with his wife Pamela Kellino he has written a number of plays. Together they have recently toured Europe, playing to the troops in both variety and straight plays. The Masons are a good team, artistically, intellectually and domestically.

Not entirely unaffected by his success James Mason is also conscious of the tremendously important part which a leading actor can conscientiously play in the reorientation of our film industry. At some future date Mason will produce his own films, for the success of *I Met A Murderer* convinced him that he can. Whatever course he decided to takes one may be sure that the determination which caused him to desert architecture for the roving vagabondage of a Thespian's life still remains part of his purposeful, uncompromising personality.

James was not perfect, not a paragon of virtue. He could be as aggravating and annoying as anyone else, but in general he was a kindly, gentle person with a capacity for loyalty and friendship not always apparent amongst the highly successful. And it was this talent for friendship which brightened and gave some continuity and happiness to the bleak and loveless years which lay ahead.

But the early years of Pam and James's partnership were both happy and fruitful. They worked together as actors in films and the theatre and they collaborated on scripts of all kinds. They were inseparable, never choosing to be apart, and it seemed that they shared the same interests, desires and ambitions. In retrospect I think that it only appeared to be so. James was single-minded in his quest for perfection in his performances, and Pam was determined that he should become a highly successful star actor. Not the same thing. I believe they ran on parallel lines, both going in the same direction but each seeking a different destination.

During the war, apart from his burgeoning film career, James managed to keep working in the theatre. He made periodic tours for ENSA and in 1944 he and Pamela found themselves appearing at Salisbury in the play *Gaslight*. It was here that an incident occurred which was to prove quite momentous – an incident which was to provoke rumour and gossip for a long while to come.

The first meeting between the Masons and a certain American Army Captain was hardly auspicious, the said Captain being very much the worse for drink, cursing and swearing against the laws governing the sale of alcohol to non-residents of the hotel in which Pam and James were staying. It was Pam, noting that the noisy and ebullient serviceman was extremely attractive, who intervened and by offering to share their drinks with him sought to soothe his temper – a ploy which brought about an immediate calm!

John P. Monaghan, Irish American, a former cop, joined the Mason household as general factotum as soon as he was released from the US forces. His original intention had been to stay on in England after the war to try for a writing career, but here was a much better proposition. Monaghan was a very unhibited character and, when sober, he had great charm. He was what later came to be called "streetwise" in every sense, tough and not oversensitive in his dealings with anyone trying to take advantage of either Pam or James. His loyalty to both of them was unquestionable and he was without doubt, with his strong physique, an enormous asset as a protective force. He certainly had a sense of his own importance, and had no fear of confrontation with those who considered him inferior as an employee and tried to treat him like a mere servant. That he most certainly was not. Johnnie, as we all called him, was part of the household and he was a devoted and genuine friend to both Pam and James. Many years later, when all the relationships were undergoing change, he sided with James as the result of friction with Pam. I don't think he found it easy to decide whom to support, but in the final analysis his loyalty was exercised in favour of James.

He became indispensable. He would accompany James everywhere and, when Pam tired of overseeing the small and tiresome details, Johnnie took over the day to day organisation of his life. Certainly, during their enforced and protracted stay in New York in 1947, Johnnie proved to be a most capable go-between. He organised the removal of goods and animals from England to New York, saw to the travel arrangements, viewed suitable houses, acted as co-host at parties and taught my mother, to her horror, that at big gatherings one offered champagne to start with then white wine topped up with soda water! A seasoned drinker, he knew how to handle alcohol. "Helene," he admonished Mama, "once you've swallowed a few glasses you don't know the difference." Mama was horrified. Hospitality in our house was offered only, as is the habit in France, to real friends, and only the best was ever good enough. But, as Johnnie pointed out, many people attending "bunfights" were professional free-loaders and had to be treated accordingly.

There can be little doubt that it was Johnnie who encouraged the Masons to embark on a tour in Germany at the end of the year for the American Red Cross Mission. I cannot see them, Pam in particular, wanting to brave the cold and discomfort of Berlin to entertain the troops, however enthusiastic and admiring their reception, without the encouragement and motivation of the dashing Captain. However, they took two plays, in a double bill, *The Road to Rome*, which Pam played the Ena Burill part, and a play of their own called *Made In Heaven,* and an original skit on the last act of *Othello,* which they also wrote. James possibly enjoyed the challenge of playing to American servicemen, but I think they were glad when the tour was completed and James once again took up the film work that was to lead him towards California.

Meanwhile, when the war in Europe ended, they sold the house in Beaconsfield and moved to Olliberrie Farm near King's Langley in Hertfordshire. It was a lovely house and it had a large garden with some wonderful cherry trees and an old apple orchard. Of course, there was plenty of room for the cats. Pam and James were thrilled by it. This was to be the background of their lives over the next couple of years as "the sought-after movie star and his clever wife". They would enjoy living there, and naturally Johnnie Monaghan would be on hand to make sure that everything went smoothly. 1946 was the year that James made the film of which he was most proud and to which he always returned when asked to name the favourite of all the films he had made. *Odd Man Out* was the story of a wounded IRA gunman seeking refuge from the law in the Belfast of the 1920s. At the time the film was made the IRA was practically dormant and in the story was only referred to as the "organisation". The director of the film was Carol Reed, whom James had admired for a long time and who was as he said "the director with whom of all the directors in the world I was keen to work". The subject matter was very close to his heart because his sojourn in Ireland had given him a sensitive understanding of the Irish question and there was a marvellous cast of Irish actors including Cyril Cusack and Kathleen Ryan to add authenticity. Robert Newton gave an outstanding performance as the drunken artist, but it was James who carried the film although he said at the time that "the Irish character actors would run rings around me". James admitted to being pleased with his own performance – a rare thing, almost unheard of with him – and more than content to at last have played in a film of some substance. He was very conscious that his box-office appeal was based on a series of popular films that he regarded privately as rubbish and of which he was not at all proud. But *Odd Man Out* he could indeed see as an achievement.

The actress Rosamund John has some light to shed on this period:

ROSAMUND JOHN

I first met James Mason, when he invited me to play opposite him in
The Upturned Glass.

To be honest the film was not a very worthy venture and I found
my part singularly unexciting, even though James did all he could to
fire my enthusiasm! I was virtually at the same time appearing in
Fame is the Spur in a role which was far more rewarding, as was the
general working atmosphere. I found James a shy and endearing
young man and an excellent actor even at this early stage of his career
– why he had embarked on a project as mediocre as *The Upturned
Glass*? Nobody knew, but conjecture had it that he had been pushed
into it by his wife Pamela Kellino and an American man John
Monaghan who was dancing attendance on Pamela and purporting
to be a script writer – on that subject the least said the better!

Suffice to say the whole set-up was extraordinary and embarrassing to all, and neither Monaghan nor Pamela found favour with the
unit. She, a not-too-resourceful actress, was co-author of the script,
which was written piecemeal in a highly unprofessional manner, and
certainly John Monaghan showed little talent as a prospective writer.

What James really thought about this episode I cannot say, but as
co-producer I can only suppose that he knew of the inadequacies of
the writing and made the best use he could of the material to hand,
nevertheless we all felt it was a pity to see such a fine young actor
being exploited into wasting his talents in an effort to launch the
careers of two, in our view, somewhat undeserving people.

Over the years I saw James play many parts and my admiration for
him grew considerably, albeit that I felt he too often agreed to
participate in films unworthy of his artistry. I shall always remember
him with affection as the diffident and idealistic young man who
tried so hard to kindle my interest in a role in which I was to be killed
off quite quickly by his wife Pamela.

Why did I undertake the part? I think I must have been charmed by
the handsome and unusual man who had already created so much
attention in his earlier films and certainly working with him was a
pleasure.

What made James decide to go to America at this point his life? It is a
question that has several possible answers. Ambition? A carefully
weighed argument as to where he would find the best parts? Money?

Or was it Pam's increasing desire to leave England that swung the balance? For Pam the lure of sunshine and warmth, plus the deference she had already enjoyed in her contacts with the American Red Cross, may have swayed her. She was never really happy or at ease in England, although it was her natural home, and I think when the opportunity presented itself she may have determined that their future lay in America. For James it was a challenge, a chance to widen his scope, to work with new directors and new leading ladies. He already had great admiration for the American film industry as a whole which he believed to be better organised and better funded than in Britain. And by 1946 James was at the crossroads of his career.

Perhaps Johnnie Monaghan had a part to play in their decision, too. I have often been asked if James really liked or enjoyed the company of the ebullient Johnnie. I'm sure he did. James may have seemed to have had an ambivalent attitude towards him at times, but he was always enigmatic about his personal feelings. With his American Irish charm, Johnnie was a very useful adjunct. Watchful, shrewd and surprisingly discreet, he protected James from those he wished to avoid. He managed to promote a feeling of bonhomie whilst giving a very definite "No" to anyone overstepping the mark with James. Pam had found him interesting and attractive from their first meeting – although in time her relationship with him would cool and he became much more James's man. How Pam came to view the association of her husband with the man who had been her admirer, and with whom she had quarrelled, is open to question. According to her, James seemed to blame her rather than Johnnie for the rift in their friendships. I myself understood that it was a divergence of views as to how Portland, the unexpected baby, should be looked after that occasioned the final break, but that has not been confirmed.

The clinching factor in the move to America was James's meeting with David E. Rose, a producer from Paramount Pictures who was hoping to sign him up. This encounter was to prove James's naivety in such dealings, an innocence he was to lose when faced with the consequences of his misplaced trust. At Rose's invitation James joined him for tea at Claridges Hotel, but he didn't have the foresight to take along a legal advisor to witness the proceedings.

As James understood it, Rose's proposal was that they should form an independent production company, with David E. Rose to take of the finances and James the artistic side. James was very tempted by the prospect of at last having the opportunity to produce and choose scripts as well as to act, and he eagerly signed a vaguely worded letter of agreement which seemed to offer what he wanted. His misunderstanding of the terminology of the agreement was to lead to lengthy and acrimonious litigation, Rose insisting that James was legally bound to him by reason of the letter and therefore unable to work for any other producer than himself in the States, and he took out an injunction to enforce this. James, who had always done everything he could to remain independent as an actor, was furious. He was also mortified to discover that Rose only wanted his services as an actor and well-known film star – not for his talents in any other department of film-making.

What was James to do? He and Pam had taken the decision to leave England, but now it seemed his career was threatened by Rose's determination to hold him to what he insisted was a legal contract. He discussed his predicament with Alexander Korda, who came to the rescue by offering him a contract for six films, the first to be made in America, with an advance payment of $50,000 to be paid as soon as he arrived in New York, which would tide him over his initial unemployment while he dealt with Rose. But James could not foresee the length of time that this seemingly handsome sum would have to last, how long it would take to get the case into court, and how long it would take for the judgement to be received.

So, early in 1947, with mixed feelings of optimism, trepidation and nostalgia for all they were leaving behind, James and Pam set sail on the *Queen Elizabeth* with a small menagerie of animals and an entourage consisting of Johnnie Monaghan, Violet Taylor from Cookham Dean who had agreed to come as their housekeeper, and a dresser-cum-valet. They had no plans and no idea what might happen once they arrived in America – but they had high hopes. As luck would have it, a fellow passenger was Deborah Kerr, who had met James when filming *Hatter's Castle* in England.

New York was a wonderful contrast to the austerity of post-war England. They took a suite at the Plaza Hotel and found, to their astonishment, that they were the target of swarms of fans who accosted them in the streets and even tried to get into their hotel rooms. Johnnie Monaghan proved a very efficient bouncer, scaring away the would-be invaders of their privacy and fielding all telephone calls. Johnnie's vigilance created a few problems, not least with Earl Wilson and Louella Parsons, the influential columnists, neither of whom was accustomed to being denied access to people they wished to interview. Earl Wilson contented himself with making a few sour cracks at James's expense in his column in the *New York Post*, but Louella devoted an entire half-hour programme to lambasting him for being swell-headed, stubborn, conceited and, worst of all, uncooperative, all secondhand opinion gleaned from misinformed gossip and press reports and the reception her "legwoman" had received from Johnnie. At that time radio had far greater influence than television and people listened avidly to their favourite programmes, so this was pretty damning stuff. But James loved listening to the radio too and in New York he found a programme he adored – and he never missed the Fred Allen Show if he could help it.

Soon after their arrival in New York Pam and James were astonished to hear featured on the show a parody of *The Seventh Veil* – but they felt it was something of a compliment to have been singled out for attention by someone they so admired. Months later James was delighted to be invited by Fred Allen to appear as a guest on one of his shows, and this professional encounter was the beginning of a very happy friendship. Fred and his wife became godparents to the daughter born to Pam and James the following year, and named after her godmother, Portland Allen Mason. As she remarked to Pam at the time, having been born into a vaudeville family where the custom was to name children after whatever town they were born in (her sister was called Oregon I believe) it was a very good thing that Portland Allen hadn't been born in Milwaukee!

But it wasn't very long after their arrival in New York that James made the depressing discovery that if and when a court heard his evidence against the claims of David E. Rose, it was not necessarily the end of the affair. The judge might not hand down an immediate verdict and James could be stuck in New York indefinitely. Because Rose had registered his complaint in Los Angeles he could only serve the injunction on him if James set foot in California, so obviously he could not do so until such time as the suit was either withdrawn or he won his counterclaim.

Meanwhile, James and Pam decided that New York was to be enjoyed, and hang the expense! James had his $50,000 and they were going to be big spenders. They frequented the most glamorous restaurants and night clubs, like the "21" Club and the Stork Club and "El Morocco" and they were staying in a very expensive hotel, so life was glamorous and profligate.

For many actors the enforced idleness and set-back to their careers would have proved very traumatic, but James was never eaten up with ambition. He took his work seriously and he regarded the Theatre and Cinema as art to which he should give always of his best and, if success followed, it was a lucky bonus. He was advised by many people, knowing the dangers of a protracted litigation, to settle with David E. Rose and find a compromise acceptable to them both. But both James and Pam were too furious to let him get away with, what seemed to them, to be little better than blackmail. For James it had become a matter of principle. So far as he was concerned he had not signed a contract and he was not prepared to accept Rose's claims. He was willing to wait for as long as need be, whatever the cost, and although he may on occasions have had doubts as to the outcome he was determined to seek vindication through the court.

During the fifteen months or so that James was barred from film work in Hollywood he and Pam took to the theatre again, for just one ill-fated enterprise. *Bathsheba* was a play about the biblical King David, written by a Frenchman noted for his comedies. But on this occasion Jacques Deval considered that he had written a serious drama and he was dreadfully displeased when the audiences reacted to it with enthusiastic laughter and, after only a few weeks, the play folded. Not a success – but no harm was done to James's reputation and he turned his attention to more work for radio, which in those days held an enormous audience right across the States. By a stroke of good luck James now found an agent with whom he had an immediate rapport. William McCaffery was a truly delightful man and he had an equally enchanting wife, Margaret, who was private secretary to the powerful John Royal of NBC.

On my first visit to the States in 1951 James, as he had done in Ireland with Mrs Brock, referred me to the care of these good friends and the kind welcome and hospitality given to me by these three charming people completely dispelled my nervousness and home-sickness.

I didn't really know who a lot of the people I met through James in New York, and elsewhere, actually were, or what they were. I never was really interested in the theatre, or the arts generally, and therefore their names, famous or otherwise, were unknown to me. I had told the McCafferys that someone I did like and admire was Robert Preston. It so happened that he was coming to dinner with them that very night so I was promised that I should have him as my dinner partner. I was absolutely delighted! He was a very nice-looking man, and he was a very good singer.

Sitting opposite us during dinner was a much older man, very dapper and well dressed, and he was introduced to me as Walter Wanger. His name meant absolutely nothing to me but, listening to snippets of conversation during the meal, I gathered he was something to do with the film industry. The subject of the film *St. Joan* came up and he looked at me and said "Did you see it?"

I said, "Oh, which do you mean? I saw the play in London with Siobhan McKenna (with our friend Kenneth Williams playing the Dauphin) and when I was in Paris I saw the Honneger one which was very interesting – a great spectacle, full of dance and music – rather exciting . . ."

He interrupted me and said, "No, no, no, neither of those. I meant the film."

I said, "Oh, God, that awful thing . . . wasn't it shocking . . . bloody awful," and so I went on.

He said, "Thanks so much. You know, I made it. I was the producer and it bankrupted me."

For once in my life I didn't say, "And I'm not surprised." I was too shocked so I just said nothing. But the silence seemed to go on and on. Of course, afterwards I did apologise and I said to Margaret McCaffery, "I'm so sorry, I made a horse's ass of myself. Who is he, for God's sake. I've never heard of the man".

She said, "Oh, he's very famous, very well-known, very big in Hollywood. His wife is Joan Bennet."

I knew that Pam and James were very attached to her and her children, and I presumed, therefore, that they were friends of Walter Wanger as well, which was pretty horrifying. But I thought, well California is 3,000 miles away and I shan't see him again! But of course, I was wrong – we met quite often in Hollywood.

Pam and James had another good laugh at my expense, entirely my own fault as it happens. John Royal preferred to drink tea after his dinner and Margaret made him a special brew which he offered to share with me. Loving tea as I do, I accepted with pleasure only to be faced with the most delicate Lapsang Souchong, which I hated. But I wanted to impress Mr Royal who was arranging an audition for me, so I bravely swallowed a second cup and pretended it was delicious.

The audition needless to say was a disaster but John Royal, dear man that he was, saw that I received a beautifully gift-wrapped present as I left New York for California to stay with Pam and James. My eyes lit as I saw the size of the box, perfume for sure, or so I thought – what did this unexpected parcel contain? A huge tin of Lapsang Souchong tea! James, I have to admit, was very pleased to receive this delicacy, as it was, along with Earl Grey, his favourite breakfast drink.

But to return to the Masons in New York. They had been spending money freely, enjoying all that the Big Apple could provide, including several changes of address – all expensive – and they had quite a household to support. To augment his now rapidly-dwindling resources, James wrote articles for movie magazines and, as well as the radio work that came his way, tapped another small source of income by selling a few *objets d'art* which had come with his household goods from England. "James Mason's candlabra" attracted interested and eager buyers and several items were disposed of at somewhat inflated prices to those in whose eyes they had the extra virtue of having belonged to the renowned British actor. Fortunately Pam was able to contribute to their finances as well by having a hit with one of her books, *Del Palma*. Then a great stroke of luck came their way. A copy of *I Met A Murderer* was discovered in the possession of the distributing company which had originally "kidnapped" the film for exhibition in the USA. Their contracts had long expired and so James and Pam were able to arrange new deals for both the theatrical and television exhibition and received a very timely advance payment against their future income from their original investment. In fact the film was shown a number of times on US television but, as they didn't own a set, they didn't get to see it.

Still, money was pretty tight and James was increasingly anxious about his situation. His lack of self-confidence haunted him, and he became nervous that he might make a poor showing in the witness box when his case finally came to court, and that he would lose.

Mama went to New York to stay with Pam and James after Christmas 1947, crossing the Atlantic on the *Queen Mary* in the company of Kathleen Ferrier. It didn't take long for her to realise that money was a serious problem. Pam controlled the finances and she kept James very short of cash, using his absent-mindedness as the excuse. She was obviously worried about the state of their affairs and, when James wanted to send some money to his brother to help buy a bike for Christopher, his young nephew, Pam wouldn't have it. One day James and "Auntie-Mummy" (as he called Mama) went shopping together and he saw a fine Black Diamond cheese which he knew would please his father. "Dad will love that – I'll buy it for him," James enthused. But he found that he hadn't nearly enough money on him to pay for it, let alone the packing and postage, and neither had Mama, so they had to walk out of the shop without it. He was terribly disappointed, and probably not a little humiliated – the famous film star without a shilling in his pocket.

One sad incident marred their time in New York. Top Boy, James's much-loved cat, disappeared. The theory was that he had been stolen by a fan, but no one came forward in answer to James's pleas or offers of reward. He and Pam went through miseries worrying over the fate of the animal and, although they tried everything to discover what had happened to it, no news was forthcoming and eventually they had to concede that Top Boy was gone forever.

Then came the really difficult decision; should they remain in New York or should they make the trek to California? There were problems to face if they chose the latter, as no judgement had yet been handed down, and David E. Rose was in Los Angeles. James would find no welcome mat there pending the outcome of the court case . . . What should they do? They made their choice, California it was. Covertly they set off, first to Arizona where they remained for a short while, sending Johnnie Monaghan ahead to scout for a suitable house, discreetly tucked away from prying eyes, in Beverly Hills.

Monaghan's choice proved to be perfect, in so far as James could find solace in painting and enjoying the garden in privacy. He was to all intents and purposes a prisoner. He had to remain unsung and unseen, any indication that he was resident in California might have enabled David E. Rose to force the issue in his own favour, the laws governing litigation being as they were so different in each state.

For James it was a trial of nerves and he and Pam used the time to write a book about cats, with illustrations by James, their by now famous affection for felines having caught the imagination of his fans. They decided to write the book because every penny it earned was needed to maintain not only the human members of their household but also a not inconsiderable number of four-footed friends. How long James could have survived is anyone's guess. But as his bank balance shrank, just in time, the Judge's decision arrived. He had found in favour of James!

This was a godsend, but one that arrived at the eleventh hour. The matter of finding film work in Hollywood became urgent and there arose the problem finding the necessary good agent. William McCaffery had recommended one of the top men in the William Morris office, Abe Lastvogel, and James found this small genial man much to his liking. But Hollywood and James didn't hit it off to begin with, at least from the point of view of the Press. Quite unjustly James was accused of having made derogatory remarks about "Tinsel Town" before he ever set foot in the place. It was all because of an article he had written for the magazine *Cosmopolitan* while living in New York. Entitled *Why I am Afraid of Going to Hollywood*, it was a classic example of James's own odd sense of humour rebounding upon him. He had thought it quite amusing to take the rumours at that time abounding about life in Hollywood, and turn them into a reason for being wary of going there. But the Press misconstrued his meaning and accused him of smearing the image of the very place he was hoping to make his reputation in and now, no sooner was he free to take up his film career, he was being labelled not only uncooperative but blatantly anti-Hollywood. Poor James! He was so often misunderstood. His dry humour, his sly little jokes, were never malicious and always funny, but I think it was his delivery of his ideas that caused the misinterpretation of his words. Oddly enough, although he was well aware of the trouble it caused, he never quite learned how to avoid the consequences of his deadpan humour. It is interesting to note that the comedian he most admired was Buster Keaton.

However, James was deemed a box office success, and notwithstanding his controversial arrival in Hollywood, he was soon at work and proving his worth although, as he came to realize later, he made an error of judgement by taking parts which didn't make the most of his screen image as a dangerously seductive cad. The first film he made, *Caught*, was edited by a man who later became a good friend, the producer Robert Parrish.

ROBERT PARRISH

I first met James Mason when we were both working on a film directed by Max Ophuls. I was the film editor and James was one of the stars. Ophuls had a beautiful office at Enterprise Studio, where the film was being shot, but he spent very little time in it. When he had trouble on the set or with the executives and/or the producer, he would quietly slink up to my cutting room, where we kept a canvas director's chair, with the name "Max" printed on it, in the corner of the room, in front of the cans of film labelled "OUT TAKES". My assistant, Mike Luciano, and I wouldn't bother him and he wouldn't bother us. We all understood each other and liked each other. Sometimes he wouldn't say anything. He'd just sit there for a while, rubbing his bald head, and then go back to the set.

One day, after Max had had a serious disagreement with an actress about her make-up or her costume or the script or one of the many other things that directors and actors disagree on, Ophuls came to my cutting room, sat in "his" chair and started to rub his head. I was working on the Moviola, a noisy editing machine, and Mike was synchronising the previous day's rushes.

"I'm not here," said Ophuls.

"I'm not either," I said and went back to the Moviola.

"I'm here," said Mike, "and it's time for a coffee break." He went out to get three coffees.

"Why is this noisy room so peaceful for me?" said Ophuls.

"Because no one knows you're here," I said.

He rubbed his head some more and finally said, "What sequence are you working on?"

"The scene with James Mason and Robert Ryan," I said. "The one you shot last week."

"How is it?", he said.

"Very good." I said and went back to work. The clatter of the Moviola kept me from hearing Ophuls creep up behind me and look over my shoulder.

When the sequence finished, Ophuls said, "He's the best actor I've ever worked with."

"Which one?" I said.

"Mason," said Ophuls. "They're both good, but James is the best prepared, the easiest to work with, the most talented and the least trouble. I wish he were playing all the parts in every film I direct."

"Even the girl's parts?" I said.

"Especially the girl's parts," said Ophuls.

California provided probably the greatest surprise ever to hit the Mason household, – the advent of an unexpected baby, Portland Allen, born on the 25th November 1948. The change of environment had indeed surpassed all expectations!

Unlike her sister, Sheila, who had married a Canadian pilot during the war and always shown a desire to have a large family, Pam to my knowledge had never voiced such a wish. Children had not figured in the Masons' life at all until the birth of the baby girl who was to conquer their hearts.

Pam was determined to see that the baby fitted into their lives and their routine, and consequently Portland was brought up without a Nanny and outside the confines of what was termed a "normal timetable". When the Masons travelled, so did Portland: their hours were her hours; the usual strictures that applied to most children were not adhered to in her case and apparently she suffered no ill effects. On the contrary she was reared in an atmosphere of love and affection albeit, to most eyes, an unusual situation which gave rise to snide press reports.

She was in fact a sweet and happy little girl when I first met her in California in 1951. I had only very briefly seen her as a baby in Paris when James was staying at the Hotel Lancaster while working on a film there. Babies did not impress me I must admit – I found them far less attractive than small animals – but I was to grow very attached to Portland during my sojourn in Beverly Hills. We did not, I may add, always see eye to eye! I had occasion to question her table manners and her propensity to give a kick or a nip to the unsuspecting visitors who seemed unwilling to suggest that anyone corrected her. I did not fall into this category and informed James that I had a few ideas of my own as to what was acceptable behaviour from children – a few lessons were on my agenda! A kind but firm hand was the order of the day in my view, and both Pam and James were in accord, which came as quite a shock – I had anticipated them regarding me as an interfering maiden aunt. I was concerned for her because Portland was, contrary to media reports, an endearing child, bright and if precocious, not in an unpleasant way.

Both James and Pam were always in demand for work, James's schedule being particularly heavy. He had early calls and late nights and it was unavoidable that the child should sometimes find herself passed over. She sought, often fruitlessly, for attention in a household not geared to the needs of a small child.

She attended a first class nursery school run by a delightful and dedicated lady, a disciplinarian with a silken touch. The children played, had lessons, ate their lunch, rested, played some more and then home about 3.30 in the afternoon . . . Portland and I would then quite often sit in the vast living room having tea on our own together and watching TV while the house was invaded by cameras, lights, script writers, agents and so on – no one bothered us, the star was being besieged in his own home and everything was geared to this effect. Leisure time for James was in short supply, even dinner parties or in fact any gathering seemed to be given over to professional talk. Not surprising therefore for Portland to be found mixing at late night outings or being in the midst of adult company at the Masons' social events.

On one occasion I had noticed that their Alsatian bitch, Lady, was full of fleas and the housekeeper, Violet Taylor, told me that the animal hated going to the dog parlour. So, having had dogs all my life, I decided to look after the flea question myself and give Lady a good bath. But Portland accused me of being cruel to their pet and wept bitterly as I used the handspray gently on the dog, and I could see she was terribly upset. Fear lay at the root of it. She had been one of those "water babies" introduced to water at the earliest age possible – a scientific process which, I'm led to believe, gave many tiny tots a love of water and proved to be of health-giving properties. Not so for little "Portie". Aged three she would neither sit down in a bath or have her hair washed without a scene. I realised her distress would need very patient handling. As a visitor I should perhaps have refrained from such interference but as I considered myself family I decided to act. A bath ritual was established and after several weeks of bribery and unending chat the bonny wee blonde took to enjoying her ablutions and her silky fair hair looking more inviting to the touch. Fear was replaced by pleasure and I felt I had gained a small victory. Thereafter she acted as assistant groom for the de-fleaing operations.

Portland and I became very close during my stay and I have always

felt a deep affection for her, and incidentally, for her brother Morgan
too, but he was yet to come on the scene.

James gave as much time as he could to Portland, but he was so
caught up with the demands of his career he was unable to devote
himself as he would have wished to the small girl who was
increasingly the butt of a denigratory press.

Pam was able to take the spiteful innuendos more philosophically,
her own tongue could be both cutting and insensitive, so the
blathering inaccuracies in print left her unimpressed. She was very
much her father's daughter – a remark she won't thank me for but
it's true. She had a total disregard for the opinion of others; she
didn't care what they thought and she lacked sensitivity herself
towards other people, sometimes giving vent to her feelings under the
guise of speaking the truth. James suffered from these verbal attacks
as much as anyone. With regard to Portland, Pam felt justified in
bringing the child up by her own standards, and certainly there was
no shortage of love for her. I believe the trauma of Pam's own
childhood was at the root of her determination not to abdicate any
authority to a nanny or governess.

James, had he been less occupied by his career might, in my view,
have had greater qualms and been more inclined to regulate the
child's schedule, but time was scarce and he enjoyed the pleasure of
having Portland eat dinner with them and be available to sit with him
watching the showing of a film late in the evening. He retained a
gentle patience with the little girl, listening to her chatter, playing
with her, helping her with her painting or whatever else she was
doing, and she definitely enriched his life. California might not have
held him for so long had there been no child to consider, or at least
that is my belief.

Apart from Portland, I had been delighted to find Roy Kellino
living in Pam and James's guest house. When his second marriage
failed he had taken up their offer of a temporary home with them in
Hollywood while he tried to make his career, and a new life, in the
States. While awaiting his work permit he had taken on the not
inconsiderable job of painting the exterior of James's house. It
seemed like old times, as Roy and I had always been good friends,
and we spent much time together. Roy was finding the long wait for
his director's permit not only tiresome but expensive, as he enjoyed
life and was used to spending, if not lavishly, without having to count

1. The Mason family home – Croft House, Huddersfield.

2. James as a baby in 1909 with his brothers, Colin and Rex, and one of the Croft House lions.

3. 'Soldiers Three' – Rex, Colin and James in military costumes made by 'Muv'.

4. James as a teenager.
5. James in 1938 with Top Boy, the cat I gave him.
6. James the Varsity Man with 'Muv'.

7. A languid study of Pamela Kellino.

8. A publicity still of Pamela and James in a domestic setting.

9. Pamela and James on the farm, with more cats.

10. James with 'Wicked Lady' Margaret Lockwood in 1945.

11.

12.

11. A scene with Ann Todd in *The Seventh Veil*.
12. *Odd Man Out* (1946) was one of James's favourite films. Here he talks to Carol Reed, the director.

TC112- KB 50.

13.

13. James brought a dashing intensity to his role as a fugitive gunman in
Odd Man Out.

14.

15.

14. The psychological thriller *The Upturned Glass* gave James the opportunity to act with Pam (1947).

15. James and Pam with Johnnie Monaghan, in Hollywood in 1949.

the pennies. Now it was different and, just as James had found in New York, there were tempting restaurants, cabarets, bars and other places to visit and the lack of ready money cramped his style uncomfortably. Through an extraordinary sequence of events, Pam had been entrusted with a small sum by Roy's ex-wife, and she doled it out to him in very small amounts.

Roy's divorce from Sue had been amicable, if rather bizarre. Back in England they had tried to run Ollieberry Farm as a CountryClub, cashing in rather on the fame of its previous occupants, but they had run into difficulties and a wealthy widowed client had offered to settle their debts if Sue would leave Roy and marry him, as he needed a companion-cum-hostess. This pragmatic solution was adopted. Sue had different plans for the long term. She had sent Pam the money as a nest-egg against the day when she could leave her new husband and rejoin Roy! In fact she never did, but she authorised Pam to let Roy use the cash when he needed it.

Roy meanwhile annoyed Pam by falling in love with a good friend of hers. Later, he married Barbara, but at the time he upset Pam's plans for him and angered her by failing to exploit a situation very general in Hollywood – one of rich ladies hunting for, or hoping to attract, an eligible man to escort them and . . . we'll leave the rest unsaid!

Pam had two or three such women in tow, divorced, well-heeled and not unattractive. Roy would have proved a tasty morsel for them and his financial strictures would have disappeared, but by falling in love with Barbara he made himself unavailable, thereby earning Pam's irritation and James's plaudits. James felt, as I did, that after two ill-starred matrimonial adventures Roy deserved to find happiness with a woman of his own choice and we wished him "third time lucky", And so it proved. Probably the happiest years of his life were spent with Barbara. She was tall, elegant and charming, and an excellent actress. A divorcee with two sons, she and her mother had maintained their home under quite difficult circumstances but her boys were well brought up and extremely nice-natured. I well remember a lovely trip to Catalina with them where we all enjoyed the glass-bottomed boats gliding over the water, the square dancing in the streets and all the pleasures of what might have been a good old English seaside holiday – but with the inestimable advantages of reliable sunshine! Sadly their life together was cut short when Roy died suddenly, in his early fifties. His death came as a terrible shock to us all. Barbara, I am glad to say, has married again and I believe built a happy and successful career – she deserves a good life.

In the Mason home, 1018 Beverly Drive, there was every comfort. James had been thrilled to discover that it had been built for Buster Keaton – his hero of the silent era. Keaton had designed it himself and by Hollywood standards it was an old, almost historic house. A Spanish-style building, it had both grandeur and an elegant simplicity of line. Downstairs there was a magnificent lounge, a library, projection room, dining room, office, bar, powder room, kitchens, store-room, freezer and laundry rooms, all spacious and beautifully planned, and a really elegant curved staircase sweeping up from the stately entrance hall. Upstairs there were five bedrooms with bathrooms en suite, and Pam's lobby and dressing-room. Everywhere was light and airy, except for the dining room. This was the one rather dark place, due in no small way to the decor at the time. It offered a relief from the constant streaming sunshine that reminded me so forcibly of my home on the Cote d'Azure. But there, in time-honoured French fashion, we closed our shutters and moved about in shaded half light.

The garden was a shambles and needed prompt attention so, with Roy to back me up, I appealed to Pam to let me go to a nursery and at least bed out the front of the house which had four or five "Cartwheel" beds bordered by tiny privet hedges but no plants. The front needed "dressing" as did a couple of side borders. My idea was to start small and gradually get permission to lash out and buy big items for the back garden, which sloped down to the pool area and the fruit orchard. James was hard at work at the time and when at home, he was a constant target for photo calls, meetings and so on, so without too much thought he and Pam gave me the go-ahead and I could start planting. I bought huge cedarwood tubs and Helen Traubel roses for each side of the entrance, a galaxy of bedding plants and spent, without as much as a blink, several hundred dollars! But that was not the real expense – plants need water and water was metered, you paid for what you used. When James saw the bill he nearly collapsed – not only had he, Pam, Roy and Violet Taylor, devoted hour upon hour helping me in the garden, but sprinklers, hoses, watering cans had been used and without stint – worse still, many of the smaller geraniums, bought by the yard, had been gobbled up by the gophers, nice little creatures in reality but unhelpful when one is trying to justify a considerable outlay. I can't say James was amused by my first attempt at improving the look of 1018, but he soon saw the fruit of our endeavours and agreed that the garden had repaid, in kind, the water rate!

In spite of my activities in the garden, James and Pam were concerned that I should enjoy my stay with them, and they integrated me into their Hollywood life. One of the first things James arranged for me on my arrival in Hollywood was a meeting with Frank Loesser – Danny Kaye was about to start recording the songs for the film *Hans Christian Andersen* and Moira Shearer, who was to play opposite him, was to have a "voice match" for the singing parts. Frank agreed that I should sing for her, which meant a duet or two with Danny and a haunting little song by the Matchgirl. Unfortunately for me, Moira Shearer was pregnant and her part went to Roland Petit's wife Zizi Jeanmaire and my voice no longer matched – I was cheated!

Nevertheless I had the great pleasure of meeting Frank and Danny, who was the nicest person imagineable to work with and really made me feel at ease. His wife Sylvia Fine was an enormously talented woman who understood better than anyone Danny's absolute genius for communicating with an audience and she was responsible for most of his original material. It was not always an easy marriage, as gossip implied he had a roving eye, but with women falling like ninepins at his feet it was little wonder.

I met most of James and Pam's friends at the constant round of parties that we attended. Groucho Marx, whom I met for the first time at a huge party, I heartily disliked. He kept picking on one unfortunate man who sat at our table of about eight. The man in question was a relative of the famous Barrymore family, a great big fellow with a propensity for drink, and no weapon to protect himself against Groucho's tongue which, although very funny, was always funny at someone else's expense. I was not appreciative and he soon saw the look of disapproval on my face. Groucho was accompanied by a lovely young girl who sat doll-like by his side while he taunted his unfortunate victim. It was a very uncomfortable meal, and when eventually he looked me in the eye Groucho said, "I guess you don't like me very much," or words to that effect.

My reply came out like a shot from a gun due to my surprise at being spoken to by this doyen of Hollywood comedians. "No, I don't like you at all," I replied, "You are rude and spiteful and in my view, not amusing." Thank God the meal was nearly over and I could escape.

I told Pam and James what had occurred and I feared I would cause them some upset. Although I was normally polite enough, I hate seeing anyone victimised. Pam shrugged off the episode casually. "Don't worry Diana, these soirees are generally given by people we hardly know – they are mainly newcomers to Hollywood, very rich, very spoilt and their status has to be confirmed by the array of stars who accept their invitations. The Studios pressure people to attend some of these 'glittering' parties because it's good press coverage. James and I do our stint if we think it will be fun, or we happen to know who's do it is."

I was mollified until I asked James if he knew the host of this particular event – "Frank Loesser," he replied. I felt awful because Frank had been so nice to me. His pianist Lydia, a brilliant lady, had helped me relax at the first rehearsals we had with Danny Kaye, and I hadn't even realised that it was his party we were attending.

As I said, James and Pam went to great lengths to make me feel at home in the nine months I stayed with them. I was included in all the party invitations they received and they encouraged me to invite my own friends to any functions held at 1018. Several of my war-time chums were already in Hollywood and, as I gradually settled into a routine existence, my circle enlarged – specifically amongst the musicians from the orchestras employed by the big studios. The composer Miklos Rozsa and his English wife Margaret became close friends, as did Prima and Ray Sinatra (an excellent musician who was Frank's cousin) and we made music together on many occasions. The Rozsas rekindled my memories of home in France as they slowly but surely replanned their lovely house on the top of a Hollywood hillside, importing marble from Italy for the floors and placing statues in the garden. They were transforming several acres of land, and I hoped that Margaret wouldn't encounter the same shocked horror over the water bill as I had with James!

Pam, most bravely, bore with several evenings of chamber music at 1018 but, quintets, quartets, Ravel, Debussy, Faure and Borodin were not her idea of bliss. James however seemed to enjoy the programmes and Portland became ecstatic.

James, at my request, invited several stars whom I admired and wished to meet – Burt Lancaster, Gregory Peck, George Sanders, Van Heflin and several others, but as I was not a great movie buff and knew little about the process of film-making I found it both fascinating and tedious when James arranged for me to visit the studios. How anyone managed intimate scenes surrounded by arc lights, microphones and cynical hard bitten professional crews I'll never know – I learnt a salutory lesson in respect for both the artists and the technicians. I must admit that James found my attitude towards his films amusing, but as he rightly said, not very flattering. My preferred artists were French, those on whom I had been brought up, Louis Jouvet, Jean Gabin, Jean Marais, Edwige Feuilleure, Simone Simon, Fernandel and Jacques Tati, and later the gorgeous Brigitte Bardot and Alain Delon. I had to admit to James that I had (and have) seen only a fraction of his movies, *The Desert Fox* and *20,000 Leagues Under the Sea* being two of my favourites.

The Hollywood film stars themselves were intelligent and charming, at least, those I met and those who made up James's immediate circle. George Sanders, for instance, played the piano beautifully and had a very good light baritone voice and a well-developed wit. And, without giving the wrong impression, he had the best legs in Hollywood – of which he was very proud. He was careful to keep them in good shape.

Zsa Zsa Gabor, George's then wife, was sensational, and she and her mother Jolie and her sisters Eva and Magda made up a family of real beauties. I remember Zsa Zsa with affection mainly because she not only pleased the eye but she had a capacity to send herself up! Her "entrances" at parties were a triumph of self-presentation. Gorgeously attired with generous decolletage to draw the eyes of the cynical but lascivious men of power in the movie world, she appeared like some fabulous butterfly, adorned richly but always with good taste, her European chic very much to the fore, enticing and flirtatious but a woman who under all the glitter was of a kindly nature.

Her house in Bel Air was quite perfect, the garden tended and planted just as I hoped one day to see Pam and James's cultivated. Subtly lit at night it owed as much to art as it owed to vegetation, and I think Zsa Zsa ordered her household with a precision and competence which her image might not necessarily lead one to expect.

On one occasion when we were invited for dinner, Hedda Hopper was one of the guests, she looked at me with utter disdain and turned to James to remark in a loud voice, "You can see she's an opera singer," James looked bemused but I knew what she meant – FAT!

James wouldn't have noticed my shape in a hundred years so I engaged her personally – "In Italy we sopranos tend to be well upholstered – we are judged on our voices rather than sizes." I was rewarded with a snort and a steely look so I continued, "It's interesting though how some people seem to advertise their trade, for instance you and Louella Parsons look typical hard-eyed, tough gossip columnists."

She never addressed another word to me all evening, which was no loss. I had been brought up to believe if you had nothing to say, say nothing, and gratuitous rudeness needs putting in its place. James had occasion to deal with one or two "monsters" who prided themselves on having sharp and scandalous tongues and he acquitted himself amazingly well – he had a turn of phrase which owed not a little to his cultural background and left many a disgruntled yob wishing he had kept his mouth shut.

Van Heflin was a dear man, albeit rather prone to overfill his glass whilst telling me he no longer had a drink problem. His wife was an extremely attractive woman and great friends with Pam. Burt Lancaster was a charmer, very handsome in a rugged way, highly intelligent and from what I heard rather a tough adversary. He had also a sharp eye for a pretty woman although he seemed to have a very secure marriage.

Ava Gardner and Frank Sinatra were regular callers at James's home, and close friends of them both – I know Pam and James were to have been witnesses to their marriage but if I remember correctly something intervened. The relationship between Frank and Ava was extremely stormy and occasionally a bust-up would enforce a change of plan. Although they would always get back together again, James once remarked to me that too much passion could be destructive, and certainly in this case there were two strong personalities. Frank had a hot Italian temper, but contrary to the criticisms of others, he was a very kind and generous man.

I remember one particularly enjoyable trip we made during this first stay in Hollywood, to La Jolla in California to see Gregory Peck at work in the Playhouse Theatre there. The glorious drive along the coast reminded me very much of the beauties of the Cote d'Azure. The red rocks of Carmel (a spot much loved by artists), the untamed wildness of the landscape, the colour of the sea and the stillness of the air brought back all the happy memories of pre-war France. The atmosphere was very professional towards the work of the theatre there itself, but very informal and friendly when relaxing over a meal or at parties.

Sadly it was in this pleasant setting that I had an unfortunate encounter with a famous movie producer whose name I best not mention, which gives an indication of Hollywood's sexual climate. One evening at dinner after the theatre, I was seated not far from him, on the opposite side of the table. The usual topic of conversation at these gatherings was sex, and I had noticed that many men in Hollywood seemed to brag unendingly about their prowess in bed and how many times they could perform, which always left me feeling that they were either totally impotent or certainly incompetent because, in my own little experience, men who can deliver don't then talk about it. So, as I ate in an atmosphere blue with alleged achievement, the producer suddenly said "You know what I find absolutely tremendous – Benzedrine makes you really good in the sack." This was intriguing, and as I looked at him I noticed that his eyes looked rather peculiar and somewhat dilated.

I jumped in with a response: "But surely, if it doesn't happen naturally, it can't be worth happening at all. It's like flogging a dead horse!" There was a ghastly silence. Murderous looks bored into me. Should I have kept silent? No. I had reacted to a situation that was to me idiotic. Here was a middle-aged man, taking Benzedrine tablets, or the equivalent, to make him capable of having a screw, which is the charming word I learnt from this encounter. To me sex was rather mysterious, and hopefully, wrapped in some sort of romanticism. Here the opposite held true. Everyone discussed it as though you were taking vitamins for breakfast or dinner, but with an unattractive childish tone. There was none of the traditional comic coarseness of English jokes: this was a ruthless competitive sport.

I soon learned not to be surprised by the tales that were passed around the dinner tables for general consumption and amusement. An English actor of note told a story against himself, about a very well-known glamorous star who prided herself on saying that no man had ever been able to satisfy her physically. He accepted the challenge and said to himself, "Hell, she's not only extremely beautiful, but I'm rather a lad myself so I shall certainly do what others have failed to do."

But, having made an assignation in Paris where they were to meet, he began to feel a little anxious about his prowess, so he asked a doctor if there was anything that could be prescribed to enhance his performance. Obligingly, the medic gave him a stimulant of a dubious sort. He read the instructions and he thought, "Oh yes, take one or two --- well, I don't know. This man-eater is going to be *very* demanding – I'd better be sure, I'll double the dose," – which he did. And to his horror, when he got to the hotel, he passed out. I though it was rather charmingly told and everyone enjoyed the joke.

I would be misleading you if I implied that all Hollywood parties were like *that*. Some were much more genteel. The Hollywood stars with families established a custom of Sunday parties for their children. The parents played tennis, swam, or just sat around chatting while the children played together. Our Sunday children's parties included Deborah Kerr's girls, the Wanger children, Danny Kaye's little girl Dena, and Geraldine and Josephine Chaplin. Josephine was Portland's best friend and she was a sweet little creature who always had her strict nanny in attendance. From England, Max Bygraves and his family were welcome guests and the focus of a very dramatic event. James, Max and Frank Sinatra were chatting together by the pool when James became aware that Max's five year old son, Anthony, was in difficulties in the water. The little boy had caught his leg in an inflatable lifebelt and couldn't extricate himself. James, without hesitation, plunged into the pool fully clothed and saved the child from drowning.

Charles Laughton would sometimes visit, and he was often included in the Sunday tea. I found him charming. James had worked with him at the Old Vic Theatre in London in the very early days of his career, when Charles was already a star in his own right, and they always got on well. Charles was a shy man, aware that he had an ungainly heavy body and that he was not "fair of face". But what a voice! What a talent! Sadly, it was obvious how easily he could be hurt, as on one scorching day he decided to take a dip in the pool.

"I'm no swimmer," he told me, "I like the shallow end."

"Me too! Don't apologise." I replied. "I cling to the sides, water terrifies me, so let's go in together."

I was first in the water surrounded by wildly splashing children but as Charles walked slowly down the steps breasting the water I heard one little girl squeal. "Isn't he ugly, isn't he fat!" Never in my life have I seen a person blush so red. It seemed to rise from his breast upwards. I felt sick for him. A thoughtless remark, albeit made by a child, had hurt and embarrassed this gentle person for whom we all had enormous admiration and liking. He bravely swam for a little while but he never again entered our pool.

Everywhere, one was reminded of Hollywood's obsession with beauty, and the demands of the camera and the public offer little respite to those whose features or figure set them outside the norm. It offers compensations in many cases for those willing and able to play "character parts" but it cannot assuage the feelings of those who are made to feal freakish by reason of their physical attributes. Thank heaven I was a singer at a time when beauty of sound was the essential – if you couldn't fill the concert hall with vocal talent and volume then ply your trade elsewhere.

Fortunately sadness such as that was a very rare visitor. My memories are, in the main, of nicer times. A tea-time treat, very popular on these Sunday afternoons, was a special banana cake made by our part-time cook. A grand Scottish lady who had, until her retirement, been Glenn Ford's housekeeper, Aggie was also famous for her cheesecake, even better than the world renowned Jack Dempsey one, which was sent to all corners of the Globe. If Aggie had marketed her two specialities she would have been a million-airesswithout doubt, but as she hadn't done so, we were the beneficiaries of her talent. This celebrated cake was a test of self-discipline for all the stars – I know many found it a temptation – and James was no exception. He imposed a very strict dietary regime on himself, rarely indulging in any deviation of his eating habits – a typical days intake would consist of the following.

James's Diet

Breakfast: Two thin slices of wholemeal toast with either orange or grapefruit marmalade – Earl Grey tea.

Lunch: when home – salad and cottage cheese, a piece of fruit or a nibble of cheese, and a *very* small glass of red wine.

Tea: If at all, consisted of tea and possibly a biscuit or sliver of cake.

Dinner: Depending on where but usually a fish or meat dish, plenty of vegetables, fruit or cheese, a little wine.

James was a strictly disciplined eater and drinker which proved fortunate as the camera is notorious for adding inches onto already slim figures and quickly blurring the contours or bone structures of the faces. The high cheek bones, that were so characteristic of the Mason features, had to be kept sharp and clear, and James was able, unlike so many of his contemporaries, to maintain both his looks and his health on a Spartan diet augmented by vitamin tablets freely dispensed by Pam, who ate very little herself but kept a hidden horde of Hershey Bars in her bedroom.

One particularly lovely lady, Lena Horne, whom James adored, was as strict with herself as anyone could be. To watch her, poured into some magnificent gown, beautiful to see and hear, could give one no idea as to the sacrifices she made so as to be the perfect performer. James told me that if she felt really hungry she would eat some cucumber! We went many times to see her at the Ambassadors Club in Los Angeles, and also at the Olympia in Paris, and I marvelled at her vitality and energy. James always said he loved her for her artistry and dedication to her work, but I believe it was her sheer physical beauty that captured his senses first and foremost.

The price some people pay for fame and fortune is a high one. James sometimes discussed with me the careers that he had seen ruined by the demands of the profession. One instance brought it home to me. Lunching at Twentieth Century Fox's studios with James, I noticed that two stars, (one was Judy Garland) had studied the menu for quite a while and then given their order. When the food arrived I looked to see what had taken their fancy. Whatever it was they wanted, they got thin vegetable broth and a salad!

I thought one of them was about to cry, the disappointment on her face was painful to see. I hissed to James that she looked like a child deprived of a visit to Santa Claus. James laughed. "Common practice, Diana, whenever someone finishes a film the wardrobe people keep a dummy figure in readiness for the next fittings – if you don't fit the measurements, it's bread and water, or as you see, broth and salad."

I gathered this order only applied to contracted artists and not to those who were freelance. Nevertheless, stars and their figures had to be perfect. I heard on more than one occasion the most unflattering, crude remarks being made about stars by producers and directors about their breasts or bottoms, often in front of the embarrassed stars themselves. It really was a cattle market. There was no place for thin skins, and it was no wonder that girls seeking their fortunes more often than not returned home wiser and sadder.

James was luckier than most. A naturally moderate man, he could adapt himself to any form of discipline and not be out of humour as a result. He applied himself wholeheartedly to whatever demands were made, and I think that his education and intellect made it easier for him to cope than was the case in many instances, when men or women achieved instantaneous success or notoriety.

When he was not filming James and I would usually lunch together. Being no great socialiser I enjoyed our quiet meals, and during our conversations I gained an insight into the myth that fame and money equals happiness – cash solves many problems, sets people free of many constrictions but peace of mind lies beyond a bank balance. Certainly in James's case this proved to be so. For Pam, it was different – her personna was geared to a more materialistic view. Being rich, being famous provided her with a sense of well-being, gave her a confidence that she was lacking previously – she has, as I have already stated, very often been misjudged, because of her manner and way of speaking, but she was at one time a very insecure and vulnerable girl. America changed all that and she came into her own, like a flower opening to the sun. On James, America had the opposite effect. On the plus side his professionalism increased as did his earnings. His prestige gained him opportunities to work with those he most admired and respected, but the atmosphere in general left him alienated.

On one occasion James took me to task – he was teasing but for a moment or so I was taken in by what seemed his stern and serious manner. "Diana," he said at lunch, "what makes you try so hard to keep the US postal services in profit?"

What did he mean? I must have looked puzzled because he continued, "Dede," (she was his secretary) "tells me that you load her down with mail virtually every day." James was not smiling.

"You double-dyed vixen," I thought to myself, Dede and I were friendly and I enjoyed her company – a very erudite lady who enjoyed many of the same pastimes as I – concerts at the Hollywood

Bowl, drive in cinemas, etc. "Dede told you what?" I sensed a
crinkling around his mouth and a small chuckle escaped him.

"Seriously Diana – How can you write a letter each day to Auntie
Mummie? What news can you have?" "We hold conversations
together, on paper", I explained, "always have done, ever since I
began my travels during the war. It wasn't always possible to post
letters then, but I wrote each day, a kind of diary, and either posted it
or took it home for Mama to read as I set off again."

James began to laugh now in earnest. "You thought I was serious
didn't you?" He seemed delighted to have caught me out, "I'm only
teasing."

The beast! But I decided to remind him that although I may have
been costing him something in stamps he, in fact, owed me dollars
galore.

"I do? What for?"

Now it was my turn. "How many visits have we made to that book
shop in the village? How many times have we nipped into Blum's?
And how many times have you borrowed money from me to pay the
bill?"

Poor James. He sat, downcast, a look of concern on his face – it
was true. He never had any cash, or at any rate enough – Pam doled
out pocket money but none too freely because she said he was so
absent-minded he lost everything!

James was absent-minded but Pam encouraged it by playing on his
vague attitude. Consequently James remained ill-equipped to cope
with daily trivialities. "Have you a handkerchief, a comb, your
driving licence?" and so on. He would be cross-examined, and
generally found to be minus at least two essentials. He never took
umbrage at being treated like a schoolboy and in truth I never saw
him lose his temper – he might show irritation, even bewilderment
and hurt if Pam was too impatient, but he had a remarkably equable
disposition.

One marked characteristic, seemingly at odds with his otherwise
gentle temperament, was his determination to win, chess, tennis or
whatever, if there was competition. Even when playing with the
children, James liked to come first. He could in truth be ruthless as he
had shown when usurping Roy's position, and he could show
harshness in his dealings with those people who failed to earn his
respect.

There is a consensus of opinion that his long association and marriage to Pam was not favourable to his career but one must never forget that they spent many happy and fruitful years together – their very different characters complemented each other, and there can be no doubt that Pam did everything possible to further James's career according to her own lights and values.

It is possible that left to take his own line and make his own choices, James might well have become a true star of the theatre as well as in films, but the fact is that in his early days, although he had all the commitment necessary to succeed, he was tentative, self-deprecatory and very shy. It would have taken an enormous effort on his part to push and thrust his way forward without the backing of a strong and self-willed personality such as Pam. Pam and James were still, at this stage, devoted to each other, but they had diametrically opposed interests and lifestyles.

Pam, to whom rising in the morning had always been disagreeable to say the least, came alive by mid afternoon and was in her element until the early hours of the following morning. She detested sport, had little, if any, interest in painting, ballet or opera – apart from any personal involvement, even the theatre and certainly the classical repertoire, left her cold. She was on her own admission an iconoclast – where art was concerned she accepted that James felt differently, and she attended galleries and performances, so as to please him. Even so, visits to Paris, or even Venice, failed to delight her!

"Had I known America existed when I was a little girl," she told Mama on one occasion, "I would have walked there immediately." I think she was right. "Tinsel Town" was her natural home and everything American proved a delight and opened a new vista for her. It fired her own ambition to be renowned in her own right, not just as a "handler" of a great star, a role which in England had satisfied her need for power.

James was well established when he made the move to America, and in California Pam's control of his career was, if not superfluous, certainly less important. She remained his mentor but she, perhaps for the first time in her life, found a freedom to express herself that hitherto she had channelled through James. In England, rightly or wrongly, she had always felt under attack which made her defensive, and many people judged her to be aggressive, which was not the case. Pam had two faces – one she presented to the world as tough, rude and pretty vitriolic when provoked. The other was what I term her "Cleopatra" side – womanly, seductive, kittenish and vulnerable. It is difficult to balance the two sides of her character, but therein lies the psychological hurt of her childhood.

Neither James or I were greatly taken with big social gatherings, but Pam sparkled and scintillated even if, as was often the case, she didn't much care for the company. At home it was different because the Masons invited their chosen friends. Some guests were "duty", in that they were important for careers, but in the main our parties were very much pleasure events.

Years later Pam admitted to me that she had decided to cut out these costly events because she found them tedious and unnecessary. I think when James had departed 1018 in 1961 everything changed to some extent. Pam had no need to promote herself, she had her group of buddies, and her own career to work on – but, when I first visited their home James was a big name and therefore much in demand, and everyone who considered themselves high up the social scale wished to have him in their circle. I think all the British contingent found it amusing to see vastly expensive parties given, with cabarets, champagne flowing, and a carefully selected guest-list quickly leaked to the local press for prestige purposes. Michael Rennie and his wife Maggie used to laugh at this with James. Interestingly, Michael had a vocabulary unsurpassed for "blueness", but he was a very amusing and nice man, and struck me as very natural and honest.

In truth, apart from one or two horrors, I found nearly all those I met via the Masons to be extremely genuine people – but many actors of both sexes struck me as being very insecure, afraid of losing their looks or their ratings, and they were very much at the mercy of the Studios' overlords and their minions, and also their own agents. The pressures must have been extreme so no wonder marriages broke down, no wonder affairs were embarked upon. Drink and drug problems were just part of the escape route.

How well James fitted into this world rather amazed me – had I perhaps misread his character? I didn't think so at the time, and later, as the years slipped by, I realised he didn't really fit in, though he went through the motions of trying to adapt to all that was alien to him. And he did have one lasting need to give him the necessary resilience, one that remained with him throughout his career. That was the need to be working, the drive to improve, which made him seek perfection. He was always honing his performance. Parts, good, bad or indifferent, were all cogs in the driving force that beset him. I think the key to Happiness for him was synonymous with work, particularly as personal happiness was taking a walk, a long walk outside.

Very few people will know that James suffered an extremely irritating and disfiguring skin complaint which affected his hands. It caused him great embarrassment, too, as it made his hands horny and rough. At home, when using various prescribed ointments he wore cotton gloves to protect the skin, but it was a scourge from which he gained little relief over many years. I sometimes wondered if his diet had caused an allergic condition but I maintained silence – my views would not have been well received by the Hollywood doctors, many of whom had left me unimpressed, as they seemed more than unduly interested in their fees to the detriment of their patients.

Whilst staying with James, I would often accompany him to the traditional exuberant and excessive festivities that made up the Hollywood calendar. Film premieres particularly were rather special events. Imagine the scene – red carpet from the kerb to foyer of whichever cinema was the venue for the night; stands, smaller but similar to those now to be found at golfing tournaments, erected on each side, packed by fans who had waited patiently for hours for a sight of their favourite performers; limousine after limousine disgorging lovely women, dressed gloriously, attended by bronzed and sleek-looking men in tuxedos, to be greeted with screams of delight from the waiting crowd; flash bulbs popping; newspaper men scuttling to and fro; the bosses of the movie industry with huge cigars and the prettiest nymphets hanging on their arms as they stood, puffed up with importance, watching with hard expressions who arrived with whom – they often showed their teeth but rarely did a smile reach their eyes!

For me it was an intriguing atmosphere, all part of a fabulous unknown world, but for James it was just a chore to be undertaken as part and parcel of his profession. He much preferred to dine at home and enjoy a film afterwards shown from the projection room above his library, and I suppose, once the novelty wears off, public appearances can become a tedious duty. One person I met through

James, who never lost interest in being on display, was Joan Crawford. A fabulous-looking woman whose legendary love of her fans surpassed the line of duty to an amazing degree, she would, according to authoritative gossips, appear at a premiere in great splendour and remain signing autographs throughout the evening, foregoing the performance so as not to disappoint her public. I gather that she never left a fan letter unanswered which, in view of her popularity, must have been some feat. As ambition and I have always been strangers, I cannot, or should not, make a judgement. I can only hope that those who are so driven achieve a modicum of contentment and happiness.

Nevertheless I must admit that my days in Hollywood were pure enjoyment – rubbing shoulders with the great and glamorous was fun and, thanks to Pam and James, I had the opportunity of enjoying the company of marvellous people. In 1950/51 there was a lack of eligible males which made life difficult for the ladies who had either parted from, or mislaid their husbands or lovers – but luckily I was never short of men friends as many of my wartime friends were now in Hollywood.

If Pam and James opted out of any parties, I and a couple of escorts would hotfoot to whoever was throwing the thrash and indulge in an orgy of entertainment. Mind you, I always wrote a "thank you" note to the hosts even though I'm quite sure it meant little or nothing to whichever social secretary had organised the soiree. Nevertheless it salved my conscience because if my friends were small-part actors they had in all probability been on enforced diets for several weeks whilst waiting for their next job, and the overflowing buffets that were provided meant they could enjoy a slap up meal, which if it didn't make them ill, would ease their empty stomachs until I could grab another invitation.

Those of my friends who were established had the loveliest houses, (even the small ones were beautifully planned) and so attractive that I was at one time tempted to become a Californian. Claire Bloom, Paul Gregory, Ray and Prima Sinatra, Hayden Rorke, Mikki and Maggie Rozsa and some of my friends from England, all tempted me to remain in Hollywood and possibly, had Pam and James's marriage not dissolved into such a maelstrom of anger and bitterness, my mother and I might have decided to remain in Hollywood when we next visited in 1959.

With hindsight I'm glad though that we never moved from Europe. My roots are too deeply embedded in the culture of my childhood and I find myself less and less sympathetic to the values of America, apart from which I hate sunshine! The rain of Wales and Ireland sing siren songs to my ears and the East Winds that blow around my small home on the Sussex Downs are all I could wish for in my old age. But the USA gave me many happy times, and I am grateful for the memories which in turn, I owe to Pam and James.

On each occasion that I went to the States I was at a crossroads in my life, when decisions had to be taken on complex issues – the time that I spent luxuriating in Hollywood gave me the opportunity to think, quietly and without pressure. Whether I made the right decision is open to question but I, like James, felt that home was where the heart is and my heart was definitely in Europe.

There were two men in Hollywood who struck me as being very much European in their attitudes, one being the fabulously handsome Greg Bautzer, whose good looks sat easily upon him, and I was told that he had escorted every well-known beauty at one time or another. He was a famous attorney, impeccably dressed with manners to match, and to any woman he spoke with, he gave his full attention, an attribute he may well have cultivated so as to inspire confidence in his clients. Whatever the reason it made a nice change from the not unusual habit of many a predatory male who, I observed, would engage their objective of the moment in conversation but continue scanning every new arrival in case they could find better pickings.

I saluted Greg Bautzer though for a very different reason – suddenly faced with this paragon of male beauty, I blurted out that I had once read all about him in *Picturegoer* when at school, "All my school friends simply drooled over you – of course we were all very young!" Can you imagine? Did I say I was gauche? Idiotic is nearer the truth – there was I, aged twenty-nine, telling Adonis that he had been a heart-throb all those years before. I could have fallen through the floor in shame, but I need not have worried – he neither looked aggrieved nor did he disengage himself at the double. Instead we had a very interesting discussion on the role of the Catholic Church, and he ended by offering to take me to Mass on Sundays as I didn't drive. Now that's what I call a lovely man!

The other was perhaps a lesser charmer, Mario Lanza – he was a frequent visitor to Prima and Ray Sinatra's home, where he could consume a mountain of food and many pints of beer whilst telling me of the horrors of dieting! He was going through a difficult time vocally and I think eating was a kind of crutch, but one which brought even more problems. As his weight went up, so the Studios nagged him to lose excess poundage. His voice, a naturally fine instrument although undisciplined, refused to function as he wished, and a vicious circle developed.

He told me that his great ambition was to sing at La Scala in a production of *Francesca da Rimini*, an opera never very popular and without putting too fine a point, hard to cast and a bloody sight harder to sing. Frankly I could not see any of the great conductors such as de Sabata, Cantelli, Capuana or Serafin indulging this young man whose musicianship was below standard and whose vocal capacity could not compare with di Stephano, del Monaco, Corelli or those who were at the height of their fame in Italy at this period. Mario Lanza could sing, but where was the elegance of Tito Schipa, the art of Gigli or the quality of Bjorling? No, he was just a singing film star. No doubt they too get hot under the arc lights but it does not compare with the sweat shed in the opera house, where the audience is as quick to condemn as it is to applaud. Anyone who knows the enthusiasm or the dislike of Italian audiences, or the freezing non-applause of the French, will know what I mean. Mariano Stabile, possibly the greatest ever Falstaff, told me in Milan how he, as his voice declined with age, had learned to use his gestures, movements, and his *mezza voce* to point and dramatise important moments. This was the art Lanza had yet to learn, and sadly he never reached that moment. A short career, spoilt by too much success in a medium which can cover one's faults too readily and left him prey to excesses which shortened his life.

To have believed one's own publicity can be a pretty heavy burden once it's proved to be a myth – the public can be fickle and changeable and therefore the build up of a star can be as easily destroyed as a fizzled out firework. A rising or falling rocket? Whichever it is, it takes courage to face the consequences.

Some of the great singers I was privileged to hear, Cigna, Caniglia, Pagliughi, Eva Turner, Sheridan and Carosio (the greatest Violetta I have ever heard) had all magnificent voices, but this alone never obviated the need to work, work, work. Every performance demanded the utmost effort, and those like Tebaldi, Sutherland, Norman, the legendary Callas, all had to sweat their guts out, and make many sacrifices to maintain their voices and their health, so as to in turn keep their places in the forefront of their profession.

In this age of a cheque book society the rewards are great, but so are the penalties for failure and it can be sad to see those who, for whatever reasons, fall by the road as they fight to hang on to a faltering position.

A very different man, who had a mastery of artistry, was Walter Pidgeon. He was no longer young when I met him, but although he was best known as an actor (and I gather considered a real ladies' man) he sang extremely well and used his voice with great charm and musicianship. Another fine singer was Robert Preston whom I met in New York an excellent actor who much later played with James in *Child's Play*, and who James swore was responsible for his own fine performance in that film. Walter Pidgeon and Robert Preston both told me that they had begun their careers in musicals and certainly it was quite apparent that they had been well trained, whereas from what he implied to me, Mario Lanza was a "natural", i.e. untrained, singer which would have explained some of his difficulties.

Whilst on the subject of song, James himself liked to sing – he often worried about his voice, which after all was a tool of his trade, but when he was relaxed or just playing around he could produce some very nice sounds. His feel for words was apparent in his occasional poetry readings, and I'm convinced that had he been given the chance to perform in a musical he would have achieved his great ambition. James as the king of a musical! Why not? All he lacked was the confidence and belief in himself to really try for it.

Some people have said they found James emotionally cold, but they did not know him as I did. Certainly they could never have observed him applauding those artists with whom he felt an affinity. He may have found it difficult to give open displays of affection, but cold he was not. With many of his closest friends, people like the directors and producers he had worked with and admired: Max Ophuls; Robert Siodmak; Jean Negulesco; Joe Mankiewicz; Walter Wanger; Robert Parrish and so on, the warmth of his personality and charm showed plainly. They, I am quite certain, would not have labelled him "a cold, austere Englishman" as did those who could not get close.

I could not argue, however, with those who found James difficult to get to know. He could be stiff, unbending and aloof, but this cool exterior masked his innate shyness. Until quite late in his life he defended himself against people and situations of which he was uncertain with a protective armour of coldness, and he was often criticised for being arrogant or condescending. But unless he was relaxed and among friends he was not an easy conversationalist, nor was he one to suffer fools gladly. An authority on his own profession he was exacting in his demands towards others, but he was also generous in his praise for those whose professionalism he admired, even if he didn't particularly like them as people. Certainly he was gracious towards his leading ladies with, perhaps I should add, a few well-deserved exceptions.

His feelings for his fellow artists were very apparent. John Woolf and the late Laurence Harvey were attending a party at 1018 given by James and Pam before the Academy Awards were to be dispensed, and both men were in great form because they had been led to expect that their film *Room At the Top* would sweep the board that night. If James had any suspicion that they were to be disappointed, he said nothing. At all events he was highly delighted when Simone Signoret was given her Oscar for the best supporting actress in that film, and I was equally pleased, having admired her and her husband, the highly talented Yves Montand, for many years. But my friend Mikki Rozsa had hinted to me that *Ben Hur* was most likely to reap the main honours on this occasion, with him personally about to be rewarded with his third Oscar for the music, so I too kept silent. But the acute disappointment felt by Laurence Harvey when he didn't get his Oscar was painful to see, and greeted with real and genuine sympathy by Pam and James. Contrary to belief there is often a camaraderie amongst artists, and the ills that befall one member of the profession are hurtful to his friends. The Masons were no exception in that both of them were extremely loyal towards their colleagues, Pam in particular offering her shoulder for many, men and women, to cry on. She had a great capacity for listening to tales of unhappy marriages, drinking problems and so on and she would run her legs off, so to speak, if called upon to intervene in quarrels, fights or violent arguments. She could indeed be a good and generous friend.

But at heart Pam was, and is, a feminist. Her views on men are spelt out in her books *Marriage is the First Step to Divorce* and *The*

Female Pleasure Hunt and feelings of sympathy were more often inclined towards women, many of whom I felt deserved all the ill-treatment they claimed to have suffered.

What did strike me about the actresses in Hollywood was how nice they all were to somebody like myself who had no standing in, and nothing to do with, their profession. They were always particularly pleasant to me and I never felt that I was an outsider. They were welcoming, they invited me to their homes, and if I talked to them they gave me the same attention that they would have done to Pam or James or anyone else in their profession.

Zsa Zsa Gabor epitomized this charm, and had the added advantage of being well brought up in an aristocratic family and her home showed this. The elegance of her decor, the discerning choice of dinner guests – all were understated. You never felt that she was showing off or being ostentatious – her behaviour was the legacy of her cultured European background.

I remember going to the beautiful house of a very lovely and charming woman in Coldwater Canyon. Her husband, in a drunken rage, had thrown a lot of their very expensive furniture in the swimming pool and it was just left there – it hadn't occurred to her that she should fish it out and try and save it. It wasn't important to her – it was replaceable. My instinct would have been to go tearing out and rescue whatever I could, pull it all out with a boathook or whatever – things that belonged to me, my home, things I'd chosen. Of course, it is possible that she hadn't chosen them. People did just call in the decorators to do the whole thing and not bother themselves with the details and thereby obtain instant designer decor. She wasn't surprised that I was surprised, but found nothing odd about it herself.

By contrast, Mikki Rozsa and his wife loved every stick and stone in their home. They'd collected it all – this bit in Italy, that bit in Spain – everything was done with care and love. They had things because they wanted them, not because they were supposed to have them. Mikki told me that, when he had won his second Oscar, he had been called to see the head of the studio and told that he had to move from his own home to a more prestigious address because he was in the wrong area for an Oscar winner. He shouldn't now be anywhere less than the "700 block" in Beverly and he was living happily on the top of a hill in Hollywood – terribly unsmart. But they loved their home. They'd battled to get the place before his big success, they were making a wonderful garden there, and they'd put marble statues and other objects they'd collected around it. It was a beautiful old house (old by Hollywood standards that is) and they had no intention of leaving it – so he refused to go.

He was virtually threatened with the sack, but he had the guts to stick them out and said, "Absolutely not. I've got my family happily settled there." He wasn't going to be pushed around. But that was the attitude. "Now you've achieved this, you've got to move there. You can't be seen to live in an area which is not smart or acceptable and which doesn't advertise your status." It was an interesting snobbism.

One little incident which has no bearing on anything but which gave us all a big laugh was when Pam and I decided to enjoy the pool one afternoon. Neither of us were true water women, so with sybaritic taste we turned on the heat and enjoyed a loll in the warm outdoor bath. Most inviting! Everyone should try it; sun, warm water and a jolly good gossip. A sip or two of Champagne doesn't come amiss either. But, there was to be a reckoning – James, the quiet man blew his top. Back home, hot and tired, from a gruelling session playing Rommel, he had looked forward to his usual ritual of a plunge and long swim to cool and refresh him – not so this time, the temperature outside the pool was in the 80s and not much less in the water. We hadn't realised how long it would take to get cold. Selfish baggages!

During this period of his career James was always in work, although it wasn't necessarily the kind of work he wanted. But I know for a fact that he was utterly determined to play the leading role in *Rommel – The Desert Fox* – so determined in fact that he was prepared to accept a lesser fee than usual. Henry Hathaway, the director, who put the fear of God into many actors and technicians with his irascible tongue, formed an amazing rapport with James and it proved to be a happy film for him – it may not have been an overwhelming success at the Box Office, but it gave James much gratification.

After *Rommel* there were other films he admitted himself pleased with: *Five Fingers* directed by Joe Mankeiwicz, and *The Man Between* directed by Carol Reed, whom he so much admired, he thought were both worthwhile. Then *Julius Caesar*, again with

Mankeiwicz directing, gave James the opportunity of playing Brutus (which he had previously played at the Gate Theatre in Dublin before the war) this time with Sir John Gielgud as Cassius. Sir John later told me how much of his own success in this film he owed to James's advice on how to adapt his theatrical performance to suit the camera. The film to me was a joy, because of Gielgud, whose voice remains the most beautiful of instruments. As a school girl I was taken to see him in *Richard of Bordeaux* and first heard the exquisite cadences of the man who remains, in my view, still King of the Theatre to this day. The actor Harry Andrews, who was a friend of both James and Sir John Gielgud, told me a very funny story about the filming.

HARRY ANDREWS

Some years before he went to Hollywood to make *Julius Caesar*, John performed the play at Stratford on Avon, I played Brutus, and in the conspiracy scene where Brutus plans to murder Caesar he says, "Let us kill him boldly but not wrathfully, let us carve him as a dish fit for the Gods." (Act 2, scene 1) but one night I got it wrong and said, "Let us carve him as a fish dish for the Gods." Fortunately it passed unnoticed by the audience but it nearly demolished the actors on stage!

John, not realising James's problems with the giggles, recounted this story to him just before they were to film the scene together, and James corpsed every time – in the end they had to abandon shooting for the rest of the day. Now half a day's shooting represents an awful lot of money, and this must surely have been one of the most expensive giggles in the history of the cinema.

Some of the other films that James made during 1951/53 were not to his liking, although I believe he enjoyed *The Prisoner of Zenda* – if only because he had such affection for Deborah Kerr and Stewart Granger.

When he was making *Five Fingers* I watched James with fascination as he practised thumbing the counterfeit notes that he had to handle as the wicked spy Cicero – Here was the perfectionist, here was the star for whom no item was unimportant, he would spend as many hours as was necessary to prepare himself for the scene to be shot, nothing was too much trouble, time spent on the most minute detail never begrudged. On occasions he would groan over some film or TV show in which he had appeared, saying how he wished the whole episode could be eradicated and sunk without trace, but honest as he was, he always accepted that he had been at fault in his judgement when taking such parts. His quirky character, his Yorkshire grit enabled him to laugh at himself and he rarely gave vent to his feelings of frustration over the inefficiency of others, although he was labelled from the outset of his career as being hostile towards producers and not on particularly good terms with the Press.

One of my last duties before I left Hollywood the first time was to keep house for Pam and James who were off to New York. They were rather anxious about leaving Portland behind, but not keen to take her out of her nursery school and routine – In any case their days were to be very full, and it seemed best if she remained at 1018 with me. All was settled, the housekeeper Violet and I were to enjoy full charge and Portie was quite content to have me look after her.

But suddenly, out of the blue, Pam announced that she had invited a man friend to live in during their absence, ostensibly as protection for us females. As every room in 1018 had an alarm call button connected to the local police (and I can vouch for their efficiency having once pressed the damn thing by mistake!) I felt there was some ulterior motive behind the decision.

I had known the gentleman in question from the war, an Englishman who had made it to Hollywood and done quite well initially. Pam and James much to my surprise had decided to make some TV films with him and they had collaborated on scripts together which to be fair were not too unsuccessful. Nevertheless I had no particular wish to have such a visitor in the place, even less so when he announced that he intended to have Pam's suite for himself, rather than use James's bedroom. Within a day of the Masons' departure I was informed that a party was being organised and meanwhile a few tennis-playing friends had come to enjoy first the court, and then to imbibe freely of the well-stocked bar.

My antennae have always proved sharp so when I was asked what food would be most suitable for about twenty people I replied that my suggestion was that he call Chasen's and arrange delivery of a buffet! They were an excellent firm and everyone used them for impromptu parties and general catering. My idea did not go down well and no more was said until Violet told me a more direct approach had been made to her – not quite an order but not far off – "Provide."

She and I had no intention of opening the doors to a group of free-loaders, or even to those who may well have been due to receive reciprocity for generous entertainment in the past. Quietly and methodically we loaded all the bar room stock onto the small trolley kept for that purpose and carted it all away to safe keeping. I left all that was already opened and in use in the bar proper, but the bulk, and there was plenty, went into hiding.

It was not well received, in fact tempers were frayed and sharp words exchanged to the point that the Masons' were to be informed of my perfidy by phone. Did I understand? Of course! I even got the number and stood alongside my erstwhile friend whilst he bitterly complained about my behaviour. When I took the phone to give my rendering of events I found Pam collapsed with laughter on the other end of the wire. Whether she approved of my stance or not, she left the whole matter to my discretion and then I spoke to James.

"Can you cope?" he asked.

"Yes, I am coping." I replied.

"Not too unpleasant?" he queried.

"I haven't noticed," was my answer, "I just won't have this place turned into a beer garden while I'm responsible for not only the house but a small girl who is in my charge."

"Good for you, do as you please."

Needless to say, I was not popular, and until the Masons' returned to release me for my homeward journey not a word passed between me and my so called Protector. In fairness I must record that our friendship was renewed prior to my departure and an apology for boorish behaviour happily accepted. Pam never alluded to the contretemps and James made just one remark, "Clever old you!"

The year I spent with Pam and James helped establish a closeness which we had not had the opportunity to enjoy before. The war and its aftermath had taken us on separate paths, but in California a genuine and caring relationship developed. We were, all three, very different in character but I cannot remember a single cross word or real argument disturbing what was for me a wonderfully happy time. In fact for many years I kept a letter from Pam, pressed into my hand as I left, in which she touchingly said that she wished I had not decided to leave and in effect, to hurry back – but as my departure coincided with Christmas, I couldn't wait to return to London, however cold and wet it would be. The thought of waking up to blue skies, palm trees and sunshine on Christmas Day filled me with longing for the sights and sounds of home! There would be no central heating, no deluxe bathroom, no Rolls Royce at the door to transport me, but these could not replace what really mattered.

James could never adjust to Christmas in California, and the following extract from a letter James wrote to Katie Searle, his god-daughter, sums up his feelings . . .

> To be convalescent is a marvellous way to spend Christmas. If ever you feel that some convalescence is due to you, apply for it at Christmas. If you step into the living room and find the place awash with half opened presents, too many people exuberating, chatting or firing newly-acquired guns, you just make like a stranger who has come to the wrong house, waddle back to your bedroom, put your feet up and ring for service, also you can act like SCROOGE and everyone will make allowances! This way I had a particularly merry Christmas. I hope you all were equally merry, in your own ways of course.

James was a wonderful letter-writer and a continual flow of correspondence kept him in touch with a very large number of friends and relatives, many of whom still treasure the letters he wrote to them. He would often decorate them with telling sketches of the people and places he described, and his elegant style and use of language exercised his sense of humour and his considerable literary talent.

I did spend a Christmas in Hollywood some years later and the generosity of the people who gave us presents was heartwarming, if embarrassing. So many gifts, such lovely wrappings, so lavish, so undeserved! At night the Christmas trees in the garden, the mock reindeers, the yuletide decorations had to be seen to be believed – Truly a fairytale to dazzle the eyes, as indeed were the decorations to be found within the home. Even so, and it sounds ungrateful, there was something missing. The holly and the ivy, the Carols, the food, all could be simulated but the smell of damp earth, snow perhaps crunching under one's feet, the sight of birds hunting for berries, the feel of cold air stinging one's cheeks, all this was missing. I wished I was back home to shiver in and out of the Brompton Oratory for Midnight Mass, before traipsing back to our house to feed the cats and dogs and turn up all the antiquated gas fires so as to heat our old Victorian pile sufficiently to greet whoever was due for Christmas lunch.

The tree at 1018 was magnificent, and the presents piled high underneath. We had each been given a small pad and pencil so as to record our gifts and the donors. There was a very practical reason for this. What was the gift and where did it come from? Why? Wrong fit, wrong size, or just wrong, you exchanged it! Saks, Bonwit Taylor, anywhere, take it back and choose again. Very sensible, but not Christmas as I understand it! However it obviated cursing Uncle Mac who gave golf tees to everyone, and Aunt Ethel who knitted granny shawls, or my father who always gave huge boxes of chocolate truffles which I hated, and well, every family knows the score. But it wasn't presents, the lack of or the overabundance, that mattered. For me the USA was not home, nor was it ever that for James. But, unlike me, he appreciated the climate – although he did admit some years later that a walk over the Yorkshire Moors on a crisp frosty morning took a lot of beating.

Not long after my return to London James came to Europe to make *The Man Between*, to be produced and directed by the man he most admired, Carol Reed. He had recently introduced me to his agent, Charlie Feldman, who was a real gentleman and a type not often, so far as I could judge, to be found representing the stars. The filming in Berlin showed every sign of being tough going, the winter being unusually bitter with snow lying heavily underfoot. Charlie, with James's welfare in mind, suggested that he take his fully mink lined overcoat as added protection but James would have none of it.

"Why not?" I asked. It seemed an excellent idea to me, I'd had experience of the winters in post war Hungary, Poland and Yugoslavia, and knew just how cold it could be, even if the Berlin hotels could offer some amelioration to the elements.

"I couldn't possibly accept". James explained that he would feel uncomfortable wrapped in such luxury whilst aware of the discomforts being suffered by the mass of the people. "Everything is so harsh, the climate, the privations, the ruins." James found the aftermath of war painful to behold. I doubt that he took the view that many people did, that the Germans deserved their fate. He was too sensitive and too charitable for that. Moreover by the mid 1950s the worst feeling towards our war-time enemy had waned to some extent, as the cold war with Russia assumed greater proportions. I did sometimes wonder how James would equate his pacifism with the sights of Berlin. I knew he had previously seen some of the devastation when entertaining the American troops but there was a fictitious excitement engendered then which would be lacking in the cold light of day several years on. I never discussed the war with James, nor for that matter with Pam. James's stand against joining the forces was a personal decision they took together and I respected them for holding to their beliefs. Nevertheless if one was in Europe during the late forties and early fifties the full consequences of the horrific holocaust left most people shocked to the core.

I use the word "Holocaust" advisedly because it did not only pertain to the Jewish people. Go to any of the concentration camps such as Majdanek or Mathausen and read the rolls of the dead, or, as I have done, travel the countries that bore the brunt of invasion and occupation and you will know the full meaning of the word. In retrospect I often wish that I had questioned James as to his feelings and reaction towards the Hitler regime. He would I know have answered with honesty and frankness, he was not devious. But because I felt to delve could only embarrass him, I desisted, also it might have led to questions regarding my own position and that was best avoided, as very indirectly and without their knowledge, they, Pam and James, had helped provide me with a "safe conduct" for war-time travel! Secrecy abounded during the hostilities and has not much changed even now, so it is best I draw a veil over that period. Although James was able to consolidate his career during the war, my feelings persist that, perhaps, he had cause to regret his decision to remain a non-combatant. Did it in any way mar his self-esteem or undermine his confidence in his own judgement? There were times when James gave the impression that he didn't much like himself, but that may have been part of his dissatisfaction with his life in the USA.

Remembering though, as I do, his determination to play *Rommel, The Desert Fox* in 1951, then subsequently Rommel again in *The Desert Rats* with Richard Burton in 1953, followed by his part of Count von Klugerman in *The Blue Max* in 1966, it would seem that James identified himself with these military roles, and he gave totally convincing and commanding performances. There were other films and television appearances where he played in uniform and assumed foreign accents, and though at heart James may have been a pacifist it would not surprise me to find in a man as complex as James, a sense of shame at having shirked his duty in time of war. It is only conjecture and I do believe that when he faced the Tribunal and stated his case, he was genuinely acting on principle. Guilt, if any, may have come later when he had more time to ponder and come to terms with his own feelings.

My own attitude to war as I look back is ambivalent and I fear, daily grows more cynical. Would that I had the intelligence, vision and trust in human nature that James Cameron possessed. A giant amongst men, one of the greatest and most compassionate of correspondents, the man I think I have admired and respected above anyone else. He once remarked that scepticism was acceptable but that one must always guard against cynicism – he had the stature to do this, alas not I.

James on one occasion, made a remark which I presume he meant to be taken as a joke, the gist of it being "that spying for those seeking a future should prove to be a good profession". A growth area? James, who was by nature, a solitary man in many ways, an insular character much given to assessing and weighing thoughts and actions, might well have missed his metier! Did he wish to be a gentleman agent of the John Buchan mould? Unfortunately he was far too distinctive in voice and looks to have blended into the grey world of espionage, but I wish now that he had expounded his theory to greater extent if indeed he were serious.

I was to observe another side of his character, rarely disclosed, when he came to London to finish filming *The Man Between*. He was a frequent visitor to our London home and he began to bring with him, increasingly, his ethereally lovely co-star Claire Bloom. He would often escort Mama to the theatre or the opera, and Claire would go too. He showed a marked interest in the young actress. There was a quality about her, a stillness and tranquillity which set her apart from most of the artists of her age, yet she had a pointed wit and a fine intelligence, virtues which appealed greatly to James – and it was quite apparent that he was in danger of losing his heart. In truth I believe his heart was lost, but due to the watchful presence of the ubiquitous Johnnie Monaghan, still always at his side, James kept his wits about him.

One day greatly to my surprise James informed me that Pam and Portland would be arriving in London very shortly and with an unblinking stare told me how glad he was that Claire and I were such "old friends" – I must have looked daft because he repeated how terribly nice it was that she and I were so close and spent so much time together! I had no objections. I found Claire enchanting, unspoiled, beautiful and amusing; a friend I was proud to acknowledge. I wasn't so sure how she was going to feel about this intrigue, but fortunately Claire proved to be a willing accomplice and in fact a real friendship that was to last to this day was born between us. She would always announce herself on the telephone with "This is your best friend speaking," and we would both collapse with laughter.

His attachment to Claire was purely romantic. They used to sit on the floor together in our house, hand in hand, plainly adoring each other. When Pam arrived in England she grilled me as to when, how and where Claire had crossed my horizon, but my wartime training by masters in the art of evasion stood me in good stead and I gave nothing away. It was only years afterwards that I tackled Johnnie as to why he had alerted Pam to the fact that she had a rival for James's affections.

His reply, in view of subsequent events, offered little good reason – "I felt it was my duty – I owed it to Pam to protect James."

Protect him? It was ludicrous – James was not in danger from some man-eating female. He'd avoided those menaces to be found so frequently in Hollywood without much difficulty – and certainly Claire Bloom was not seeking to inveigle an unwilling victim into her life. Quite the opposite – She was young, lovely, talented and much sought-after. There was no shortage of admirers, no lack of would-be courtiers, but whatever relationship might have been established between James and herself was laid waste and there was to be but one loser – James. Claire Bloom remembers the period very well.

CLAIRE BLOOM

In 1951 I went to Hollywood to make *Limelight* with Charlie Chaplin and one day I was pushing Josephine, his three-year-old daughter, in her swing when Portland – her best friend – arrived in the garden with James. I pretended not to be impressed but, like everybody else, I had worshipped him ever since *The Seventh Veil*. Even there in the garden he had a kind of aura about him, and his beautiful voice and face were quite stunning. When I went to Berlin to work with him on *The Man Between* he still looked absolutely beautiful but I thought his life was strange. He had his minder, Johnnie Monaghan with him all the time and I was surprised that a man of James's enormous intelligence and quality should need a companion like that. Of course I was only 22 then and now I realise that going on location all over the world can be immensely lonely and it is useful to have someone around to protect your interests. James and I enjoyed the same things and we talked a great deal about ballet and the theatre and, although he never said a word against Pamela, I do remember him saying rather sadly, "She doesn't want to do any of the things I do".

He completed the film and returned to Hollywood where he settled back into a life that left him dissatisfied and generally disappointed. The US was still for him an alien land. He was not willing to give up his British passport. He was not totally enamoured, as was Pam, with the lifestyle of California, although he did enjoy the sporting facilities, the warmth of the sun and the companionship of his cronies. Nevertheless the kernel of discontent was within him. He was bored.

Although he made film upon film, and was feted and flattered, with money and fan mail pouring in, the seeds of unhappiness were firmly planted – Why? I have no desire to rake over old gossip or rumour but the collapse of James's world coincided with the change in the relationship between Pam and himself. What was to outsiders a secure and long-standing happy marriage had become nothing but a charade. If blame there be then, sadly, it must lie at Pam's door, not because she deliberately set out to destroy the fabric of the marriage, but because she allowed her contempt for James to become too obvious even for James to ignore. It signalled her dislike for a man who refused by word or deed to intervene in her relationships – both parties told me that the marriage had been in name only for several years yet neither had anticipated or desired a separation – Again the question "Why?" is paramount and there are no easy answers, only speculation.

If I presume to give the answers, it is because I saw both sides to the question, and by trying to understand how two such people could continue to live together, seemingly in harmony, reached the following conclusions.

James clung to his marriage because he could not rid himself of feelings of guilt. Having deliberately broken up the Kellino romance, he had now to face the behaviour of his wife without complaint. What he had once done was now being done to him. I think he saw it as a kind of judgement. Portland was a factor of enormous importance and when he was born in 1955, her brother Morgan too became part of the balancing act. James felt that he had an important part to play in the upbringing of these children; he could widen the youngsters' horizons. He feared they would otherwise see too narrow a world, with the emphasis on material success: success that he, having exploited his own talent, found unsatisfactory. He was rich in monetary terms but lonely in spirit.

Pam's behaviour may have offended him but was there also a guilt of his own – the guilt for failing to satisfy her emotional needs? Many women are driven to seek the solace of other men's attentions solely because they feel unwanted, unloved, by the object of their true affection. Some men are incapable of showing their wives that they do care and take for granted that the unspoken words or the touch that denotes affection are understood. No relationship stands still, there is an ebb and flow at all times and in the Masons' case affection, and perhaps most importantly, respect for each other, had ebbed beyond recall. It can be no flattery for any woman, much less for a talented and beautiful one such as Pam, to find her husband perfectly willing to accept her behaviour without demur.

Flirtations, flattery, compliments and sexual encounters were the norm in Hollywood. I was often surprised to hear some of the other wives in her circle, apparently with solid marriages, discussing quite openly their desires, their regular infidelities, and their means of satisfying themselves, which struck me as being unrestrained – and their all too frank descriptions of lovemaking I found indelicate. Nevertheless it was an accepted way of life, and no doubt the husbands behaved in the same manner.

One little incident that caused great hilarity was due to an inadvertent remark made by Tyrone Power.

Pam's gynaecologist Red Krohn (a dream of a man, immensely kind and a very good friend in time of need to his patients) had a house-warming party to christen his new home which had been built to his own specifications and was quite inordinately luxurious.

Red and his wife Esther had thrown a no-expense-spared event, and I, after dinner, found myself in the company of Hugh Marlow, Tyrone Power and Esther. We'd dined well and drink of every kind had flowed freely hence, I presume, the rather crude words which were to give Pam great amusement when I told her what consternation I had caused!

Ty Power's then wife, the beauteous Linda Christian was pregnant at the time. Like a magnificent ship in full sail she carried all before her whilst maintaining the loveliness for which she was famed, but I noticed that Ty was having a good look about the room and eventually his eyes alighted on Pam.

Turning to Hugh Marlow he said, "Now there's a woman I'd like to screw."

"I think she'd be delighted to hear your words, Mr Power," I blithely chipped in, "Pam's my sister so I'll give her your message – I know she's fancied you for ages!"

Deathly silence followed for a second or so then I was begged to forget the whole business.

Having assured the by then worried actor, that I would not relay his message to Pam, I waited until we were home and then of course out it came.

James found it as funny as Pam and I, but whether Pam pursued the offer or not history doesn't state and it was not for me to enquire.

I had quite a number of similar happenings, few people associated me with the Masons and a clanger or two were only to be expected from the type of open conversations that were the norm.

Hollywood is not a very discreet town and gossip abounds – I found it hard to believe that many a very private matter would find its way into print, often causing great upset and unhappiness. Parties were always a source of misinformation, some malicious, but much of it just chat. None the less reputations could be marred as easily as the next drink swallowed. There were few verbal inhibitions and not many of the other kind either to be frank, but what happens between individuals I believe should remain private and the salacious appetite of voyeurs and diarists strictly curtailed. But, who has the power to do so? Sadly it would seem, no one.

I find it hard to believe that James found the situation in his house or his marriage to his liking. As he has admitted to several close friends, the last few years in California were the loneliest, saddest years of his life. Again one wonders why he took no action. He had recourse to as much as any other person faced with the breakdown of a relationship. Was it a refusal to acknowledge defeat? A poor reason to continue in a life that you have admitted offers you little if any pleasure! Was it a refusal to see Pam go free, to extend her burgeoning career as chat show hostess, writer, businesswoman and so on? I think not. James was never an ungenerous man towards those he loved and he had loved Pam, no doubt of that. They had spent more than 20 years together, moulding and influencing each other's careers. Success had been won the hard way and each had made sacrifices on behalf of the other – if love had turned to hate, or if not hate, dislike and distaste, why not part amicably?

The ultimate break-up of the Mason marriage shows some of the reasons. Though it may be argued that my theories are too simplistic, I base them on my knowledge of both Pam and James and the motivation behind their actions.

What are of interest, and must in fairness be recorded, are James's own amorous adventures. Not many, and always discreet, the impression that I gained was that the recipient of his affections had to come under the heading of real romance – a sex-only relationship was not what he sought and the few ladies (who shall remain unnamed by me) who offered romance caught at James in a way that was more dangerous than he realised. Dangerous in so far as he was unable to remain uninvolved, he did not only wish for sexual fulfilment, he needed to feel that he had some importance in their lives. He could, as many others would, have found a call-girl to satisfy his physical needs, but he was fastidious and, by the 1950s, no longer a callow young man. Whatever the options, he chose to have a relationship. He was searching for someone to fill the emotional void in his life. It may be that he kidded himself into believing in his own views that love and sex should go hand in hand. Possibly the women in his life may not have wished to disillusion him for he had, even in middle age, a kind of "little boy lost" appeal, and what woman would have the heart to wound unnecessarily someone they purported to care about?

But the turmoil in James and Pam's private lives was interrupted by an unexpected and thrilling professional opportunity which came out of the blue and which James came to view as a great landmark in his career. In 1954 Tyrone Guthrie, his old friend and mentor from as long ago as his undergraduate days, was directing the second season of the New Shakespeare Theatre at Stratford, Ontario, and he invited James to join him there, offering him the challenge of performing once again classical roles in the live theatre – Angelo in *Measure for Measure* and the title role in *Oedipus Rex*. This opened a whole new vista for James and he accepted with a mixture of high excitement and uncomfortable misgivings.

At first the enterprise was difficult and not very successful for him. It was so long since he had performed in the live theatre. Not only was he lacking in confidence, he also found that his voice, so excellently attuned to the microphone, was not the instrument necessary to penetrate the far corners of the huge tent which was to be the venue for his Canadian debut. He got no help from Pam with this dilemma because she had from the first been against his taking what she viewed as an unnecessary gamble. She was unhappy about having to leave California for a protracted stay in Canada and she had no interest in the Shakespearean repertoire. But the challenge came at a moment in James's life when he was ripe for change so he took it up and persevered against considerable difficulties. He had more success with Oedipus than with Angelo, but *Measure for Measure* was the first of the two plays so he hadn't had time to get into his stride when it opened and *Oedipus* was a very spectacular production with marvellous costumes which no doubt helped give him confidence.

Some who remember his appearances during that season speak highly of him, others more critically, and once again it is the cold, off-hand manner which was his defence against the world and which, without his meaning it, gave the impression that he was arrogant and dismissive. At the time James himself felt that he had failed to make any real friends within the circle of theatre artists and stage technicians, but there are plenty of people who were in that company with him who speak of him with affection and admiration. Elspeth Cochrane, who was Tyrone Guthrie's stage director, has kindly given her thoughts and recollections of this period and her insight into James's fears, failures and successes offer a far better view and balanced opinion than I am able to do. But now let her speak in her own voice.

ELSPETH COCHRANE

The first Stratford (Ontario) Season was enormously successful and Tyrone Guthrie decided that a big star, a famous name, preferably English would be an added asset for the second year's performances.

So he decided to invite James to join the Company for the 1954 Season.

The offer coming out of the blue, took James by surprise and, finding himself thoroughly fed up and dissatisfied with his work, it gave him the impetus to take a chance and move back into the theatre – he felt he was at the turning point of his career, and the opportunity to play under the direction of Tyrone Guthrie who was his god tipped the scales in favour of Stratford.

Having made his decision and signed the contract James admitted later that he was beset by sheer terror at the immensity of the undertaking, not offset by his wife's dire warning that "You'll fall flat on your face and make a complete fool of yourself."

There was no doubt that it was a momentous move for James to make, not only would he face the competition from the highly talented performers in the company, but he would have to face the critics, adapt to the new environment and atmosphere of live theatre, iron out the problems he was having vocally and, horrifying thought, accept that the eyes of the artistic world would be trained on him to see if he was capable of making the transition from movies to the classical theatre repertoire, a daunting task.

It was no sinecure, and James admitted that he questioned himself over and over again as to whether he should have risked his reputation, and why had he chosen to do so.

As the opening night drew closer so his confidence waned, and his diffidence and uncertainly created more and more doubts in his mind. Fear grew stronger, and although he worked and worked, bearing all the shouting and harrying heaped on him by Guthrie in his effort to drag out all the latent talent screwed down by nerves, I have to admit that his debut in *Measure for Measure* was neither good nor promising, in view of the Oedipus that was to be next role.

Tony Guthrie, I and all the company were willing James a successful first night, we knew that he was capable of giving a fine performance, his talent was obvious as we saw in rehearsal but nerves conquered him and the penalty was poor reviews and a less than admiring response in general.

It was for James the moment of truth. Hours after the perform-ance, when he failed to attend the dinner party given to celebrate the opening of the second season, I was sent by Guthrie to see what he was doing, and I found him still sitting despondently in his dressing

room. I had established a rapport with James early on. He knew
something of my background as a stage director, the job I still held
when he arrived to join the company. As a friendly gesture James had
offered me a bag of liquorice allsorts, one that he had just bought for
himself. He was so shy, so tentative when making this overture,
pressing the bag into my hand, that I hadn't the heart to say that I
simply loathed the horrible things. Later on we were to laugh about
it, but at the time I knew he would have felt rejected had I refused
and there was no denying that he was very much in need of
sympathy.

I know that James felt that he had failed to establish any contact
with the other actors and actresses, nor indeed with the technicians.
This was not so – everyone admired his capacity for work, his
"un-grand" manner and his willingness to muck in. I heard nothing
but praise and genuine liking for the man whose reputation had
preceded him from Hollywood as being highly professional but
remote and austere in character. Once he had relaxed and gained
confidence I believe the camaraderie became more obvious to him,
and he was able to enjoy the working partnership which was so much
part of the company's strength.

An example of his eagerness to be part of whatever went on was
his delight at being allowed to join the company's baseball team. He
was no player, but he took endless trouble to learn the rules, and he
practised like mad in the hope of being good enough to play,
although he never was. Nevertheless he spent many enjoyable
sessions, and I can honestly say not a season passes, even to this day,
without mention being made of James, whose memory is held in
affection by virtually one and all, for being a kind and simple man, a
generous actor and a highly talented performer.

His failure in *Measure for Measure* could have sent him scuttling
back to Hollywood, many a lesser person might have chosen to
abscond and run for cover, but it was not the way for James. The
issue was not to be shirked, this doughty fighter from Huddersfield
girded himself up and began to work like a fiend until he was satisfied
that he could do the company justice and incidentally justify
Guthrie's belief in his ability.

The outcome was triumph. A personal triumph in *Oedipus Rex*, a
great vindication of everyone's conviction that James had within him
the attributes of a great actor, the press gave him rave notices and

Stratford remained a highlight never to be forgotten for the rest of his life. It was not just the approbation from his colleagues or the critics, it was the knowledge that he had conquered fear and partial failure and come through the experience successfully.

I think we had all been aware of James's feeling of insecurity and his vulnerability in regards to the pitfalls that faced him in adapting to theatre work after so long an absence. We all recognised that he plainly was suffering the grip of stage-fright, that he was terrified would not be putting it too strongly, but what we could not know at the time was that he was facing a personal dilemma in his private life.

James's return to the live theatre revived his longing to be part of a musical show, but his vocal shortcomings had been borne in on him more unavoidably, and he now decided to embark on a long and protracted period of voice-training which gave him the confidence hitherto lacking. His unusual vocal timbre was as much a part of his allure as his dark and brooding looks but he had for many years felt dissatisfaction with his voice as, when under stress, it tended to sound husky, but that was not necessarily in my view because of bad production.

Frankly I felt that all James required was an understanding of breathing. The microphone being so sensitive allows film and T.V. actors to use the minimum of effort, whereas in the theatre projection is a first necessity. Centre the voice and give it a solid sounding board, i.e. the diaphragm, and you are half way there. Breathing for classical singers is the basis of their vocal art and in Italy it is the first and foremost lesson one must learn.

In any event he undertook to study and after two or three years with Mrs Holmes working on his voice James emerged as a satisfied client with far greater confidence than before. I used to think how wonderful James would have been as Coriolanus or Othello, but because opera was my genre I would then picture him as Andrea Chenier the revolutionary poet, or as Calif the brave prince in *Turandot*, or Cavadorossi the painter in *Tosca*. If only he could have sung! He would have been superb.

1954 was a year of great endeavour for James. As well as the Shakespeare season in the theatre at Stratford he made two of his best films, *A Star is Born* with Judy Garland, and *Twenty Thousand*

Leagues Under the Sea for Walt Disney. *Twenty Thousand Leagues* was one of his favourite films; it appealed to the child in him, a quality he never quite lost, and in Captain Nemo he had a ready-made part; dark, mysterious, handsome and dangerous – a perfect combination.

A Star is Born was something different, a role which demanded a great deal more from James's talent and indeed his personal resilience. For many years he had been a fervent fan of Judy Garland, considering her to have talents as near to a "Chaplinesque" genius for wringing the emotions as any performer alive. His sympathy and genuine liking for her gave him an insight and perception of the problems that had dogged her for so many years – her health and her weight which had caused her such anguish, and had earned her the reputation for being unreliable and unpunctual. Traits which in others would have been an annoyance to James, were, in the case of Judy, recognised as the true reason for her being temperamental and difficult. Her predicament touched James's heart. As a sensitive man, it pained him to observe a fellow creature being torn apart by the demands and stress of their profession and aroused in him great pity and understanding. Not only did he make allowances, but he tried as best he could to minimise and cover any lapses which might have interfered with the filming schedule.

As it so happened it was James himself who was the first culprit. He caused consternation by disrupting the first few days of shooting. The man known for his professionalism, exact time keeping and 100 per cent reliability was, unbeknown to anyone, suffering from Meniere's Disease, a malady affecting the inner ear, causing dizziness, nausea and lack of balance. It was a condition which came as a great shock to James and to the film-makers, but fortunately the symptoms can be controlled medically and the problem was overcome.

Oddly enough, although both Judy Garland and James were nominated for an Oscar, the film itself was regarded as disappointing by Hollywood, and neither of them received an award. In his usual dry, laconic way, James shrugged off any personal regrets he might have felt at not receiving the prestigious little statue although, quite apart from the kudos, the fillip to the Box Office receipts and the rise in one's professional standing and one's all important fees, James simply loved prizes and winning! It was a trait he never lost –

perhaps a relic from his schooldays when, according to him, he was a bit of a duffer who failed to win any distinction? Was he always trying to prove himself, or was he truly "Bulldog" Englishman determined to succeed? I could never decide. Only once did James confide to me that he had never realised just how ambitious he was, until he saw his popularity as a star declining. It was an admission made during a period of great stress, but I believe there was more than a grain of truth in his words. For all his success James was not satisfied with his career – Yet he chose to make so many poor films, made so many unsuccessful incursions into TV and admitted he should have known, or chosen better, that one has to question what drove him on. I wonder if he was not beset by some demon whose aspirations could not be satisfied.

An interesting remark made to me recently about James begs the question – were the 1950s the worst time for someone like James to have forged his career in Hollywood? The industry was beset by change; TV was beginning to fill the minds of those who had been the frequenters of the cinema, and the audiences were staying at home with the small screen, so the movie Moguls were having to look for more gimmicks to attract attention. Would he have done better to have signed a contract with one of the big studios than to insist on freelancing? It is difficult even with hindsight to know if he might have fared better had he gone to Hollywood later.

James was a law unto himself and not easily swayed – he chose his parts, he was responsible for his decisions and generally accepted the blame when he'd made a mistake. But the streak of stubbornness I've mentioned before was always there below the surface and I doubt that even Pam's blandishments would or could have forced him into a situation had he set his mind against it. There lies the paradox, the enigma. James was not weak or vacillating, he was intelligent and critical, and his knowledge of filming exceptional, so why did he perform in bad movies or TV knowing that they could bring him nothing but discontent and even a sense of failure? He needed the challenge to be found in acting, or as he hoped, directing or producing.

He longed to direct a re-make of *Jane Eyre* and I remember very clearly his chagrin and disappointment when he was politely but bluntly told that such an investment was not viable. He did not want, as might have been expected, to play Mr Rochester, although to get the project accepted he would have done so – and been ideal in the role. But the subject was considered too uncommercial to appeal to the vast American public, unless he could conjure up a big name (however unsuitable) to play Jane, as he alone was not a sufficient draw. It was made painfully clear to James that, in spite of all his success, his name meant little compared with Gary Cooper, John Wayne, Joel McCrea, James Stewart or Gregory Peck, for such stars could have sold their audiences anything from the classics to the Presidency of the United States.

Box Office appeal brings home the dollars, and James knew this perfectly well, but the blow to his ego – always fragile – increased the aggravation of living in an alien environment, surrounded by things he didn't value, striving to maintain the facade of a marriage that in the full meaning of the word was a sham, and seeing his stardom and reputation sliding away. I must confess, I felt very sorry for him. Unhappiness was eating into his soul.

Would he have been happier if less committed to his career? He had fought against his insularity and his innate shyness and he strove for perfection right up to the end of his life, so the question remains, was fame important to him? Was adulation necessary food, admiration sustaining to his psyche? I only wish I had the answer but I haven't. Yet one small memory lingers which in itself shows the measure of James's sensitivity.

In the course of a desultory conversation James mentioned *Pandora and the Flying Dutchman* – I think he was teasing me because I had admitted to having seen so few of his films! As it so happened Pandora had tempted me into the cinema and I told him so – his reply was an anguished groan about the awful close-up of his very discoloured teeth at the end of the film – "So ugly, ghastly," and so on. I was surprised, I'd never thought James was vain, in fact I had wondered many times why he hadn't had his teeth fixed to disguise their lack of enamel which disfigured his otherwise exceptional good looks.

In my efforts to assure him that it had been of no importance we touched on several sore points, not least one which took my breath away. I was really confounded, not only by James's memory of so inconsequential a matter but because this little episode had occured during the mid 1930s.

James spoke of an old and rather grumpy Aunt of mine who had remarked testily that he looked a very scruffy young man, and she had her doubts as to his talents, or that he might become a future star. I remembered Aunt Minnie's tirade very well. In fact she and I got on famously, being two of a kind, dotty about dogs and gambling on the horses. It was she who introduced me to the vagaries of "Yankees", "Canadians" and "any to come," just as my father completed my education at the roulette tables of Monte Carlo. She was an irascible old Tartar with a vinegary tongue and James had received its full flavour and obviously been hurt by the encounter.

Poor James, he had come down the road to see us riding a bicycle, shirt sleeves rolled up, tatty old trousers and a piece of cloth tied Indian fashion across his forehead to hold back his hair which was rather long, very fine and prone to fall in his eyes. "Goodness gracious," Aunt Minnie cried in her stentorian voice, "Is that a man or a woman?" We told her who it was, but she remained unimpressed. "Tell him to get his hair cut and smarten up", she snorted with indignation, her view of actors befitted her generation, and any slackness or untidiness showed a lack of moral fibre. Lying abed after eight in the morning was virtually a mortal sin, and appearing in a peignoir, as we did in France, smacked of immorality of the worst kind!

I managed to assure James that he had earned Aunt Minnie's unqualified approval before she died. I don't know which, if any, of his films she saw but I know she enjoyed boasting about how she had known "the boy had talent and would go far." Her old tabby friends were very impressed, needless to say.

I reminded James of an incident that happened in Paris, in 1956. We had a good laugh over it, but it shows how very protective he still was towards Pam, even at this juncture. I could be labelled a tiresome and annoying hag, but not she! The Masons had arrived in Paris en route for home from the Venice Film Festival, where James had taken Pam and the children for a holiday, mixing business with pleasure – or so he had hoped. But Pam, apart from the initial impact of the beauty of the city, considered it a smelly place. Morgan was too young to make anything of it at all and his nanny had proved to be an uneasy traveller, but at least James and Portland had a consistently good time. I went to meet them at the station when they arrived in Paris and found them all tired and hot, Portland, Morgan and his nanny, baggage galore and wilting bouquets which had been pressed on Pam (no doubt by lovelorn Italian admirers!) who was not in the least enthralled by the beauties of Venice. Smells and half-starved cats had firmly rooted themselves in her mind, and her one desire was to get back to California and civilisation.

We traipsed off to the Hotel George V and were ushered up to the suite set aside for the Masons – I had dutifully tagged along, although I was booked into the Prince de Galles for a couple of nights before leaving for Menton. I wanted to hear all the chat about the Festival, but what first assailed my ears, was Pam announcing that she couldn't possibly cope with a bathroom that hadn't a loo en suite -- "It would mean coming out into the lobby, Diana, it's quite impossible."

It was all beautifully equipped and very private, but for Pam it was quite unacceptable – I thought grimly of some of the so-called luxury hotels I'd been stuck in behind the Iron Curtain – what wouldn't I have given for some soft loo paper and a fluffy bath towel and for that matter a loo that worked! Nevertheless, Pam was used to the best and she had to be considered. "Ring down and ask if they can move us." James pushed this duty on me, "My French is not yet up to such an explanation." I felt a bit puzzled as the desk at the George V rarely, if ever, is troubled by French not being spoken and anyway the staff speak many languages, English for certain.

Still I duly spoke to the reservation clerk and explained Mrs Mason's needs, and soon afterwards porters arrived to manhandle the baggage, with an Under Manager to bow obsequiously to "Madame" as we were escorted, to another magnificent apartment offering a huge living room, two rooms and bathroom for the children and .Ma, as nanny was called, then two bedrooms and bathroom for the Masons themselves.

All seemed well, or so I thought, then I heard Pam's voice – the loo this time was sited accurately but there was but one bathroom for the two bedrooms. "Impossible." Pam's verdict, which in a way I could understand – she liked to spend a long while doing her toilette and if she had the bathroom, James hadn't – so what to do? Walking into the sitting room I heard James on the phone and the following words fell on my ears . . .

"I'm really sorry about this, but my sister-in-law will not share a bathroom. Can you move us again?"

"Your what?" I screeched at James who sat, a disconsolate heap looking as if he were about to cry! Not bloody likely. No, he was chuckling. His shoulders heaving, his eyes moist and eventually, through the mirth, came an apology. "I couldn't let them think it was Pam complaining again – now could I? You don't mind."

"I do mind, I'm not even staying here," but I didn't want to appear a sour old grizzler so I had to laugh as the third and final move was made, and Pam approved of all the bathroom facilities at last.

Portland decided that as I had twin beds in my hotel room she would stay with me (even if it did mean sharing the bathroom) and we quickly buzzed off together to have a nosh up at the Pam Pam on the Champs Elysee – Martha Miller, (Ma the nanny) was a delightful soul, right up my alley, an inveterate gambler who very quickly cottoned on to the intricacies of the pari-mutuel system, and when I next met her in Beverly Hills she returned the compliment by explaining the betting arrangements in California. Neither of us ended up winners, needless to say, but what fun we had picking losers!

But, in spite of the gallantry James still showed towards Pam, it was clear that all was not well with the marriage and so, in this same year of 1956, James was glad to accept the offer of a film which gave him the chance to escape from his increasingly unhappy domestic life in Hollywood. *Island in the Sun* was filmed in the Caribbean on the island of Grenada where he found the kind of refuge and tranquillity that was balm to his troubled soul. The whole unit fell under the spell of the sea and sand, whilst the Caribbean people themselves contributed in no small way to the delight of filming on the island.

James found the absence of colour bar a particular bonus, he not only liked black people but numbered several amongst his friends at a time when many would not, and he abhorred the injustice of segregation. It offended his sense of decency and smacked of the old Colonialism which he so heartily detested. He found the ambivalent attitudes towards colour a particularly ugly part of the American scene. The States operated their own form of apartheid. Petty rules in certain States worked against Blacks, Red Indians, and Jews, and certainly James viewed the politics in both the USA and Britain with contempt for the cynical attitudes and hypocritical proclamations of Democracy with a big D whilst bad housing, poor education, rotten health services and a bar to certain jobs, existed with the support of governments. James was not a political animal, but he was a champion of fair play, decent standards and open minds – the McCarthy trials in the USA disgusted him, as indeed they did all fair-minded people, and again it was to prove just one more disillusionment, the great country offering freedom to all comers showed itself to be as biased and vicious when faced with opposing views as any other place and the "own best interest" dealings with Central and South America caused James to see politics as a particularly dirty game.

Certainly Grenada found a lasting place in James's heart, in fact I think he always hankered to return there but feared to do so lest he shatter a dream. The film itself, starring Harry Belafonte, James and Dorothy Dandridge, was well enough received. Even if no earth-shaking success, it nevertheless offered James a prolonged period away from Hollywood and allowed him to enjoy a complete sense of freedom in the atmosphere of *laisser faire* endemic to the Islands. Life and love were there to be enjoyed and anxieties and worries were left behind, until it was time to return once again to the vacuum of Hollywood where James found himself not only bored but even more aware of the emptiness of his personal life. Incidentally, when in 1961, James went to Tahiti to make the film *Tiara Tahiti* he surprised me by saying that the island could in no way compare or compete with Grenada. In the past my French naval friends had vied for a posting to Tahiti, (preferably without their wives tagging along!) because of its ambiance of flowers, sun and beautiful girls.

But James found the place spoiled. Whether because it had been geared to tourism I cannot say, but he did enjoy the opportunity of practising his French on the local inhabitants and also the company of his co-stars, Herbert Lom, Claude Dauphin and John Mills, all tremendously talented actors. An added bonus was that the producer was his old friend Ivan Foxwell.

Tiara Tahiti received mixed reviews, praised for wit and panache by some, but generally it brought little reward to James although his sparkling partnership with John Mills was admired, both men being masters of their craft. I suspect that *Island in the Sun* and *Tiara Tahiti* caught James in very different moods. He was undergoing much deeper personal problems when filming the latter and this may well have coloured his appreciation, or lack of it, for both people and places in general.

In January 1959, James's parents paid a visit to Beverly Hills partly to avoid the rigours of the English winter and partly to give James the opportunity of welcoming them to his Californian home. John Mason, his father, was not in good health and stayed only a few weeks before returning to Yorkshire but "Muv" stayed on a while longer. It must have been difficult for her to adapt, and none too easy for James to maintain a peaceful atmosphere in a divided household. I don't imagine that Pam found it a bed of roses either.

Although the breach between James and his parents had been healed and he was firmly back in the family fold, the differences that had caused the friction, even if abated, had not entirely gone away and I can imagine that wife and mother-in-law met each other politely but not warmly. "Muv" Mason loved flowers and gardens and was hoping to see some fine landscapes during her stay, but she was disappointed by the similarity of the plants to be found in most Californian gardens. It is true that luscious though they are the variety of plant life they contain is limited. Certain things such as bouganvillia, poinsettias, canna lilies and so on grow magnificently, but manicured lawns and organised shrubs cannot compare with the gardens to be found in England or in any climatic conditions that offer the same seasonal changes. Daffodils, tulips, crocuses in spring, roses, herbacious borders with lupins, golden rod, sweet peas in summer, the wondrous colours of autumn and the bleak beauty of the trees in winter – where better can we see this marvel of nature than in England?

I had been impressed by the gardens when I first arrived in California and some of them were indeed spectacular, but somehow the pleasure waned as the abundance and similarity seemed theatrical. It was all so cultivated, as of course most gardens are, yet some continue ·to seem natural as if they had planted themselves without the hand of man. "Muv" Mason would have loved, as I did, the dogwoods on the drive from New York to Long Island, a sight I've never forgotten, spare and beautiful as only such trees can be. I cannot say if the Masons really enjoyed their visit to 1018 – it may have come too late in their lives – but James's return to England to film gave them great feelings of happiness. He was coming home.

When James returned to London in 1959 to make *A Touch of Larceny*, it struck me that he was more relaxed and a little happier in himself. Finding old friends such as Ronald Searle and his wife Kaye Webb, Maggie and Al Parker and a host of others gave him a sense of well-being and comfort – of "belonging".

Johnnie Monaghan had accompanied him as usual, and through my mother's good offices, James had taken on a secretary-cum-dresser who was not only a great fan of James's but an extremely competent and useful little man – Frank Essien, whose wife Bobbi had been our dressmaker and had died suddenly of cancer while Frank was in James's employ, an event which bound him even closer to James, his home life having disintegrated. A sufferer from diabetes, Frank was also to die a few years later, but his time with James gave him enormous pleasure and satisfaction. Half Ghanaian, Frank also spoke good French, an added bonus to James, who had hopes of producing a film in France. With Frank he could practise and polish up his knowledge of the most beautiful language in the world. James found the French language much to his taste. It has a certain elegance, and even rude words implying the worst, never sound as crude as they do in Anglo-Saxon.

On one occasion I earned Frank a rocket from James, and received one myself for which I took him to task. It was a trivial matter but James was at the time still smarting from the disaster that had overtaken him in the divorce suit Pam had brought against him. I shall deal with this event at length later on, but my little contretemps which involved Frank was over a donation to an animal charity. In the normal course of events James would willingly have supported my appeal but at the time he was abroad, so I got Frank to dig in the coffers and fetch out a very modest sum. He showed some reservations but for friendships sake he gave me a cheque.

I wrote to James thanking him for having allowed me to twist his secretary's arm and received in return, as did Frank, an angry and sharp rebuke, the gist of which was, I quote approximately, "In future, apply to the rich, ex Mrs Mason for donations – it is she, not I, who has the money." I could understand the bitterness he felt at being left penniless, though he seemed less aggrieved than I would have been in such circumstances

Nonetheless I tackled him when we eventually met, and tore a strip off him for being mean – in spirit (not cashwise) – lambasting Frank and incidentally myself. As always James showed his capacity for turning away wrath. He apologised and made a joke about his short fuse – over the years I suppose we did have the odd clash of opinions but I can never remember any real anger or disagreement.

Only once did I see James lose his temper and there, again, he was abject when apologising.

It occurred during my next visit to Hollywood in 1959 when I remarked whilst having lunch with him and Johnnie, that I was anxious, because they both looked so ill. Six months earlier, when they had been in England for *A Touch of Larceny*, I had found them fit and in good spirits, now a short while later, the change was worrying. These two men, both in their early fifties, looked like old men. They had suddenly gone to pieces – James so odd and distrait, and Johnnie looking white and pasty, thin and ill.

A fist crashed down on the table and James shouted, literally "Don't ever make such remarks again, Diana – I forbid it – say no more on the subject." Johnnie looked pale and embarrassed, James red-faced and furious.

I was so taken aback that I left the table quietly, only to find James about half an hour later sheepishly waiting to talk to me and say how sorry he was for his outburst. All over in a second and no harm done. I liked the man, I'd known him then for over twenty years so I understood some of the pain he felt, and I'm sure with hindsight, that the bleakness of his personal life over so many years had been borne with real stoicism. His reasons may have been faulty, but his intentions had been of the best. The sad fact was that everything he had hoped to avoid crashed upon him, leaving him lost and bewildered by events.

A Touch of Larceny brought James and Vera Miles together. A delicate blonde girl discovered, so I'm told, by Alfred Hitchcock and James certainly enjoyed filming with her. Gossip implied they were more than friends and maybe that is so but although I saw them on many occasions, I cannot say that I was aware of any special relationship. James, as it happens, was not a man to keep his affections under wraps, but maybe on this occasion, if the gossips be accurate, he was playing "Brer Fox".

The few times that I joined them the atmosphere was warm and friendly and we used to prowl around various clubs, mainly run by black people for black people, but where lovers of jazz of any colour were welcomed. I was not particularly enamoured of such music, but I enjoyed meeting the artists and seeing James so happy and at ease gave me a great deal of pleasure.

Those who disliked James, or upheld Pam will say, if they read this book, that James had many affairs, that he was a hypocrite, that he was mean and only kept up the appearance of his marriage so as to avoid a division of property. Not so! James had loved Pam, as Othello loved Desdemona, not wisely but too well, and that in a nutshell lay at the root of the problem. To let go is never easy, and after years of partnership and commitment it demands a lot of courage to cry "enough".

A *Touch of Larceny* provided a number of pleasures for James and not least amongst them was the chance it gave him to play comedy. The producer, Ivan Foxwell, had known James from his very early days in the British cinema, before the war, and had long admired him. In happier times James and Pam would sometimes rent a small theatre in Hollywood and, for the amusement of themselves and their friends, perform together Victorian melodramas like *Murder in the Red Barn*, *Sweeney Todd* and other over-written horrors. They never made any money out of it, probably just managed to cover their costs, but it gave them a lot of fun and kept them occupied when there was no film work. Ivan Foxwell had seen some of these family shows and knew that James was a very accomplished comedian – something which few other people recognised. Convinced that James would be the perfect casting for the lead in the light comedy he was about to put into production, Foxwell fought tooth and nail to persuade Paramount that James could do it and, in the face of strong opposition from the studio chiefs, he won. It was the start of a new phase in his career.

Towards the end of 1959 I went with my mother to stay again for some months with James and Pam in Hollywood. The purpose of the visit was to allow me a necessary period of convalescence, after an illness, in the warmth of California. But by now the atmosphere in the Mason household was anything but warm. I found many changes had taken place in the intervening eight years since my first visit both in the social and working life of Hollywood and in the marriage of Pam and James. Most immediately obvious were the changes they had made to their home. They had sold off the lower part of their land to development and new houses now replaced the area of their gardens that I had planned to cultivate as velvet lawns, thick shrubberies and luscious fruit trees at a later date. It did cross my mind that perhaps James, fearing that I would indeed return to Hollywood and put my plans to work, had decided to rid himself of the land before I could descend on him again with my blueprints for herbacious borders and huge rose gardens. But I must confess that the improvement was miraculous. An unmaintained garden in the heart of California soon becomes a sad and sorry sight, a prairie without flowers, burnt and patchy. But the new garden was now as well stocked and cared-for as those of any of their friends and neighbours.

Having shed the burden of the upkeep of so much land, James and Pam had made alterations to their home which had greatly enhanced it. A smaller pool had been built on the patio that fronted James's library, a tennis court dominated the area overlooked by the dining room and a huge conservatory and long terrace gave the cats a delightful indoor/outdoor salon of their own − not that they stayed there, one or two especially favoured felines would find their way to Pam's bedroom and Violet, the housekeeper, had her own cats in her quarters which made for accusations of favouritism! But they were a particularly happy aspect of the household. Everyone loved the animals and Pam was forever rushing off to rescue an unwanted or abandoned creature. As far as I know she still does, which is a big plus for her in my book.

It was good to see Violet Taylor, whom James and Pam had first met in 1937 while making *I Met a Murderer*, and who had accompanied them to New York and then to California as their housekeeper, still in residence with them. She was a real character, fag ever in her hand, bright red hair which over the years was never allowed to dim and she remained a devoted retainer up to the time of her retirement. She loved James with a fierce protective love, but after the divorce she remained with Pam − torn by divided loyalties and her need to keep her home and her cats! She was already an elderly woman when James finally settled in Switzerland and she had established a life in Hollywood which suited her and enabled her to enjoy the climate, her card-playing friends and her four-footed felines. In my time there, on her days off, she would summons a yellow cab and rush off to shop and visit her buddies, a smart trim little woman who drove Pam mad at times with her constant chatter whenever she could pin her down in her bedroom. Pam used to lock her door and refuse to open it until Violet and dreaded Hoover removed themselves. How Pam was supposed to listen above the whirr of the machine I don't know but it was Violet's ploy to try and get access to Pam's suite. "Mrs Mason, Mrs Mason, I must do your room, please open the door," a cry from the heart which was left unanswered needless to say. When dressed, Pam would fly out of her room, tear down the stairs like a bat out of hell, leaving Violet screeching after her whatever bit of gossip she wished to impart. To no avail – Pam's ears were not for bending.

When Morgan was born, the fifth bedroom and bathroom were required for him and his nanny, "Ma", so a small wing was built on to the side area overlooking the tennis court. This was Violet's domain and was close enough for her to watch out for cat fights or marauding racoons. The garden of the late Tom Mix's property backed on to the Masons guest house and offered a haven for quite a few animals who naturally enough bundled over the boundary walls to enjoy the tit-bits available at 1018. My mother and I loved our stay in the guest house, two bedrooms, bathrooms, lounge and open plan kitchen/dinette plus patio. It was ideal, and I had the added pleasure of being able to observe some of the variety of birds that nested in the trees that overhung the patio. I had never seen a Golden Aureole until I was in California, a truly lovely bird.

One trip my mother and I enjoyed to the full was to Las Vegas – Pam arranged for us to fly while she and James drove there, because at the time Pam had not yet conquered her fear of aeroplanes or of being enclosed. She had battled for many years against this form of claustrophobia and I remember how she dreaded journeys on no-corridor trains during the war years. When we arrived in Vegas we were installed in a gorgeous bungalow set in the grounds of the hotel. We had a bedroom and bathroom each, and the living room boasted a massive open fire with burning logs, plus a huge TV with dozens of channels. It was the height of luxury, and my delight, having ordered breakfast, was watching it delivered by smart young men on motor scooters! Everything reached us piping hot and beautifully laid out on trays.

Prima and Ray Sinatra had their home in Vegas at this time as Ray was permanent conductor at one of the Casinos. Prima had become an expert blackjack player and knew many of the croupiers. Whether her benevolent eye had an effect on the roulette wheel I know not, but I enjoyed a run of luck and playing with silver dollars was an added thrill – better than coloured chips!

James was not a man to chance his luck. I don't think gambling had any appeal for him, but Mama and I sat glued to the roulette tables, the type as yet unknown to us in Europe, small, seating six to eight people with only one croupier in charge. Pam too quite enjoyed a turn at the wheel, but her particular delight were the fruit machines which proved very lucky for her. I believe a jackpot came her way on one occasion some years after our visit when she spent quite a while working in the town. She took an apartment there where, needless to say, she found a few cats requiring a loving home.

But to return to my visit. The air was intoxicating after Los Angeles – pure and clean, and the prairie flowers were a delight to behold. Contrary to most peoples ideas, the town and surrounding countryside offer every pastime, golf, swimming and riding. We made a tour of Boulder Dam, which I found a somewhat frightening experience, the vastness and complexity of the engineering feat was most impressive, but water and I are not compatible (only civilised hot baths or showers).

Of course Las Vegas is known for its night life and therefore those who go there are not so interested in seeing the amenities available to residents. Most of the hotels are open for gambling day and night, the Strip offers every kind of game you can imagine and I watched goggle eyed some people, women in particular, plonk themselves on a stool in front of their favourite machine and from a bag feed the beastly clanking thing for hour upon hour. I was told that fortunes could be won and often were, but it struck me as a soulless pastime.

In every lounge there was entertainment, a trio of musicians, a singer, a pianist all performing so it seemed on a twenty-four hour rota, and I must add, all to a very high standard. The Chuck wagons, laden with food, allowed people to eat as much as they wished for a minimal sum, while the most lovely, scantily clad girls, dispensed free drinks to those playing at the roulette or poker tables. The crap tables were the most exciting as the watchers grew as hepped up as the players, and vast sums of money were won or lost on the throw of a dice.

Freddie de Cordova, a producer friend of the Masons was a terrific player, and though not known for throwing his money about in general, Las Vegas and the crap tables knew otherwise. Pam used to read him the riot act on the occasions that he returned to Hollywood sadder and wiser to face his mother Maggie, an irascible Irish American who adored him but felt he needed protecting against the evils of gambling (and women). As he was an incredibly handsome man and one of the few bachelors in town, I suspected that he was a far shrewder man than most allowed for. In any event he was a devotee of the dice and seemed to be drawn to Las Vegas by an irresistible magnet. I fully understood, the touch of green baize and the clink of the roulette wheel is music to my ears, to be able to depart this world over a table at Monte Carlo with a large pile of chips in front of me would be a joyful end.

James and Pam loved the shows that were the draw to the non-gambling fraternity. The opulence and talent to be seen there was unequalled anywhere in the world with fantastic costumes, the best performers, dancers, singers, comedians, conjurers, troupes and speciality acts. You could sit and have dinner at any of these performances and every Hotel Casino provided entertainment of this kind. I don't think there was a real celebrity in the States or from elsewhere come to that who hadn't done a stint in this desert paradise.

Rumour had it that some of the "resident" performers were bound to the managements by virtue of their gambling debts – Unable to repay their losses they were fixtures until such time, if ever, they were able to settle them. Meanwhile they did their turns, lived in comfort, and no doubt added to their outstanding account, because you simply could not avoid having a flutter – wherever you went, between shows, etc., a game of one sort or another was in progress. The only hope was to live near the golf course, do sport all day and go to bed early without visiting the Strip or the tempting luxurious hotels – but how many could pass up the chance of winning a fortune?

For James the enjoyment was seeing all his favourite artists within a stone's throw of each other, Sinatra, Peggy Lee, Dorothy Dandridge, Johnny Mathis and scores of jazz musicians. One particular favourite of the Masons' was Max Bygraves, who held James in special esteem, since, as we have seen he had been responsible for saving his son from drowning.

Some of the comedians, Milton Berle for one, I did not enjoy. I found him crude and vulgar, but maybe I'm just not in tune with American humour, because I could have sat through hour upon hour of Max Miller who was hardly Mr Clean!

The only shoddy side of Vegas visible to me was the Matrimonial

Halls and Churches. You could marry anywhere, at any time, under any conditions. Divorced and re-married in a helicopter if you so wished within the hour, a production line, gaudy, opportunist and needless to say financially advantageous. Nonetheless these ceremonies offered the kind of service demanded and therefore they were part and parcel of a very special place. James found them very funny.

When I went back to Hollywood for this second time I found that the atmosphere and the whole way of living had changed totally. We no longer had such huge parties at the house. This was partly because James and Pam had changed, and James of course had been making a lot of his films abroad and moving out of Hollywood rather than working there. Pam had become much more her own person. She had got a lot of work (television chat shows and books) going on. She was in demand within her own sphere. But of course the more obvious change was in the relationship between them.

"Would you consider James an eccentric?" How many times have I had this question put to me! Numerous times, and the answer is "no". He was not the dithery vague Englishman so beloved of writers and so ridiculed by foreigners. I who can look back on nearly fifty years of Jamesian behaviour will go a little way towards conceding he was unusual, an original, a "one off", a mixture of the unexpected.

He certainly drove like a madman. A couple of hair-raising drives across Coldwater Canyon in Hollywood in his sports car quickly decided me to opt for Pam and her Rolls! James loved birds, harsh bleak paintings, sweets, parkin and liquorice allsorts in particular, and at one time he had a rather hippy period when he slung a guitar round his neck and wished to take Portland and Morgan on picnics with the children belonging to his then girlfriend, an idea hardly likely to pour oil on the already troubled waters at the Mason home.

He also had a desire to return to the simple life – planting organically-grown vegetables in the garden of his lady-love, who I feel would have preferred a somewhat less basic gift. An installed swimming pool or some lasting monument to their relationship might have proved more beneficial!

A dreamy man cast into a *modus vivendi* at odds with his temperament, he was ill at ease in a non-compatible materialistic world, yet one which he chose. For reasons I feel sure he never fully understood, he remained in the environment that in so many ways he despised. His brusque manner, his direct gaze unnerved many, he seemed unfriendly and aggressive, and I've known him to quite often walk into a room, encounter a sea of faces, even if they were familiar, and leave without saying a word! Was he rude, or was it part of his innate shyness? A mixture? If he had nothing to say, he said Nowt. As simple as that!

But if you could engage his interest, you found an erudite, intelligent person, never belligerent, never forcing his views, but giving carefully weighed opinions on a wide variety of subjects. He drew his conclusions but never dismissed other people's attitudes. His Yorkshire common sense was much to the fore in argument. I cannot deny that at times his abruptness could create the wrong impression, which led to some of the criticisms levelled against him.

I once suggested to James that he write studies of some of the actors, actresses and directors with whom he had worked, but he only laughed and said he hadn't the patience to sit and write. Not true. He was a great letter-writer and in 1981 his own autobiography was published, although he said he found writing it a chore and was not best pleased with it. "Too dry and rather dull," he told me was his own verdict. It certainly revealed little of James himself, but that was to be expected. Not for him the trumpet-blowing, self-admiration or the tittle-tattle that accompanies many such books. That was not James's way. He kept his own counsel, looked on with amused and sometimes bemused gaze at the antics of his fellow men, but he would not allow his tongue to injure or denigrate anyone. He might occasionally let fall a few critical remarks and, if he did, it was more likely to be the women of his acquaintance who would be the recipients – he tended to be harder on them than the men.

It has been said by those less well disposed towards James that in England he enjoyed the company of sycophants more readily than he did in Hollywood, a view which I totally reject. He didn't have many real friends in Hollywood, and no one who was a particular soul-mate, and this must have contributed to his loneliness when his marriage to Pam was breaking up. His main friends were in England, mostly in London, and they were very different from the people he knew in Hollywood. In the late 1950s he began to mend fences, and whenever he was in London he would pick up the telephone as soon as he arrived to contact all those people whom he regarded as *his*

friends, and arrange to see as many as possible of them while he was
there. Of course he preferred the company of people who were
sympathetic towards him, and more of these were to be found living
and working in Europe than there now were in Hollywood. But James
didn't choose his friends from the sychophants, he had great affection
for certain people whether or not they supported his views and
arguments.

Where sycophancy is in question I remember some amusing
moments when Pam's suitors called at 1018. James, often as not,
would collar them and take them off to his lair for chats about filming
or tennis, leaving Pam somewhat irritated and frustrated. "Who does
he think "so and so" has called to see? ME, not him!" Quite likely, but
as "so and so" was usually considered to be a friend of both parties,
who is to say?

James was no fool, he could be a fierce adversary when professional
conduct was called into question, and he was never inclined to give
praise easily. It had to be earned and his standards were demanding.
He applied the same stringency to himself too, his critical faculty was
acute and nowhere more so than when viewing himself. "Not bad was
it, not bad at all". That was the most praise I ever heard him say in
relation to his own performances, and even that was rare enough.

My only criticism, if that not be too strong a word, is that he tended
to regard actresses with a harsher eye than he did their male counterparts. I believe he felt that women stars were given an advantage by
dress, make-up and their sexuality, often to the detriment of their
talents. He didn't blame them, rather their exploiters, but it gave
James cause to weigh the real value of the actress against the build-up
which so often preceded their performances. I know for a fact he
simply adored Margaret Rutherford, admired Flora Robson, Simone
Signoret, Wendy Hiller and others who (I say without wishing to seem
uncomplimentary) owed their success to their craftsmanship rather
than their beauty. It's true to say James was captivated by comedy, and
his greatest joy was being made to laugh, and male comedians were in
the ascendancy over the ladies, in his opinion. When it came to
musicals the honours were more equally shared and James was highly
appreciative of the stars of both sexes competing, as they did, on pretty
equal terms. Nevertheless I did feel that he was a trifle hard on some of
the screen beauties who failed to measure up to his search for
perfection.

I hadn't realised until years after James made his home in Vevey that he was such a great admirer of my friend Kenneth Williams. Ken was sheer delight, a very serious person who viewed the troubled world with compassion and great anxiety, his public face and private face were poles apart and though he gave few people the opportunity to get close to him, those who were able to do so, as my mother was, held him in great esteem and deep affection. I can well imagine that his zany humour must have reduced James to tears of laughter on many occasions. *Pieces of Eight* remains in my mind as being a show that allowed Ken to offer his vast array of talent, but I suppose I remember him best as a unique personality and a very troubled spirit who cared too deeply.

I could perhaps place James in the same category to some extent, he found the ills of the world-disturbing and ugly and chose to set them aside as being too painful to observe as a daily diet, but he, fortunately, had someone to cherish later in his life and with whom he could share his innermost thoughts. Dear Ken, I believe, found this less easy, another very private man who took his refuge in farcical performances so as to mask his fears.

For James, the breakdown of his marriage realized some of his own worst fears. But why did he continue to live with someone for whom he no longer cared and who, by her general behaviour, held him in contempt? I taxed him with this subject before the divorce was finalised and I asked him why he had condoned Pam's behaviour. His reply was evasive and he seemed troubled by his own inability to answer. His only words were "After the initial shock, it didn't seem important."

Surely this was not the response one would expect from a man who had loved his wife? Jealousy may not be a pretty sight, but it is surely quite natural. Anger and resentment also, and I would suggest that James felt both those emotions, but love had gone.

Knowing Pam's propensity for speaking her mind without reticence or delicacy, James must have been made to jump through the flaming hoop many times, and this kind of hurt would have affected many a tougher man.

His indecisiveness was in no small measure to prove his undoing in the divorce, when he seemed unable and unwilling to offer any resistance and consequently allowed Pam to have her own way. She stripped him of everything he possessed in California and, as he later told a friend, he just "walked out of the house in the clothes I stood up in, and that was that." He never went back, and he took nothing with him.

In the final analysis I suppose one could say that Pam had created James, but once having achieved fame and success, in her own right, she chose to discard him like an unwanted plaything.

Just at the moment that James had to recognize that his marriage to Pam was over, there came the offer of the part of Humbert Humbert in the controversial film *Lolita*, which was to be another milestone in James's career. A book acclaimed by many, disliked by others, it offered James a role which might have been regarded with distaste by the average viewer. Yet he brought to it all the sadness and pathos that lay at the heart of this story of a middle-aged man enthralled by a nymphet. The part of Humbert Humbert was a challenge, one that for a while James had considered refusing. He was torn between accepting Stanley Kubrick's offer (although he knew he was not first choice) and waiting for the chance of a Broadway musical that was in the offing. He had prepared himself for a singing audition with his main party piece "Oh what a lovely bunch of Coconuts" (a song that I used to sing with him and we made a grand pair of duettists!).

When it finally came to the crunch though, James opted for *Lolita* much to the relief of Pam and many of his friends, who all felt that it would be wiser if James stuck to his own metier – particularly as the film would attract as much attention as Nabokov's controversial book had done.

The role itself was difficult because he would have to present a study of a man undergoing a traumatic and obsessive experience of a nature repugnant to most people. The male menopause may not always be taken seriously as a mid-life crisis, nevertheless it can be a strange and even tragic event for the man suddenly assailed with-temptations and odd predilictions hitherto unknown to him. The psyche that we all have and probably keep hidden well beneath the surface can suddenly explode, as I believe it did in James himself, in a moment in his life when bleakness of spirit was spreading rapidly through his veins. I am not suggesting for one moment that James himself was attracted to very young girls. But the part of Humbert Humbert required the understanding of a man facing a trauma that lay within himself – the pitfalls of such a part, which so easily could provoke disgust, called upon all his talent, and he had no scruples about playing a role which some actors had refused. He did not shrink from the possibility of offending his fans, but chose instead to explore the complexities of a character intent on gaining sympathy for what was in effect, on the surface at any rate, a sordid and manic obsession. There were plenty of his friends who could not understand why James had decided to take on such a controversial subject, which most people found distasteful and felt to be quite outside his normal sphere. He'd done a very wide range of work, from the classics to outright rubbish, but he'd never done anything seedy or sordid. The reason he chose to do it, I think, was that his own life was in such disarray that he could identify with the trauma that Humbert Humbert was undergoing.

Years later James was discussing the film with his friend and fellow-actor, Victor Spinetti and, when Victor told him what a wonderful performance he had given he replied "That was the director, old boy, it wasn't me. If you remember, I wore a white suit in the film and Stanley Kubrick said to me "Smile when you speak your lines and be charming, but all the time be thinking that if anyone dares to lay a finger on your suit and soil it you'll kill them. Keep thinking that and it will come right". That was direction – he gave me an inner dimension for the character". "You see," said Spinetti, "he was always so generous about other people – always gave credit to others if possible and was modest to a fault about himself."

It had been said that the part of Lolita herself required a younger girl than Sue Lyon, but James defended the choice and was full of praise for the way in which she handled an extremely difficult role. Sexual deviations do not, in general, carry much sympathy from an audience and I believe the measure of the success that *Lolita* enjoyed was in no small way due to the freshness and wayward innocence shown by the young actress – I had no doubt that James would find the means of touching a spark of understanding for his part. He had all the necessary experience, his age was right and mentally he had to be in tune with a character reacting to unknown feelings both exciting yet frightening. The human mind and body can so easily become a battlefield and James was enduring a personal war of his own when he undertook this film. I think too that he was perhaps swayed by the fact that shooting was to take place in England, his spiritual home, even if at this juncture he was still going through the motions of living in California.

The final curtain had begun to fall on the marriage before my mother and I arrived in California in 1959. As I mentioned before I had been ill and after an operation it was decided that Beverly Hills would be the perfect place for my convalescence. Pam and James had generously offered us the use of their guest house for as long as we wished to make it our home, paid our fares, and we duly set off.

On arrival we were met by Pam and her brother Vivian (who had for some years been working for James as a financial adviser), then the children duly appeared, but there was no sign of James. Pam said he too was unwell and had been for some while – that was all we were told. I believe in correspondence between Pam and Mama, mention had been made of James's ill health. I must confess however to having been too preoccupied with my own illnesses to pay much note of the ills of others, and it came as a shock to me when eventually I was able to leave my couch and walk across to the main house, to find James in a hospital type bed in the library, now turned into a sick room. He was surrounded by books, papers and medicaments, and wired up to all manner of machines which enabled him at the flick of a switch to turn on radio, TV and even a screen movie if he so wished. Whether any of these contraptions were also monitoring his health I wasn't sure, and his general demeanour did not encourage questions. He looked frail and strangely hectic, with his hair straggly, his face blotchy and of a livid hue, his manner uneasy and nervous.

I found it very disturbing – possibly I was more sensitive to his mood than the others who were in good health themselves – a sick room has a special atmosphere and does not necessarily bring out the best in those who find illness hard to cope with. "What has happened? What is wrong? "We received rather vague stock answers to our questions, which gave the impression that the whole business was being allowed to continue for far too long a period. Pam showed marked irritability in her dealings with James which surprised me, I had expected her to be sympathetic and worried by his condition – worried she may have been but sympathy was "non est" – at least by the time Mama and I had arrived on the scene.

Portland and Morgan were of course at school but when home they spent a lot of time with James and as he gradually took up a more active routine so they enjoyed sessions of playing either chess or pool with him and we gained the impression that the household was returning to normal. We were wrong.

As my own health improved I began to see more and more of what was going on in the house and how bad things really were between them. Their relationship seemed to hover between indifference and dislike, yet on the surface they still were able to enjoy outings like our trip to Las Vegas together and to appear at social functions.

The bubble burst one afternoon when Pam informed James that he was expected at a dinner party with her that evening. Rather uncomfortably he told her that he just couldn't make it because he had already made arrangements which he couldn't break.

She attacked him physically and verbally, with great violence. I believe some women, having decided that they no longer want someone, become determined that no one else is going to have them, and this seemed to be the likely explanation of her behaviour.

In her hysterical outburst she screamed terrible and wounding insults, accusing him of sexual and emotional incompetence and devaluing all his achievements. The things she said to James shocked him dreadfully as she destroyed for him the picture he had had of himself, and of the way she had thought of him in their relationship. Perhaps his preference for avoiding conflict had allowed him to deceive himself about the reality of their life together, but he was devastated to hear her say such things out loud. Much later, when Pam described James to me as a lousy lover I asked her how good a lover she had been for him. Why should he always have to live up to her requirements? Many men go through periods of diminished perform-ance, especially if they are under stress. If they are very sensitive they need more than just a quick sexual release, and if they are a bit nervous as well, they, like any woman, need careful and tender handling. James was always nervous and he wasn't a man who had experimented with sex in his youth – he had not been a mere kid when he had his first experience at twenty-six or so with Pam.

These were bad times. I watched the painful disintegration of a relationship that had endured for too long. I heard, with distress and anger, the vicious and insulting words that Pam poured forth against a defenceless man whose bewilderment was that of a child. James simply couldn't understand Pam's sudden change of attitude – from mutual toleration to frantic abuse. I witnessed the harm that Pam's outbursts did to the children's view of their parents. At twelve years old, Portland realised what was going on, she could figure it out and was an intelligent child, but at that age it was natural for her to be closer to her mother than her father. Morgan was only five and it was terribly saddening to see so small a boy so confused and upset, for he couldn't understand at all what was happening and why his mother was so tearful. I remember him rushing at James and hitting him with his fists crying, "Why are you making Mommy cry? – why are you making her cry?" It must have been quite terrible for him to hear the recriminations and abuse that Pam hurled at James when these screaming fits took place, but Pam's outbursts were so distressing that it was natural for him to blame James for having caused his mother's unhappiness.

James never had outbursts. He was the silent victim, he even wept soundlessly, and I shall never forget the sight of his standing, defenceless, with the tears coursing down his face and his body slumped in misery. Before this awful moment they had never really quarrelled and there hadn't been any tremendous rows because James would always withdraw from any confrontation. Of course he would fight his corner professionally, but never against Pam. He collaborated on films and scripts with Pam and her friends. He would also embrace everyone who came to the house and into their lives and work, regardless of their designs on Pam, or hers on them. It was as though he didn't want to be separated – to be put outside the family circle, and my own feeling is that he feared being alone. I think that's why he loved his friends so much and whenever he came to London he would phone them, and if he didn't get one he'd get another. He wasn't making use of people, they were just terribly important to him. This is why he kept in touch with me – I had a privileged position with him, because I had known him before he became famous, and he knew that I would make no judgements. He also knew that if he told me something in confidence he could trust me to keep it – and so did Pam. If she told me what she was up to in confidence I would never have gone to James and told him what was going on. For me they were two people living a quite extraordinary existence but, if that kept them happy and they were content to live in this way it was not for me to try to change it – I couldn't have changed it anyway.

But now this extraordinary existence had reached the point of no return. Pam's behaviour continued and the atmosphere in the house was charged with misery. You could feel the unhappiness when you walked inside – you could almost touch it. One evening, soon after Pam's first outburst, a visitor arrived to take me out for the evening. My very dear friend Paul Gregory, the talented and brilliant man who had been responsible for the successful *Drama Quartet* in which Charles Boyer, Sir Cedric Hardwick, Charles Laughton and Agnes Moorhead performed came to collect Mama and me for a dinner engagement. He was a great admirer of James and very fond of Pam, so it was natural that I should tell him about my anxieties and the dreadful scenes which had unfolded about my ears. "That's kind of sad, Diana," he said, "but it does not surprise me – I've noticed the atmosphere in this house". I suggested anyway that he might like to call in at the main house to greet Pam and James before we went out. We went across the garden but we got no further than the front door because, as he stepped over the threshold he shivered and said, "The atmosphere in here is dreadful, I just can't go inside," and he left without speaking to either of his friends.

Like so many others who knew and liked them, he hoped they would be able to sort out their differences without too much misery. But it was not to be. Misery was to abound, for James in particular, although I believe Pam suffered as well. She could have solved the whole unhappy mess quietly and without rancour, for nobody would have been more reasonable and generous than James in the circumstances. But she chose the other option, an option that was to secure for herself everything she wanted and to strip James of everything he possessed, leaving him emotionally and financially drained.

This trauma was to remain with James, an unhealed wound, raw and painful for much of the rest of his life. He thereafter feared unemployment and felt desperately the need to be constantly in work to earn the money he needed to meet the ruinous terms of the final divorce settlement. It was a near-phobia which left him edgy and tense between films. The bruising to which he had been subjected left him unsure of his personal relationships but this he could cope with providing he was not threatened by lack of work.

An artist's life always carries great uncertainties, fame today, failure tomorrow, and actors and actresses are vulnerable at the best of times. For James, facing the collapse of his private world, it was absolutely essential to find solace in work, taking on film after film.

Suitable or unsuitable, he was prepared to chase his agents, directors, producers so as to get a job.

If left in the doldrums for any length of time he became anxious and aggrieved. One has only to study the list of films he completed between 1953 and 1964 (twenty-seven or more) to realise how driven he was to remain busy. Any likelihood of a curtailment of his career assumed quite unnatural proportions even before his marriage fell apart and after the event work was imperative. I don't know whether or not it is fanciful to say that James's self-portraits were indicative of his own true view of himself? Possibly so, certainly none were flattering or complimentary. Caricatures tend to overstate oddities or defects and James was never one for vanity – even so there was an underlying bitterness in his drawings of himself, one in particular was disturbing in its intensity – a sketch of himself holding a gun to his head plainly showed the depth of his depression. But it would be quite untrue to imply that James lived under a black cloud at all times. However unsatisfactory his home life he still showed signs of enjoying the children, sport and of course, above and beyond all else, WORK.

His emotional sensitivity was rarely seen, he hid his feelings from virtually everyone – maybe he felt ashamed of admitting weakness or failure – he was in a sense the victim of his reputation. A critically hard man, a professional outspoken actor with a tough, uncompromising wife – difficult to feel sympathy for someone so successful, so well endowed, a lovely home, happy children, fame, money and a marriage of long standing. The world judges what it sees and James by any standard was to be envied. Poor fellow, how far from the truth can one get?

The fact that he was able to confide in me may seem strange, but remember that at the time he was *in extremis* and I was close at hand and he knew he could trust me. I could listen and I could take a cool detached view of the situation, I had affection for both Pam and James but I was not blind to the effects of what was to be a war with no holds barred.

Pam's resentment of James's visits to Mama and me at the guest house caused a breach between him and my mother, solely as a result of the tirades by Pam – she wanted him isolated, forced out and James was greatly upset by what he saw as an unfair and critical stance in regard to his behaviour. "Why is Auntie Mummy so against me Diana? *You* don't blame me, do you?"

16. One of my favourite images of James, as Rommel in *The Desert Fox* in 1951.

17. Peek a Boo! James playing with Portland in 1951.

18. Round the piano, Hollywood 1951. Left to right: James; Portland; myself and Pam.

19.   20.

21.

19. James the Pitcher, during his season at Stratford, Ontario in 1954.

20. Another part that really suited James – Captain Nemo in *20,000 Leagues Under the Sea* (1954).

21. James with Judy Garland in *A Star is Born* (1954).

22.

23.

22. James, Sue Lyon and Shelley Winters in the controversial film of the novel *Lolita* (1962).

23. James relaxes with Alec Guinness on the set of *The Fall of the Roman Empire* (1964).

24. A Mason family group, 1965 – Colin and James with their parents.

25. In 1969, James made *Age of Consent*. This is a photograph of the cast and crew, with Clarissa next to James.

26.

27.

28.

29.

26. James in *Spring and Port Wine*, the film he made with Susan George in 1969.

27. James and Clarissa at the races – The Melbourne Cup.

28. *The Faith Healer*. James and Clarissa with director Jose Quintero.

29. James returned to Yorkshire in 1976 to film *The Water Babies*, with Bernard Cribbins and a donkey!

30.

31.

32.

30. and 31. James and Clarissa created a beautiful garden at
Vevey, incorporating one of the lions from Croft House. Even
James's favourite car, when past its prime, was put to ornamental
use, covered with clematis.

32. James and Clarissa at their home in Vevey, Switzerland, with
'Michael' the rocking horse.

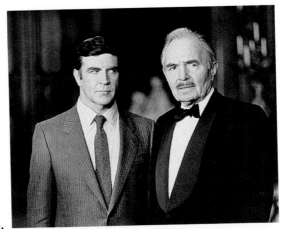

33.

34.

35.

33. James's penultimate role was as the lead in *Dr. Fischer of Geneva*, which also starred Alan Bates.

34. Clarissa acted with James in *Dr. Fischer*, and away from the cameras, they made sure that the cast had plenty to eat, bringing food from their home.

35. James's last film, *The Shooting Party*, followed immediately after *Dr. Fischer*. As the aristocratic host James won universal acclaim.

Of course I didn't, neither did Mama. Blame had no part to play –
I tried to explain that it was difficult for a mother to side against her
daughter, if forced to choose it was not unnatural for her to support
Pam – it was a choice she would have preferred not to make, but in
any event she felt that James's reasoning was disengenuous
altogether.

How could he have hoped to maintain his marriage and keep a
mistress? What kind of woman would be willing to remain shunted
away in the background without having any form of security on
social standing? Particularly as no doubt the lady in question was
fully aware of the situation that existed between Pam and James.

The marriage was a farce, it was up the creek, there was no basis
for continuing together and what I found more than puzzling was
how James could have ever considered remaining tied to Pam after
the violent scenes that had left him reeling with shock and weeping in
anguish. Did he enjoy being a victim? There are some characters who
choose that role, they desire to be punished – The "nanny" syndrome
is not uncommon, but in James's case I think it would be wide of the
mark. He tended to overlook, or fail to see, the faults in those he
cared about, and chose to ignore the more obvious problems that
needed sorting out. His introverted nervous character made him
desirous of peaceful co-existence and the rages that shook his
household left him appalled when the storm burst.

It struck me that some of Pam's most uncontrolled outbursts were
the result of too much to drink. I was concerned for her because I was
aware of a slackening of self control, her moods were mercurial and
I knew that drinking was not a good or safe way for her to get a
"lift".

"Tinsel town" can be a demanding place and Pam, diamond bright
a person as she was showed signs of being prey to the pressures that
are synonymous with success and being in demand. On the surface
she had everything, beauty, wit, a fine home, children who loved her
and definitely no lack of admirers. James was an excellent provider
and her own business acumen saw that there would be no shortage of
financial security in the future.

When I left her in 1952 none of us drank. But I had noticed in
London, when Pam came over after that, she had developed a habit
of nipping vodka. She told me that she had been drinking brandy
before that, but it made her feel so ill and she had been warned that it

was dangerous so why the need for booze? Was Pam perhaps as dissatisfied with life with James as he was unhappy with her? If this was the crux of the matter either party had the means of ending the partnership – in Pam's case it would not have meant any sacrifice. She would not have lost her home, her children or her investments. True, under the Community Property laws she would have had to share but James was no hard bargainer, quite the opposite, if Pam had wanted the house and the blocks of flats and so on.

When cash became the prize, loyalty, honesty and ethics were discarded as quickly as a snake sloughs off its skin, and it was Pam who decided that divorce was the answer. She held all the cards and James, for some quite inexplicable reason, refused to fight for his rights – I taxed him again and again as to why he hadn't countered the lawyers claims and his answers were veiled and evasive.

The divorce was finally completed in September 1964. James and Pam had been married for twenty-three years and their love affair, which had begun with such fervour and success twenty-eight years before, ended in great bitterness. The final settlement had taken nearly four years for their lawyers to agree and it left James homeless and penniless. Pam had sued him on the grounds of "habitual adultery" but James, true to his own standards, refused to counter-claim or make any reference to Pam's own adultery. His declared reason was that he wished to protect the children from being dragged into the humiliating and public court procedures with all the awful publicity this would attract. Knowing that she had won Pam agreed in court to drop adultery charges (in which she had named three Los Angeles women) and was granted the divorce on the grounds of desertion and extreme mental cruelty. She and James had actually separated in 1962 when James had left the USA but Pam was an American citizen and she now stood to gain everything they had worked for together. Not only did she get the marital home and everything in it, she took the apartment blocks and every investment and possession they jointly owned. James was required to pay her a large sum each month for maintenance until both children should have reached the age of twenty-one, and since Morgan was still only nine, that was to be a long-term commitment. James was stripped of everything he had.

But who was really the loser? In material terms it was James, and at the time he was also the loser emotionally, for he had to leave in

America the children who meant so much to him and who had, for so long, been his emotional anchor. Their loyalties lay with their mother and the less they saw of him the stronger their ties to Pam became. For years James would make great efforts to keep in touch with them, to have them visit him in Europe and make the journey to California himself to see them. But they lived with Pam in what was now Pam's house and he found small welcome there. James said that he felt the children needed him but I think he was wrong – I think he needed them.

James had few really close friends in Hollywood. Plenty of good professional friends with whom he shared a common interest in work, but no real soul-mates or supporters. Because it was hard for people to get close to James he found himself at the end of his marriage with no one who could console him. He longed to be close to people, he cared about people, and he hated to be alone.

In Europe, and especially in England, things were different. Towards the end of the 50s, and while his marriage was irretrievably deteriorating, the work James was offered took him more and more frequently out of America. With every trip away from the States he made contact with old friends and his relations in England, and began the process of mending fences with his family. He had made his first visit home to see his parents at Croft House for the Easter holiday in 1953, after a gap of more than fifteen years. His own diary provides an account of his first sight of the familiar landscape of his home:

> Genuinely moved by the scenery. Denby Dale, Cawthorne. Trees hunched against the heavy weather, huddling in copses, sheltering in tiny valleys, beginnings of spring buds, heavy beads left by the rain, bright green lichen. The country houses square stone boxes, the heavy blockhouses of lodgegates. Little isolated neatly dressed people walking. The drama of Cawthorne Park ripped open by outcrop coal mining.

He was plainly deeply affected by the loving and unceremonious way in which his parents and his brothers all welcomed him quietly and generously back into their home and their domestic circle. They were genuinely glad to see him for his own sake, and to put aside for ever the differences and neglect of the previous eighteen years. His diary goes on to describe the joy of discovering that Croft House had not changed, things were as he remembered from his boyhood, familiar furnishings and fabrics, books and pictures – even the intense cold in the badly heated old building – all brought back to life the memories and experiences of his childhood. James had found his roots, and from now on he would never lose sight of them again. He had also found a source of strength and comfort to which he would return again and again.

In London there were friends, real friends, whose affection had been fed and nurtured over the years by the letters which had always been his pleasure to write and their delight to receive. James's artistic talents had found their natural expression in his drawing and painting, his enjoyment of music, poetry and literature but, above all, in the prolific, stylish and descriptive prose in which he couched his correspondence with his friends. He made the Dorchester Hotel in London his regular base and as soon as he arrived there he would pick up the telephone and call everyone that mattered to him and make arrangements to see them all. He filled the days when he was free from work with lunches and dinners and outings in the company of the people whose friendship and loyalty now became the most important ingredient in his life, a constant consolation in the privately bleak years which followed his divorce.

When he realised that his marriage was past salvaging James decided that he would have to make some kind of alternative base for himself on his own and he began to look around. He would dearly have liked to settle back in England but, as he pointed out to me, he had to consider the problem of the English tax laws which would make it impossible for him to earn enough to meet his financial obligations to Pam and the children in America. So he decided finally that Switzerland would be the answer, as there was already a fairly large colony of Hollywood tax-exiles in residence. He knew he could afford to live there, it was well placed for travelling to England and anywhere else in Europe that he might need to go to for work, and there were familiar faces from the film industry living in the vicinity. He didn't have to look for very long before he heard of a small flat, three rooms with kitchen and bathroom on the ground floor of a house overlooking Lake Geneva at Vevey. Without hesitation he took it. Now he had a base of his own from which he could begin the next chapter of his life.

At this point, in the early 60s, my path and that of James divided – purely as a result of geography. We remained good friends, but I returned to my home in France whilst he began rebuilding his life and career elsewhere. We would always meet when our visits to London happened to coincide but these perforce were fairly rare occasions – my main recollection of those days is of luncheon parties with too many guests and far too little food!

James at that time took rented apartments, and Frank Essien, the dear little butterball of a man, who had replaced Johnnie Monaghan as his aide and companion, took charge of the catering. This task was no easy one, as six guests more often than not became twelve, leaving Frank to scuttle back and forth to the kitchen and, with whatever help he had laid on, chop sausages into bite size nibbles scrambled with whatever ingredients came to hand so as to conjure up sufficient "snacks" of exotic odds and ends Ghanaian style! All the while James would sit like a potentate holding court at the head of the table oblivious to the frantic efforts being made in the culinary department – it says a great deal for James that our enjoyment was never clouded by the paucity of the fare provided – mild pangs of hunger might have assailed us on occasions but we had so much verbal entertainment that they passed unnoticed!

His greatest pleasure at this time was to bring his closest friends together and watch them become friends through him. He was thus creating his own "family circle", knitting together the people he liked so that they should in turn know and like each other. In this way he made a network of communication and recognition amongst them with himself at the centre and to which he could feel he belonged.

At this stage my personal memories will seem both scrappy and uninformative, my meetings and contacts with James were fleeting and perforce our friendship to some extent dwindled. His life and mine no longer had any common ground. We kept in touch and of course I read of his travels. His capacity for work had, if anything, become even greater and his films were too numerous to note. Narrations and TV appearances were also undertaken, and my impression was that he kept loneliness at bay by filling his life, as he had always tended to do, by working. Between times he enjoyed the company of his friends and relatives, but I suspect that what happened in Hollywood left James very wary of trusting anyone. His confidence, so meagre at the best of times, had been shattered, and even while he sought a personal relationship he felt unable to feel confident in his ability to make the right decision.

James's friends and colleagues who have so kindly contributed to this book will shed a better light than I on James's state of mind from now on, and perhaps they will confirm my observations of this complex man. Whatever bitterness he may have felt he kept to himself, he had tasted fame, riches, joy and sorrow, but one had to know James very well indeed to see beneath the surface of his well maintained facade.

To see James at ease amongst his friends was rewarding, easing my memories of the bewildered, defeated man I had observed in Hollywood. Yet stripped though he had been of all his worldly goods, and incidentally, his *amour propre*, he was not the loser – the ranks of his family, his friends and colleagues closed firmly around him, and the loyalty and affection felt for this quiet, even austere man, was tangible from all sides. The sadness, gall and bitterness that James must have felt was assuaged by the warmth and sympathy so freely offered.

Naturally enough, from time to time James would dwell on the collapse of his world, even a world built on straw had its compensations, but he disguised his pain from prying eyes and forced himself, through work, to find the solace he needed to allow the wounds to heal. What caused him the greatest heartache was not having Portland and Morgan near enough to see on a regular basis – as a result of this, James made several journeys back to California so as to keep a close contact. Understandably these sojourns were a source of irritation to Pam and I doubt that the welcome mat was much in evidence. Too much had happened, too much harm done, too much bile spewed out in the heat of the moment for any meetings to be comfortable.

Portland was able to make fairly regular visits to James, and Morgan too, though more rarely, and I know their welfare was always uppermost in James's mind. He had no doubt of Pam's love for the two young people, but he feared that left solely under her influence they would subscribe to her values, or to put it more generously, the values inherently American, with the emphasis on money and success. It was not that James scorned these attributes but the experience of the divorce and his natural inclination towards the basic precepts of his upbringing gave him greater cause for anxiety about the children than he might otherwise have felt.

By now his home base was the little flat in Vevey and his visits to

California became few and far between. The flat was sunny and nicely proportioned, but it was pretty bare of furnishings and possessions, for he had very little. It was whitewashed throughout, and there was a wonderful view of the lake through the windows. An outside door from the small sitting room gave access to the garden, but apart from perhaps using it as a place to sit James had neither the time nor the interest to do anything with it. He grew to be very fond of his downstairs neighbour, an elderly English lady called Mrs Cresswell, and in time he got to know the landlord (a banker named Fleury) who lived in the upstairs flat. It was pleasant and convenient, and it served the purpose for which he needed it.

One unexpected pleasure James found in Vevey was the revival of an old professional friendship. Jack Cardiff had worked for Gainsborough Films before the war and at one time with a certain camera operator called Roy Kellino, so he and James had known each other from very early days. Jack had been the cameraman on *Pandora and the Flying Dutchman* and the two men had found a rapport and liking for each other during the making of that film, so when James took the flat in Vevey and discovered that Jack was living only half a mile away, he was thrilled. Having their interest in the film industry and their ex-pat status in common, they soon became good friends. They both loved to play tennis and they would go off to Montreux quite often for a game together and spin out the day over coffee or drinks. They enjoyed dining together in the evenings and discussing their work. Jack had great admiration for James's professional integrity and he would sometimes ask him for his opinion of potential projects. James loved to talk over these possibilities and he would go over to tea to read the script and play all the parts for Jack and spend hours discussing it in detail. He was always tremendously interested in other people's career and work opportunities, and would happily give his time and energy to them. He loved reading aloud and he adored to get hold of a script and bring it to life. They both enjoyed and valued the companionship they could offer each other.

Charlie Chaplin was another friend from California who had settled nearby and who welcomed James to his home. He had brought his family to live in Switzerland and his children were growing up as Europeans, but they used to share the Sunday afternoon tea parties when they all lived in Hollywood and they had many memories in common. Charlie and his wife Oona kept themselves very much to themselves but they made an exception with James, who shared their dislike of uncourted, invasive publicity.

A change in the American tax laws in the mid sixties sent many of the American exiles scurrying home again, and gradually the Swiss film colony dispersed. But James stayed on. In time he bought the rest of the house from his landlord, and as he built up his financial resources he and Fleury began to invest in building apartments nearby as a business venture – as he and Pam had done in America. When they divorced his money was mainly in property and Pam reaped the benefit of all those investments. James never liked or understood the stock market; he distrusted it and all those who manipulated it. He had never been money-conscious as a young man, and he was never seriously interested in it until after the divorce when the settlement forced him to provide regularly very large sums for the benefit of Pam and the children – and then he became continually anxious about it. But he knew that property had been a good investment in America and he thought he couldn't go wrong if he put his money into the same thing in Switzerland. So Switzerland became the place from which heoperated, but it was England that he came to regard as home, because it was there that he knew he would find friends and family who would welcome him with open arms.

After that first visit back to Croft House in the Spring of 1953 James began to make regular efforts to see his parents and his brothers. His niece Val, Rex's daughter, remembers that if her uncle James was in England for half-terms and holidays he would be included in any outings that were organised and, as his visits home became more and more frequent, he would always try to get to Yorkshire for important family occasions. He was there for her twentieth birthday and, after taking her out to dinner, they went off to the Masonic Hall in Huddersfield for a dance – admission four shillings. He loved to plan things that he knew would give real enjoyment. Val's growing up coincided with the breakdown of James's marriage and in her he found an unexpected and welcome companion. She was family and, in the same way that I had been a "comfy relative" to whom he could relate without difficulty, he found in her a willing friend. When she came to live in London he arranged for her to stay with his friends Al and Margaret Parker, and she had a room above their premises in Park Lane. Al Parker, the man who had discovered James and given him his first job in films, was now his agent. They had never lost touch and Al had always been generous with his advice and guidance as James's career had progressed, and now he was handling all James's work. James and Val got to know each other very well while they were both in London. They used to go for long walks along the Embankment by the Thames and talk and talk while she filled in for him the family history he had missed while he was in America. Val was a little older than Portland, but she helped to fill the gaps in his life created by the absence of the two children he had lost.

There were other friends who became constant factors in his life. Kaye Webb, founder of Puffin Books, had known him since the Second World War when he had appeared on a radio programme with her, and he was godfather to her twins from her marriage to Ronald Searle. They might have lost touch when James and Pam went to America, but her babies had been born in the U.S.A. and James had taken a great interest in them straight away and asked if he and Pam could be godparents. Kaye tells the story of how, when she arrived in the New York in 1948 just before the twins were born, James, indulging his own sense of the ridiculous, took her to lunch at the Stork Club. Her shape left no-one in any doubt as to her condition and little jokey presents, like large diaper pins, were brought to their table as a friendly gesture. Dining nearby was the columnist Walter Winchell who couldn't believe his eyes and certainly couldn't contain his curiosity as to who the lady might be and what her relationship to James really was. So they had a lot of fun leading him on and gently teasing the poor man who was sure he was on to a really hot story. The babies turned out to be a pigeon pair, John and Katie, and while they grew up back in England James kept in touch through letters and saw them when he could. Katie was only slightly older than Portland and James took great pleasure in spending time with Kaye and Katie on his visits to England.

A nice example of the way in which James liked to involve his friends with each other ties up two friendships. As Katie said, after her parent's marriage broke up, James took his role as godfather very seriously and she came to regard him as a very important part of her family. One winter, when she was still in her teens, Katie took a job

as a demonstrator with an exhibition that was being held in Basle.
When she arrived there she found that the only place available for her
to stay was simply awful – freezing cold, flea-ridden and miserably
depressing. She stuck it out for as long as she could but finally she
could stand it no longer and rang James to tell him that she was
stranded and broke. He immediately drove from Vevey to Basle,
collected her, told her employers what he thought of her treatment
and took her back to his home. He looked after her for a week, fed
and cared for her, cheered her up and finally, having bought her
ticket, put her on a plane for London.

Val Mason, his niece, also found James to be a wonderful friend in
need. She was injured in a riding accident on a weekend holiday in
the West country and, after hospital treatment, had been sent home
to London. No-one realised that she had been quite badly hurt and
when James, despite her refusal because she felt so ill, persuaded her
to meet him at the Dorchester she went, only to pass out in the foyer
at his feet. Immediately he booked the vacant room next to his and
had her taken to it. She was put to bed and he summoned the help of
an emminent brain specialist to examine her. On Mr. McLellan's
advice he kept her there, at his own expense, for three weeks until he
was sure that the injury had been properly treated and she would
recover completely. And while Val was lying in her bed at the
Dorchester, James got Katie, who was a talented artist herself, to go
secretly with him to Val's flat and paint her plain white walls with a
marvellous mural to give her a happy surprise when she was brought
home. She had recently had a holiday in Greece and was fascinated
by Greek mythology, so James's design for the mural was based on
the gods and goddesses in a classical landscape, with lots of owls for
her special amusement, because he knew she loved them. When,
much later, she finally had to leave the flat it took her nearly three
weeks to clean the walls, but the paintings had looked wonderful.

Thereafter James and Val saw a great deal of each other and Val
was able to provide the family companionship that James so badly
missed. He had always made an effort to include his godchildren and
his nephew and niece in what he was doing when he was in England.
He would invite them to visit the sets of the films he was working on,
and when he had to improve his ice-skating for *The Man Between* he
hired boots and skates for them and paid for their lessons at the rink
where he was practising. When he moved to Switzerland he invited

them out to join him for ski-ing holidays, always paying for everything. Sometimes he would have Portland or Morgan visiting too, so the younger generation were not strangers to each other and this gave him a sense of belonging.

Val went out to Vevey to see the flat soon after James bought his first stake in the property there. James could relax with Val because, having the Yorkshire family as a common bond, they had much to talk about that had nothing to do with his work and the other stresses and problems which weighed him down. But while Val could give him her easy companionship from time to time, she could see that he was desperately in need of someone to look after and care for him.

In 1964 James went to Spain to work on *The Fall of the Roman Empire*. He said he took the role because it gave him the chance to ride a horse, which he enjoyed and it proved to be a very happy location. Alec Guinness was in the cast and they were able to renew the acquaintance begun in the theatre in London before the war. Christopher Plummer became a lasting friend, and James took a great liking to Sophia Loren. For the sequences that required a studio setting they worked in Madrid, and while they were there Val went to stay with James for a short holiday. In her twenties, she was a very attractive girl and her arrival caused a flurry of gossip in the local press. This had happened before, but the joke appealed to them both and they played along with the press, tantalising the persistent reporters by making no denials about their relationship. James loved a joke. He was not a practical joker or a great teller of tales, but he adored other peoples' funny stories and he saw humour in all kinds of situations, and he enjoyed telling stories against himself. Val remembers being with him one day in the Dorchester Hotel when a film fan engaged him in conversation. Unfortunately the fan wasn't much of an expert on the cinema and he had in fact mistaken James for someone else – like John Wayne. James didn't put him right and hugely enjoyed himself by answering, inaccurately, all kinds of questions about the life and work of the other actor and keeping an absolutely straight face all the while. He graciously received the fan's final tribute of admiration to the absent actor and bade him a polite farewell as the fan took his leave with an enthusiastic "Goodbye, and thank you so much Mr. Wayne". And James loved to tell the story about an interview he had heard on the radio with an old man who

had worked for 35 years as the attendant in the gentlemen's public
lavatories at Marble Arch in London, who, when asked if he had ever
recognised anyone famous making use of the facilities, replied
without hesitation "Oh yes, James Mason".

James was more relaxed and happy in Spain than he had been for a
long time; geographically removed from all his problems and in the
company of people he liked, the warmth of the Spanish sun seemed
to cheer his spirit. Val remembers that he had taken up the guitar and
loved to sit on the balcony of his flat there gently strumming in the
sunshine. They used to sing together to his accompaniment and they
perfected (sadly never recorded) their own unique if tuneless version
of "Does Your Chewing Gum Lose its Flavour on the Bedpost
Overnight".

The base for the outdoor location work was a small Spanish town
called Segovia, and James loved it. Set in wonderful scenery with
beautiful old buildings, it even had its own fairytale castle and, on
Sunday evenings, the *Passea*. Between six and eight everyone who
lived there would promenade around the town in their best clothes,
nodding to each other as they passed or stopping for a gossip in the
street and filling and cafes where they settled for refreshment and to
meet their friends and relatives – even the mayor and town dignita-
ries would turn out in style. James found it all enchanting and the
way of life, so simple and complete and different from anything he
had come across before, attracted him strongly. And then he found
the house. It was a kind of terraced manor house, built around a
courtyard. The main part of it was quite old, but bits had been added
to it over a long period of time – Romanesque, Roccoco, Spanish
traditional, Spanish Colonial – and it was a wonderful jumble of
architectural style and period. James fell in love with it and he saw it
as an idyllic home in an idyllic place in which to make a totally new
life – so he bought it. Frank Essien, who was of course out there with
him as his aide, negotiated the purchase of the house. It was owned
by two brothers who sold it to a Mr. Neville Mason – James quite
rightly thinking he might be taken advantage of if he used his more
famous first name and, indeed, the brothers were annoyed when they
discovered his identity – they would certainly have doubled the price
if they had known who he was. Behind the house there was a lovely
garden and inside the house, in the basement, lived the family who
looked after it. Their windows should have had a marvellous view of

the garden but the previous owners had bricked them up so that they were not only deprived of that pleasure, they were deprived of the daylight. The first thing James did when he took possession of the house was to unblock the windows, transforming the living conditions for the family and winning their undying gratitude. But although James now had the house of his dreams there was something missing. George Murcell, a fellow actor working alongside him on the film, remembers how thrilled he was with the house and how, before he bought it, he was so excited he wanted everyone to come and see it. It wasn't a castle, the real one *El Cazar* was on the other side, but he called it HIS castle. "You must come and see me at my castle" he would say.

George's wife, Elvi Hale, had joined him in Spain with their three month old baby, Jamie. James took to Jamie in a big way and he and the Murcells struck up a friendship. They spent a lot of time together and shared an enthusiasm for sightseeing. They dashed off whenever they had time free from filming to look at the places of interest and the ancient architecture with which the area abounded. They also shared a great enjoyment of jazz. George played the trumpet and he was very knowledgeable about the kind of music James liked. James knew Louis Armstrong and Duke Ellington, he had met Sidney Bechet in Paris and he had a large collection of records. He adored Ray Charles and used to listen to his records for hours, but he used to make a point of sitting down to listen – he wouldn't use it as a background for anything else. George played New Orleans Jazz, and that was something James really liked so they used to talk about and listen to it endlessly.

They appreciated each other's sense of humour. George thought James was actually quite a funny man. He used to send up the people he knew in Hollywood who took themselves very seriously and make wry jokes about people that they wouldn't understand. He was very peverse and used to introduce Mel Ferrer (who was also working on the film) as Mel Torme – because he knew it would irritate him – and he would introduce an English friend to some unsuspecting Spaniards as "The Duke of Windsor". In his turn, James enjoyed George's flair for funny stories. One evening they were dining in a restaurant together when Elvi's low-cut dress slipped as she leant across the table and bared her bosom to the public view. James took great delight in using the occasion to tell one of the stories in his own repertoire – about the waiter who helped a lady in a similar situation by carefully replacing the exposed breast in her dress with a spoon and napkin, and was fired by the head waiter for not warming the spoon first. James liked that one.

But Spain was not going to provide the princess as well as the palace and although he had great plans for entertaining his friends there on a baronial scale it never really happened. There was never anybody much in the house and the parties he had were for just a few friends – after all he had always hated the big parties he and Pam used to give, so there was no reason for him now to do it if he didn't really want to. He had ambitious plans for the way he would furnish and redecorate the house, but he wasn't there for long enough to do much and it was never really furnished properly at all. The film came to an end and he had to leave Spain, and in the end he sold his castle with all his dreams for it unfulfilled.

But back in London James's friendship with the Murcells continued. They had just moved into a Edwardian terraced house near Kew Gardens, close to the river and open space and near enough to the Dorchester for James to be able to visit them easily, so a few days after they got home from Spain James turned up for lunch. It was chaos in the house, cases half unpacked, nappies and baby paraphernalia everywhere, the builders' work half-finished, bare plaster inside and bricks, rubble and old beer bottles in the garden. But it was a very hot day and James said "Can we have lunch in the garden", took his shoes off, rolled up his trousers and sat happily with them in the sun amidst all the muddle and mess. He had the ability to be at home almost anywhere and, if he liked them, to make people feel at home with him. He obviously enjoyed being with this young family and they decided, it being a lovely day, to take Jamie for a walk in his pram in Kew Gardens. They set off, but the afternoon was soon spoilt for James as people began to recognise him. He had hoped for a quiet and anonymous outing but his was a famous face and it was impossible for him to be private in a public place. He hated it so they turned round and went home.

George and Elvi assumed that, like so many 'film' friendships, theirs would quickly fade as their professional paths were unlikely to cross again. But whenever he was in London James would ring them, as he did all his friends, and ask them to meet him or join him for a meal. Elvi remembers that when he called he would always begin by saying "I don't know if you will remember me, my name is James Mason".

Very often when they met he would have a lady with him, and it seemed that he was looking for their opinion and approval of her. He was uncertain about his choice of female companions and needed to feel that his friends would accept them. As George said, they were not always of his calibre. He was an educated man, very knowledgeable and interested in history, architecture, art and literature and current affairs and perhaps it was hard for him to find someone with similar interests among the women he met through his work. Paul Grunder, who was the manager at the Dorchester Hotel, tells how he would occasionally see James accompanied by a lady, and think to himself "Oh dear, what a pity, not for him."

There was never any scandal about James. Though he always stayed at the Dorchester when he was in London, he never looked for any special treatment and he never wanted anything more than an ordinary room – no grand suite for him. He came and went unassumingly, checking in and out and going about his business quietly. As a guest he was a very private man, keeping himself to himself and not, as many well-known people did, forming friendships with the hotel staff. After the divorce he seemed to them to be a very lonely man, but he was always courteous and polite and they liked him for his natural decorum. He didn't behave like a star, he behaved like a gentleman, though perhaps a rather sad one.

Meanwhile, work was the palliative and, when he was working, he kept his social life very simple. *The Pumpkin Eater* followed *Fall of the Roman Empire* and, because it was made in England, he had several months in which he could refresh old and valued friendships. His fifty-fifth birthday came in that Spring, and Kaye Webb decided that it should be properly celebrated so she organised a surprise luncheon party for him at her house. The weather was lovely on that Sunday in May so the party was held in the garden and Kaye had invited a wide selection of James's old friends with a number of the cast of the film. It was a complete surprise for James, who thought he was just going to have lunch with Kaye and his godchildren, and he had such a wonderful time that the party lasted well into the evening.

But outside the security of his chosen circle of faithful friends

James sometimes found the world a pretty cold and lonely place. The next film he did, *Lord Jim* took him to Hong Kong. He was there for the New Year celebrations but it didn't suit his mood to go to the party organised by Peter O'Toole and the rest of the film unit, so he decided to see the New Year in alone on the ferry boat crossing the harbour. But at midnight he found he was not alone, he was sharing the deck of the ferry with a stranger who was horribly drunk. This unpleasant man recognised James and accosted him belligerently, and the discovery that he was English upset James even more. It made his lonely situation the more poignant, and keeping company with this drunken stranger in a foreign country with no family or friends to comfort him made this the worst turn of the year he had ever endured. He was at a very low ebb indeed.

However, less than three weeks later he was back in England travelling back to Huddersfield for an extraordinary family event. His parents, both now eighty-five years old, were celebrating their Diamond wedding anniversary and friends and relatives gathered at Croft House to give them a wonderful party. The presence of their famous son attracted the attention of the local press to this family gathering, but the reporters were received courteously by John and Mabel Mason. It was not so long since James's divorce had been dealt with very publicly by the newspapers and while he stood beside his parents someone asked insensitively "Mr. Mason, in the sixty years of your marriage have you ever contemplated divorce?" With his own sharp wit John Mason replied "Divorce never – but murder . . . quite often".

For James it was more than a party, it was a refuge from what he increasingly felt to be a hostile world. The old familiar house and the faces remembered from his boyhood gave him comfort and the knowledge that, if nowhere else, he still belonged in Yorkshire. He longed for Portland and Morgan to get to know and understand this background to his life, and occasionally he managed to take them there, but too seldom for it to mean very much to them. Just a few months earlier he had taken Portland to visit Howarth Parsonage, the home of the Brontes, to give her a taste of the literary heritage and the landscape that he loved and which was so vastly different from the life that she knew in Hollywood.

But his own working life was a foreign land to his Yorkshire family. Like me, they had never been particularly interested in or impressed by his fame and career, and there was no point in discussing with them his plans and projects for the future or asking for their advice in professional matters. So it was back to London he went for the consolation and encouragement he needed to help him make the decision about what he should do next.

He was now approaching his fifty-sixth birthday, and clearly he had to face up to the fact that the work he would be offered from now on would be of a different nature to the kind of parts he had played up to now. He was long past the heartthrob matinee idol roles that had brought him such success in his thirties and early forties, and he would soon no longer be a candidate for the attractively mature heroes that he could still, until quite recently, have played quite convincingly. *Lolita* had started a change of direction for him but he had then been scarcely out of his forties. *The Pumpkin Eater* had provided him with another interesting and rather unattractive role and in *Lord Jim* and *Genghis Khan* he had been heavily disguised in scene-stealing cameo parts – supporting the bigger names in star-studded casts. But where could he go now? There was always the problem of the money he had to make to fulfil his legal obligations to Pam and the children before he could begin to live himself, so it was essential that he keep working and earning. He couldn't afford to stop and he certainly didn't want to. After all, what else was there for him to do? Although he had always been fascinated by television and had made a brief appearance in a couple of experimental plays in the early days of live transmission from Alexandra Palace just before the war, his forays into that area had never been very successful. Before he left America, he had hit a professional low by appearing as the host of a series called *The Lux Video Theatre* which culminated in a spectacular disaster when the teleprompter failed leaving him speechless and helpless in front of a live audience and millions of viewers. He had done a couple of plays for television directed by Sidney Lumet, whom he admired very much, but for him it was very much a medium to be feared, and despite his success in *Oedipus* at Stratford Ontario, and the fun he had had with the melodramas in the little theatre at Beverly Hills, he believed that he no longer had the voice or the presence to fill a theatre. He was most at home in front of the film cameras, and that was where he wanted to stay.

Before long the problem was solved with an offer from Otto

Plaschkes to play the role of Lynn Redgrave's fifty year-old suitor in
Georgy Girl. The age was right for him and the film turned out to be
a good career move. But he had had severe doubts about the wisdom
of taking the part and took a while to decide to do it. Elspeth
Cochrane, his friend from Stratford Ontario, remembers accom-
panying James on a trip to Chichester to see the Canadian company
performing at the Festival Theatre there. She knew he was wrestling
with this problem on the journey, but he was determined not to spoil
the outing by discussing it. He had taken infinite trouble to make it a
special occasion and had ordered a wonderful hamper from Fort-
num's for their picnic on the way, choosing everything that went into
it with the greatest care and enjoyment. He loved to organise treats
and to make an ordinary outing something quite special. Elspeth was
by now a successful literary agent and James liked to discuss ideas
and projects with her. When *Lolita* was published James bought a
copy for her the day it came out and sent it to her for her opinion –
long before he was offered the role he had been fascinated by
Nabokov's novel. But she realised that he was very worried about the
choice he was going to have to make and didn't want to spoil the
pleasure of the excursion by chewing the problem over with her. It
wasn't until the return journey that he began to talk about his
dilemma. He knew that he was standing at another crossroad in his
career, that there wouldn't be many others and that he simply had to
make the right decision. In the event, he did. *Georgy Girl* marked the
beginning of a new phase in his working life.

At one point in the sixties James had gone to Moscow hopeful of
finding sufficient cultural material to enable him to make a film of
James Elroy Flecker's, *Hassan*. He had envisaged using the Bolshoi
company set against the panoramic scenery available in the vast
Russian landscape. To mount such a project, unless partially funded
from outside interests, would have cost millions of dollars, but James
left London buoyed up by the knowledge that the Soviets were not so
conscious of the profit motive, if by utilising their own resources they
received rewards of outstanding artistic merit. James departed
Heathrow during the baggage-handlers' strike, and seeing a woman
struggling with her suitcases he offered to help as he was carrying
only one bag himself.

When he arrived in Moscow he sent a card to a friend who had
driven him to the airport saying that once they had boarded the plane

the grateful lady had thanked him profusely for his kindly act and then left him to enjoy a peaceful flight unmolested, as she had not recognised him. "I'm wondering now, in retrospect whether I should have felt relieved or very unflattered!" he wrote.

Frank Essien, who had gone ahead to see that everything was in order, and he, terrified lest he be overheard to make what might be construed as a derogatory remark about the Hotel or the city, sent cards to all his friends saying "this place is wonderful" or words to that effect and for good measure, in case his room was bugged or searched, left messages and little notes in his drawers and in his clothes praising the food (!) and the general atmosphere. I laughed so much when he told me how nervous he had been, even in the hotel. Having spent some time behind the Iron Curtain myself, when indeed it had been "Iron", I could understand how oppressive it must have seemed to Frank. He had spent years in the clublands of Paris and London, he enjoyed the sleazy, seamier environment of dives, and the easy freedom to be found in the European capitals. Not so in Moscow. At that time, a coffee-coloured face would stand out in a crowd and in any case all foreigners came under close scrutiny. For Frankie it was an excursion he had no wish to repeat and for James it proved a wasted effort.

He was, as befitted his standing, accorded all the courtesies reserved for artists of renown, but the necessary backing was not forthcoming. James somewhat wryly, told me that one of the cultural directors had listened carefully and politely to his outlined plans, but crushingly ruled out a co-production.

"Why?" I asked, "What was the reason?"

"Simple" James replied, "He pointed out that in Russia, fairytales and fantasies abounded and that they had no need to import other people's subjects to exploit."

That, sadly, ended the episode, as *Hassan* is a wonderful piece, and James would have brought his distinctive voice to the storytelling to great effect. As usual he took it philosophically, but I always nurse the wish that James could have succeeded in a huge musical, his lifelong ambition. Had he been a young man when Andrew Lloyd Webber's line of huge hits occurred, who knows what might have happened? But then few of us are born at the right time or in the right period.

After *Georgy Girl* came *The Deadly Affair*. John le Carre's thriller had the added attraction for him of a reunion with old friends. Produced and directed by Sidney Lumet, the cast included Robert Flemyng, whose wife Carmen had witnessed his wedding to Pam, Simone Signoret, and Harry Andrews. One of the pleasures of the advancing years was that his work provided new encounters with long-lost colleagues, and he loved to dine with them and chat about mutual friends and acquaintances and to catch up with the details of their lives.

Then came a small change of direction in James's career which he took up with great enthusiasm. *The London Nobody Knows* was a documentary film about the forgotten corners of London and the areas of building, trade and endeavour which still survived the bulldozers of the sixties. Acting as narrator and guide, James explored the city in which he loved to live and made new discoveries about its history and buildings. He also made new discoveries about himself, finding that here was an area of film-making quite different from anything he had previously done, which gave him great satisfaction.

The following year he went home again to Huddersfield for his mother's ninetieth birthday. In all the years he had been away, living in London, America and Switzerland, the one thing that had remained constant, unchanging and uncompromising was the firm family base in Yorkshire, and this special birthday celebration in June 1968 was very important to him. It must have seemed to him that the values and ties to which he now clung for emotional sustenance were vulnerable to the frailty of his now failing parents. There had been a succession of ladies in attendance in the years after he left America, but none of them had been able to provide all the qualities he was searching for. As George Murcell said, "the only thing they all seemed to offer, apart from being decorative, was the virtue of being small". James was not a very tall man himself, and would not perhaps have been comfortable with a very large lady. But setting aside the question of size, in none of them could he find the soulmate he so much longed for.

It was on one of Portland's visits to London that I first learned that "Dad" was becoming over-involved with an American lady who was his neighbour in Switzerland. I gathered that she was divorced from an Italian Count and that she lived in style and comfort, but reading between the lines I came to the conclusion that the relationship was viewed by Portland with a jaundiced eye. In so far as I can judge, the lady in question sounded to be beyond reproach but certainly at this point in time she did not have Portland's blessing, who doubted that her way of life would be compatible with James's.

I cannot comment either way, but I could understand Portland's attitude. I think we all had to admit to having some fears on James's behalf. Here he was, a man alone, having experienced a traumatic break up of his marriage after more than twenty years, and if not actually lonely he was most certainly having to adjust and contemplate the future. Should he remain *celibataire*, or should he consider remarriage? My view is that Portland would not have encouraged the latter decision and for all I know she would have been proved right in this instance. In any event the relationship did not develop into so close a tie.

Nineteen-sixty-eight – next year James would be sixty. With what apprehension did he view the emotional wilderness he now faced I wonder? But work would distract him, and work now took the form of a project in Australia. As early as 1944 James and Michael Powell, the director, had wanted to work together. During the war Powell had asked James to take a part in his film *I Know Where I'm Going*, but that had come to nothing as had their joint and enthusiastic plans to film Shakespeare's *The Tempest*. But on this new venture, a film based on a novel by the Australian Norman Lindsay, they were working together as co-producers, star and director. The film was called *Age of Consent*. The occasion was the most important meeting of James's life.

He arrived in Sydney to start work on the film towards the end of the pre-shooting preparations, just in time to attend the final casting session for a few of the small parts. One of these James rated as extremely important, although limited to a single sequence, and he was concerned that they should find the right actress to play it. They found the right actress and James, without warning, expectation or premonition, found the right woman with whom to share the rest of his life.

THE YEARS OF FULFILMENT

CLARISSA Kaye was thirty-six when she met James, nearly twenty-three years his junior, and her background couldn't have been more different from his protected, well-provided and carefully organised childhood. She had been born into a very poor and disadvantaged family in what she readily describes as the slums of Sydney. Her mother had great ambitions for her and she was taken to dancing classes from the age of two. At four she was started on a career, beginning with local concerts which included, forever imprinted on her mind, the terrifying experience of entertaining the prisoners in the city jail. By the age of twelve she was working as a contortionist, travelling with an act that played in circuses, clubs and cabarets. Her formal education was pretty well sacrificed to the rigours of this existence, but that didn't affect her own lively intelligence and natural interest in the world around her. She was married at nineteen, a disastrous mistake which lasted for only nine months, and she then embarked on an eight year relationship with an American actor/director.

During this time she learnt about the legitimate theatre and exchanged her career as a dancer (she had in her early twenties been the principal dancer in the long-running musical *Kismet*) for that of an actress, and she was a founder member of the Ensemble Theatre Group. From Australia she went to New York for a few years, returning to Sydney again in 1966 where she went back to her family and found work again as an actress. In the year that she met James she received a special award from the Australia Film Institute for her outstanding performance in a film made for televison based on a story by Henry Lawson, *The Drover's Wife*. But awards don't necessarily generate work, and her success in *The Drover's Wife* didn't bring her the kind of offers she could have expected thereafter. So being the practical and down-to-earth person that she is, she began the usual rounds of auditions for work and kept herself going between jobs with her winnings on the racecourse, for she adored horses and was an expert on racing form. And then one day the telephone rang and she was summoned to audition for a small part in the new Michael Powell/James Mason film.

In his autobiography, James describes his first sight of Clarissa as she was ushered into the room where the casting session was taking place. "Here was a good-natured woman with big expressive eyes, a generous mouth and no pretensions – a woman whose face was a window rather than a blind." She was also small and delicately made, with the grace of a trained dancer and a warm, confident, outgoing personality.

They didn't actually work together until the film was nearly finished and James returned from the location on the Great Barrier Reef to complete the work in the studio in Brisbane where, as he put it "I had a rendezvous with an almost naked Clarissa Kaye to shoot the bedroom scene." Clarissa proved to be a finer actress than the part required, because she managed to conceal from James at these close quarters that she was suffering from pneumonia and had a temperature of 104. She should never have made the trip from Sydney to Brisbane, but she was determined not to lose the opportunity of working with such a director and such a star. As James said, they both survived the encounter and on this and many other daunting occasions Clarissa Kaye proved indestructible.

With the film finished James prepared to go home to Switzerland and the entire cast and crew of the film went to the airport to see him off – including Clarissa. With regret she waved goodbye to the departing plane, certain that there would end a very pleasant but, by definition, passing acquaintance. Frank Essien was remaining behind for a few days to clear up some last-minute business for James and, as she turned to go, Clarissa was intrigued but not convinced when he took her arm and said mysteriously, "You know, Mr Mason is enamoured of you". Back home again she thought no more about it, there was little point, until the day came when her luck changed in a most spectacular way, by a marvellous betting coup.

Work had been a bit thin on the ground for her for a while and she used her spare time to study the local racing form until she knew enough about bloodlines, times, distances and so on to be able to count on a small profit to fund her visits to the course. One day she took a reliable tip to back a horse called General at 7 to 2, but was interested to see that the price was gradually going out and that the horse, which was a long distance runner, had been entered for a five-furlong dash. She kept her bet as the odds changed to 9 to 1 until she caught sight of a magnificent chestnut also set to run in the race – Lady Cleves. Without stopping to think any more she dashed back to change her bet and forecast Lady Cleves and General and, in a moment of madness doubled both with a horse in the next race, a rank outsider at 40 to 1. The first race ended with a photo-finish between Lady Cleves and General, with Lady Cleves winning by a whisker and the second was won by her 'no-hoper'! In that instant her life was changed.

For the first time in her life she was suddenly and comparatively rich. The need to find work was removed for a while and she had the means to do what she enjoyed most – travel. She planned her trip with care, to America and then Europe. Before he left Australia, James had invited her to visit him in Vevey, as he said to her "If ever you are in Switzerland". It was an impossiblity at the time and seemed a suggestion best forgotten. But now, astonishingly, there was a chance. She knew that James was away more often than not, but by the greatest good luck, when she arrived in Vevey after her visit to America, he was home.

Something very special was established between them while she stayed there, but eventually she felt she had to go back to Australia. Her life and her work were based there and she couldn't remain a visitor in a foreign land indefinitely. James perhaps could not see any good reason for her to return to the far side of the world, but she was an independent spirit and knew she should make a move to take up her own career again. So she went, but she left her heart behind with James and he found life without her colourless and empty.

At the end of 1969 James went to Hong Kong to work on a film and to her surprise and delight Clarissa was offered a part in it too. She flew off from Sydney to join him there, but the joy of their reunion was cut short by the death of James's mother. She died in January while filming was in progress, and on such a tight schedule that it was impossible to release James to fly to Yorkshire to be with his family for the funeral. He was heart-broken, but Clarissa was there to console him and he found her concern for him and his family a comfort and a revelation.

When the film was finished they went their separate ways, but this time they both knew they had found something too precious to let go. When James asked her to go and live with him she agreed without hesitation and a little later that year she moved permanently into his home at Vevey.

James was transformed. He was gloriously happy. At last he had his soulmate, friend, companion, lover in one constant and truly loving woman. Their relationship became a voyage of discovery — how much they had in common and yet how much they each could teach the other. Once Clarissa decided to share his life she set about enriching it in a hundred ways. She was a good home-maker, she loved cooking and providing him with all kinds of comforts to make him feel cherished. She made cushions and arranged furniture so that the rather Spartan surroundings in which James had previously and unenthusiastically lived became warm and comfortable, and she filled his house, as she filled his life, with colour and with love. In the couple of years before her arrival he had purchased first the other ground floor flat and then the whole building from his landlord so that he now owned quite a spacious house. The garden that surrounded it was large, but quite bare of trees and flowers for he had not had the time or interest to put his imagination to work on it. After all, he had always been looking for things to do that would take him away from Vevey instead of finding reasons to stay there. Theresa, his Spanish housekeeper, took to Clarissa at once, thankful to see James at last so complete and content.

Three times James asked Clarissa to marry him, and twice she refused. He was very aware that, in committing herself to their relationship so completely, she had virtually given up her career and the family and friends which had been part of the fabric of her life for so long. In Australia she was recognised as a very considerable actress and had managed, in spite of the limited opportunities Australia had to offer in the infancy of its film and television industry, to achieve more success than most. He knew that he was removing her from all that and it would be hard for her to make a new career for herself in Europe. But he wanted her to be his wife.

It was true that Clarissa valued her own independence and professional achievements highly, and she was loath to give them up.

But James's own professional standing was so different from her own, his experience and reputation so far outstripped hers, that she felt she might be regarded as a gold-digger and an unsuitable match for him. She was also very aware of the difference in their backgrounds and education, and his trained intellect and broad knowledge of so many subjects made her wonder if she could ever be a wholly satisfactory companion for him. As she said, "I knew who I was and didn't see how I could fit completely into his way of life, and I couldn't believe that he would be permanently satisfied with someone from my so totally different way and experience of life."

But these were less important reasons for her hesitation than her belief that James couldn't seriously want to be married again – to anyone. She knew he had spelled out his views on marriage to the press, and she'd read those papers. She was pretty sure that Portland and Morgan wouldn't accept her as a stepmother and she didn't want their opposition to spoil things, for James was still very attached to them and this would hurt him. Her own early marriage had been such a bad mistake that she had never intended to tie herself to anyone else again, and she couldn't believe that James would really and truly want to marry her. Things were good as they were so what need was there to make an actual commitment which he might in the end regret – why make any changes? But for the time being, having made her decision to share his life, Clarissa concentrated on his happiness and welfare. She didn't whirl through his home like the wind of change and alter things to suit her, but gradually and carefully she made suggestions that appealed to him and together they began to make a home that was theirs and not just his. She loved to sew and knit, and it thrilled him to see the things she made adding colour and comfort to the place. The walls, which had been bare of such things, were covered in time with photographs of their friends and the places they visited together, and pictures, paintings and hangings of every kind that they chose together. They took delight in discovering new artists and sculptors and collecting their work – not as investments but purely for the pleasure of acquiring together things they both liked. They shared the same enthusiasms and they did everything together, all the time. They became inseparable.

Then James returned to England to make *Spring and Port Wine*. The story was set in the industrial Lancashire mill town of Bolton, and James played the intractably severe patriarch of a troubled working-class family. He drew heavily on his own North-country roots and experience, and produced a portrait very different from anything he had played on the screen before – and very different from the happy and contented man he had become himself.

Susan George was the young actress who played his daughter and the character who was central to the story. She was only eighteen at the time, and she found working with James one of the most significant experiences of her early professional life. The thing she noticed immediately about him was the quality of physical stillness that he had, something that Sir Alec Guinness had recognised in his stage performances at the Old Vic in 1933 and which, when I asked him for his recollections of James, he mentioned at once.

She learned from him that on film, where the image is larger than life and out of proportion with reality, gestures and actions must be kept to the minimum and the performance concentrated and given from within the actor. She regarded him as "the ultimate professional" and he taught her by example. She admired the quiet and dignified way he conducted himself on the set, demanding nothing but always getting the results he wanted so that everything ran smoothly around him, and the total control he had of his own performance.

By this time his relationship with Clarissa was secure and established and for the first time in his life he was secure in himself. Susan George remembers him as a man who seemed to know himself very well, who was not soul-searching and who had a great clarity and contentment about him. He and Clarissa seemed to be "at one" and in complete harmony and, unlike many people in their position, they were absolutely genuine in their dealings with others – "What you saw was what you got".

What a change had taken place in James's personality in the short time that Clarissa had been with him! Gone altogether was the uncertainty and pain of the lonely man. There was no need now for the shield of remoteness he had for so long carried as a defence against the world.

On Friday 13th August 1971 James and Clarissa were married in Vevey. In Europe Friday the 13th is considered to be a very lucky day and it happened to fall the day after their application to the local authorities for their wedding was finally approved. They had bought the ring months earlier from Aspreys, but the procedures they had to follow which would allow them as foreigners to marry in Switzerland had taken ages to produce the necessary permission, and so when James heard at last on the 12th that everything was in order he dashed to find Clarissa and say "We can get married tomorrow." So they did.

The weather was beautiful for them, and the day bright and hot as they walked round to the local registry office in Corseaux for their quiet wedding, accompanied only by Joseph the gardener, Theresa their housekeeper, the Fleurys who had been James's landlords, Mrs Cresswell who had been his neighbour in the downstairs flat, and Jack and Nicky Cardiff who still lived nearby. After the short and simple ceremony they all went back to the house for their wedding breakfast, which Theresa had laid out in the garden. The single day's notice had given her no chance to make any great preparations so they sat down to a plain salad lunch in the sunshine. The guests stayed for quite some time, for the day was so relaxed and happy, but as dusk fell they finally left, and James and Clarissa were alone in the warm garden watching the star-filled night sky above them. And then, quite incredibly, shooting stars began to streak across the darkness over the lake beyond them, raining down out of the sky in their hundreds and providing a natural and spectacular gold and silver firework display to celebrate their wedding. Clarissa remembers that James said "That's a good omen for our marriage." – and it was.

James had already taken Clarissa to Yorkshire to meet his family. He had stayed at Croft House with his father, while Rex and his wife, Halo had welcomed her into their home. They had never come across anyone quite like her before, and at first they found her blunt and forthright Australian manner quite difficult to understand, but they could see how happy she had made James and they soon became very fond of her. This lady was clearly not going to divide James from the family, and they were glad that she was enthusiastic and interested in them and their surroundings.

The day after they were married James telephoned his father to give him the news. The old man was not too surprised because James's contentment had been very evident to him, and he was more than happy with his new daughter-in-law because, as he said to Rex and Halo, "James has got the right girl at last."

When I knew he intended to re-marry I felt, rightly or wrongly, that we who had been so much part of his previous life should retire into the background, but I wrote to congratulate him and assure him of my continuing friendship. At the same time I made it clear that I did not expect him to maintain contact, although I hoped we would not lose touch entirely.

We didn't, I'm glad to say, and I was always pleased to hear from him, particularly as it was quite obvious that he was enjoying a full and contented existence with his wife, Clarissa. In this second marriage James gained a new-found freedom of expression, but he was never an independent male – he needed the bolstering, the comfort and affection so freely given by his wife, and through it he found the happiness that had for so long escaped him.

Much to the relief of James and Clarissa, the press had failed to pick up the story of their marriage and so there was no need to tell anyone else until, several weeks later, they met Portland and Morgan in Berlin and were able to tell them themselves. The news was greeted with silence, followed by polite congratulations. Clarissa's greatest anxiety had always been that they might not want to accept that she was going to be a permanent fixture in James's life, and she went out of her way to try and show them that as far as she was concerned they were James's priority and his interest and affection for them was something that she wanted to share and would never diminish.

The children were now more or less grown up. Portland was twenty-three and Morgan sixteen and James had not lived with them for eleven years. He had kept up a flow of letters and money for them across the Atlantic and seen them whenever it was possible for him to do so in America, England and Switzerland, but their life was in California with their mother and his was now in Europe with Clarissa. Surely they couldn't begrudge him this happiness?

Whatever the young people might feel about their marriage, it could not affect the strength and joy that James and Clarissa found in one another. Money was no longer the crushing problem it had been for so many years, and the need to find the next job was not so pressing. But work there was in plenty and wherever it took him she went too. They both adored to travel and now they lived like a couple of happy gypsies. James had always loved the prospect of another film and a new location, and Clarissa shared his enjoyment of these adventures but, as their marriage became so central to their lives, they loved coming home even more. Margaret Lockwood met James again, and vividly recalls the change.

MARGARET LOCKWOOD

I was asked to present James with the Evening Standard Award at The Winter Garden Theatre and we greeted each other like long lost friends – as we hugged and kissed I realised that James was overcome with emotion and that he had tears running down his cheeks. It surprised me because I had never thought of him as being vulnerable or emotional, and as the evening progressed I was struck again and again, by the change in him. His second wife Clarissa accompanied him. I reminded him of his first big hit with a heroine who bore the same name in *The Man in Grey* – a coincidence?

"I've come full circle then," James laughed "the beginning and the end."

I saw him as a supremely happy man and I could not resist saying how changed I found him.

"Changed," he said, "In what way?"

"You've mellowed," I replied. "Softened, warmed, as different as chalk from cheese."

He still seemed surprised and uncomprehending so I continued. "To be truthful, in those early days you were a bit of a pain, always grousing, rather pompous and a bit stand-offish – and that's only for starters!"

James's expression was one of amazement. "Extraordinary," he kept repeating, "I can't believe it – those were lovely times, some of the happiest of my career."

I truly believe he had obliterated those memories from his mind, he was a changed man, at peace with himself and the world in general, sharing his life in a loving and devoted relationship with his Clarissa, enjoying his home in Switzerland, secure in the knowledge that he had fulfilled all the promise of his youth and I may add, in the process he had become a charming and delightful person.

Had a suitable vehicle presented itself I think I might have really been tempted into playing once again with the "new" old James Mason, and this time without any trepidation whatsoever.

At home they had the time to explore the countless interests they shared and to concentrate on each other. By definition if James was in Vevey he was not working on a film so he could relax and immerse himself in their domestic life without any distractions. Although Clarissa was twenty-two years younger than he, she was thirty-nine years old when they married and a mature woman, but he called her his "child-bride" – sometimes even, rather to her dismay, addressing her simply as "Child". But in her company he was discovering pleasures and aspects to his life that had long been suppressed and forgotten, and his own delight in these things was like that of a child.

They both loved sport of all kinds and, whereas Pam couldn't have been less interested, they watched it whenever they could. On the subject of sport I must refer to an item which gave my mother and I many a laugh. James's brother Colin was a top class sportsman and on the occasion that he received his first "cap" as an International Hockey player James was bursting with pride when he announced that "dear old Col" had achieved this honour.

"His what?" Pam's incredulous expression left us in no doubt as to her reaction.

"How ridiculous!" She was not impressed as people chasing, kicking or hitting balls were outside her realm of understanding. The honours and intricacies of sporting parlance and attainment were lost on her. James still enjoyed playing tennis but it wasn't Clarissa's game, so they took up cross-country ski-ing in the winter months, and for as long as the weather permitted they would walk for miles in the mountains. They were both mad about football and on Sundays they would go to watch the local team play in Vevey. James would follow the English football too, for he was a Chelsea supporter and would get very excited about the FA Cup, especially when Leeds and Sunderland were winning. He loved the annual University Boat Race and of course supported Cambridge, and when they watched cricket and rugby on television and England was pitted against Australia, they would have great fun taking sides against each other. They were glued to the Olympic games when these were televised, especially the track and field events, and remembering his own efforts on the ice rink James was spellbound by Torville and Dean. They both enjoyed music, and although James's preference was for jazz, brass bands and the Scottish pipes and Clarissa's was for opera, they shared a love of the classics that they freely indulged.

But it was the garden which became their passion. James of course had spent his childhood in a wonderful garden which had been tended by a full-time expert gardener, but when he and Pam had lived together they had always been too busy to take much care of anything they'd had. That was why he was glad to let me get my hands on the garden in Beverly Hills and provide him with something he could enjoy, even if he did have to pay through the nose for the water it needed.

Although Clarissa's childhood home had been without any kind of garden she had always had a tremendous feeling for nature. She grew up close to a grandmother whose almost mystical knowledge of the healing powers of plants had influenced her considerably and who had taught her to respect all natural things. When she first went to Vevey the garden was barren – a large square lawn with a couple of straight-edged rose beds plonked at either side and a few trees near the uncompromising wall which bounded it. James had never had the time or the expertise to do much about it, but once Clarissa was able to lavish her love and enthusiasm on it she wrought a transformation. Gradually she made suggestions to James about what she would like to see there, and he discovered that she had an abundant knowledge of plants and flowers. He marvelled at the way their Latin names came easily and naturally to her, how she knew what would smell good, or climb well, or thrive in certain corners. The wisteria he had planted against the house grew for her as it had never done for him, and she planted fruit orchards and a vegetable garden that would provide for their needs for much of the year.

She asked him if he would tell the gardener to stop using pesticides and poisons, and once these things were banned natural life of all kinds flourished there and the garden and orchard abounded with rare insects and butterflies so that, after seven years, even glow-worms had taken up residence. More and more birds visited the garden and in one year they counted more than forty-nine different kinds. A flock of rock-doves came to live there, and martins and other birds made their homes in the nesting boxes under the eaves of the roof and the garden was loud with their song. As the trees they planted in the orchard began to grow and bear fruit James thought it wonderful to be able to pick and eat it fresh from his very own trees.

Every May, when the young crows were fledglings, the very high winds would blow some of the nests out of the trees and the casualty rate was considerable. They would find the nestlings dead on the ground underneath, but one year they found one still alive. So

Clarissa tried to rear him. She fed him each day on raw meat (and kept him safe in a box) until he thought she was his mother and, when he was able to hop about, he would follow her around like a dog and sit beside her on the lawn for company. Finally she persuaded him that he was a bird and she taught him to fly, and in time he joined the other crows in the trees, though he was happier sitting on her shoulder or James's head. In time Churchy (named from the cartoon character Churchy la Femme) turned out to be female and produced her own family which she brought down to the garden to be fed. She liked an extraordinary range of food herself, including cheese and fruit, and one day they watched her carefully burying a cherry stone in the earth at one side of the house. The next year a tiny tree began to grow there and long after Churchy was gone from the garden the cherry tree she had planted flourished and flowered.

As more and more birds took up residence, James found observing their habits utterly enthralling, and he spent hours filming the nestlings' progress from birth to flight. But he wasn't too keen on sharing the fruit with the wildlife, and one day Clarissa heard him shout in fury from the garden, "The buggers are eating our cherries". She found him fuming at the sight of a flock of small birds feeding on the cherry tree and had to point that, unlike him, they could scarcely pop down to the market to buy a kilo for themselves. He saw her point.

Away from home they went everywhere together. When he was filming she would sit in his dressing-room knitting, sewing or writing the flow of cards and letters that kept them constantly in touch with their friends. She seldom went on to the set, because she felt if she wasn't working herself she had no place there, but James loved to find her waiting for him when he had finished a scene.

A film which received a great deal of publicity for quite the wrong reasons was *The Last of Sheila*, made in 1972-3. During the shooting of the film some very sharp ripostes were reported, and James was accused by one of the leading ladies of "ungentlemanly conduct", which, let me hasten to add, referred only to verbal misconduct.

James had been driven to make a few acerbic remarks in regard to the lady's unprofessional behaviour and she had taken the criticism amiss. From what I have heard not one word uttered by James could have been considered impolite or out of place, the consensus being that she deserved everything, if not more, than she got. The final outcome of the film gave James a deal of satisfaction, the aggravations which had detracted from the atmosphere while making the film were put behind him, and he was able to enjoy a good laugh at the nonsensical coverage given to what was a storm in a teacup.

Nonetheless, at the time James had shown a modicum of real irritation and annoyance because the original screenplay was an interesting one by Stephen Sondheim and Anthony Perkins, whom James very much admired, and he felt that his co-star, by her inefficiency, drew attention away from what was a serious and good script, not to mention her showing a marked lack of respect towards other members of the cast and crew involved in the project.

I am unable to say whether or not the film was a success, all I know is that James, in his usual manner, put the episode behind him without rancour or grudge, although I rather doubt that he would have rushed to appear again with the said lady without careful thought and much weighing of the outcome!

His friends and colleagues accepted Clarissa's constant presence beside him with gladness because his happiness with her was so apparent. Paul Grunder remembers how different he was when they came together to stay at the Dorchester after their marriage. Clarissa was lively, full of fun and very demonstrative and soon came to regard the manager of the hotel as a friend. When they arrived there she would rush off to find him, and her effervescent and genuinely affectionate greeting was a great contrast to James's previous behaviour, though nowadays he would stand by quietly smiling at his wife's show of friendliness. Paul Grunder felt that Clarissa had brought out in James qualities that no one else had found before, and he saw him as a different man now that Clarissa had given him the confidence and security of her concentrated love.

As his garden had blossomed under her care, so did he. She looked after his health and devised a low-cholesterol diet for him. She worked out a fitness regime too and together they would jog round a four and a half mile circuit of the land behind the house and then do a work out on the exercise bike. In London they would jog around Hyde Park and then use the bike that was provided for them in their room at the hotel. James had never been in the habit of drinking much so there was no need to do anything about that, but he decided to give up smoking and he gave his collection of pipes away to his

friend Jack Cardiff. An indication of the improvement in James's
physical well-being was the disappearance of the skin complaint he
had suffered from for so long. Remembering what she had learned
from her grandmother Clarissa would gently rub castor oil into his
skin each night, massaging and soothing away his nervousness.

Although James would discuss his work with Clarissa, ask her
opinion of new projects and get her to hear his lines while he was
learning them, she decided not to take any part in his business life.
She felt that he had been, as she put it, "de-balled" by the constant
interference and manipulation of other people in the past and that
his role as "man of the house" should be respected. She kept out of
all his business dealings and left his career decisions to his own final
judgement. His secretary dealt with everything but their personal
correspondence and his agents, Al and Maggie Parker, looked after
his contracts and negotiations. When the routine work for the day
with his secretary was finished James would find Clarissa in the
garden looking at their private mail and they would go through it
together, reading aloud the choicest bits for each other's
amusement.

Clarissa found that living with James was like living with an
encyclopaedia. He had a grasp of so many different subjects that
she could ask him almost any question and receive a better
explanation than she would get from the reference books. She never
tired of listening to his voice and in the evenings he would read
aloud to her his own choice of poetry and literature, or they would
listen to music together.

In the years before he met Clarissa James had kept sparse diaries,
which were no more than a record of appointments, but they
showed how really lonely he had been then. He would fill his time
with lunches, meetings and dinners out with friends and acquaintances and he would visit Pam and the children in America to feed
the illusion that he had a home and family out there. As the years
proved increasingly how wrong he was to cling to that, he tried to
arrange to be crossing the dateline at Christmas (or maybe Hong
Kong harbour at New Year) to avoid spending these family festivals
alone. The caricatures he had drawn of himself then revealed how
he felt about his life. There was a dark, almost nightmarish mood
about them and a terrible sadness about the eyes and mouth, and
there was even one he had done of himself holding a gun to his

head. When Clarissa found it she asked him why he had drawn himself like that and he said "Oh well, that was how I felt."

He would never feel like that again. He relished every moment he spent with Clarissa and everything they did together was precious to him. He kept everything she made or wrote for him, even little cards and notes, and he was tremendously proud when she took up painting and discovered she had a natural flair for using colour. His architect's eye recognised a complementary talent and he displayed her work on their walls next to the paintings by the artists he most admired.

Less than a year after they were married James's father died. They were actually staying at Croft House at the time and were able to stay there to be with the rest of the family for the funeral. For James it was more than just the loss of the father whom he had loved and admired for all his sixty-three years and who had been such a constant factor in his life, it was the end of the family home to which he had for so long returned for solace and reassurance.

Croft House and its one and a quarter acres of land had to be sold. It was bought by property developers who eventually built thirty-two two-storey homes on the site. James did not benefit under his father's will because the old man had felt he would not have the same need as his two brothers, whose lifestyles were very modest in comparison. Rex and Halo in particular had shouldered the burden of caring for the old man after "Muv" had died, for they lived only six miles away, and they also cleared up the house and did the necessary work in selling it. But James, in effect had the lion's share for, with his brothers' agreement, he shipped back to Vevey something which represented Croft House and all it meant to him. He brought home to Switzerland the two great marble lions that had for so long mounted guard outside the front door of the old house, a permanent reminder of everything he had known there.

But he wanted something more and he decided to commission a painting that would keep the picture of the house forever fresh in his mind. There was an artist in Yorkshire whose work he had admired for some time and from whom he had already bought a couple of landscapes. So he asked Peter Brook to visit the house with him before it was demolished. It was a meeting that Peter Brook remembered vividly.

It was a very cold day and there was a sprinkling of snow on the ground. James was wrapped up in a greatcoat and he was in mourning. The house seemed dark and mysterious, like James in his black clothes, and the contrast of the whiteness all around intensified the melancholy atmosphere. It was a sorrowful place that day, full of the past, redolant of its recent bereavement. But at the same time it held the echoes of the life it once had contained; the joy and energy of growing families, happy Christmases and children's laughter. Now the lovely gardens were overgrown, the tennis courts neglected and rhododendrons rampant and soon, when the house was pulled down, there would be nothing left.

So Peter Brook made some preliminary sketches and set to work on a painting which delighted James. It was a sizeable work and covered perhaps a third of the wall at one end of his sitting room in Vevey. It was a stark picture of the house in the snow, rather bleak perhaps, but a marvellous interpretation of the house as it was on that cold January day when the artist saw it. James loved it.

He also had a deep and abiding love for his native Yorkshire. He liked the misty grey weather, the farmers and their dogs, the open fields and traditional farm buildings, the wide moorlands and old drystone walls. He enjoyed the local pubs and he identified with the local architecture and, like John Betjeman, he thought Huddersfield station was magnificent. Towards the end of 1972, the year that his father died, James returned to Huddersfield to make a documentary film for Yorkshire Television called *Home James*. It reflected his own personal view of his home town and was an account of all the things he loved about it. When it was transmitted he was criticised by some of the people who actually lived there of taking too sentimental a view of the place and portraying it as he might have remembered it to have been from his rather privileged and distant experience. It was, after all, a North Country textile town and had its fair share of poverty and unemployment. Fair comment, but James preferred to think of it in his own way.

At this point he found his career diversifying. As well as a steady stream of films he was in demand as a narrator and reader of poetry. He made any number of public appearances and appeals for charity and it seemed that his popularity had not been so great since the days of his early stardom. But how much more he enjoyed it now! He returned to Yorkshire whenever he could and he was delighted to do some bible readings for the YTV religious programme *Stars on Sunday*. He narrated a documentary about the Treasures of the Vatican which involved a trip to Rome and, knowing what it would mean to his faithful Spanish housekeeper (who was a devout Catholic), he took both Theresa and her sister to Rome with Clarissa and himself.

His natural generosity could now assert itself without restraint. He was never the really wealthy man that his long-standing star status might have led people to expect, but he was open-handed whenever it seemed right to him.

Years ago, during the making of *The Fall of the Roman Empire* in Spain Frank Essien had mentioned to him the situation of the young man who looked after the horse he was riding and who, having damaged the car belonging to his girlfriend's family, was facing a bill he couldn't possibly pay. James sympathised strongly, knowing only too well the pressure of impossible financial obligations, and wrote out a cheque for half the amount the boy needed at once. He gladly and spontaneously contributed to anything that seemed worthwhile to him. In 1968/9 he visited his old friend George Murcell when George was building an Elizabethan Playhouse inside the shell of an old circular church in North London where he was going to present Shakespeare's plays as the author had intended. The proportions were quite small, about the size of the playhouses of Shakespeare's day, and James thought it was wonderful. Perhaps he remembered the vocal problems he had had in the huge tent at Stratford Ontario when he said, rather wistfully, "Well, of course, I could have played Angelo here . . ." He knew his Shakespeare and he always wished he could have done more work in the classical theatre, and he admired very much George's vision and determination. He knew the enterprise was badly underfunded so he asked George what he needed to repair the leaking roof so that at least the building could be kept dry inside. "About £3,000 to £4,000" George told him sadly. "Well, here's £1,000 to start it off" said James, reaching for his chequebook. He liked in his quiet way to help friends who were in need, perhaps to tide them over a difficult time or to give them the means to start a new venture, and he was always generous to the charities that appealed to him.

He took a particular interest in 'Animals' Vigilante', a small organisation set up by one man in 1965. Its founder, Ted Cox, heard that James and Clarissa were interested in his kind of work so he wrote to invite their support for what he was doing. They responded with their encouragement and a donation, and then became actively involved in raising money and public awareness of the plight of neglected and abused animals, and in helping to find the necessary support for the new and larger premises the charity needed. In recognition of their work the new centre was named James Mason House, and they made sure they were present at the opening ceremony in 1976. They became joint presidents of the organisation, following Spike Milligan, and in 1980 they started a fund to help owners who could not afford the cost of unexpected vets' bills in cases of accidents. They kept up a constant and lively interest in its work. And there were many other deserving causes that found generous support from the Masons. But let Ted Cox speak for himself.

TED COX

I first became a "fan" of James Mason in the days of 1945-46, when he appeared in those early films in our London cinemas. It was those films which made him a household name. I well remember *The Man in Grey*, *The Wicked Lady* and *Fanny by Gaslight* to name but three films, which made this young man my idol of the screen. I saw these and other films in which he starred many times.

I think the thing which attracted me most of all was his keen love and compassion for all animals. No species was excluded. Remembering this I wrote to him in 1973, eight years after I was privileged to launch Animals' Vigilantes, and invited his support for our work. I received an encouraging reply and his keen interest and support for our cause was backed with a generous donation. James not only encouraged us with a promise to support our work, but his wife Clarissa also said she would be delighted to join James to help Animals' Vigilantes. I invited James and Clarissa to become patrons, and they said they would be happy if their names were added to our Patrons' Roll.

They have not only supported us financially since those early days, they have worked in a practical way in speaking up for our work and animal life on radio and television, and also handed out leaflets and raised signatures for our petitions. With international petitions he carried the signature sheets to many countries which he and Clarissa visited. In 1974 we had to face a problem. Since Animals' Vigilantes was founded in 1965 in a small room we had moved twice, into larger premises each time. However by 1974 we realised our third premises were still not large enough so the problem facing us was to find premises that would be large enough for our ever-growing work and to raise funds to buy them and so save endless years of paying rent and have nothing to show in the end. So after consulting James and again getting his support and approval, I launched the James Mason Appeal to raise funds and purchase suitable premises when such became available.

During the period of the appeal I did a sponsored ten miles walk and James headed the sponsor list with a further generous donation. It was James's name which made the appeal so attractive to many. I found two-storey shop-fronted premises in Salisbury Street, Fordingbridge, but whilst raising the necessary money the property was sold.

We were not discouraged, for James was behind us with encouraging letters and a generous donation. I so wanted the building just mentioned and was very upset when it was sold but James said keep going. Strangely the property came back on the market and although the asking price was £17,500 I offered £15,000 for a quick sale to which the owner agreed.

The next question was how were we going to pay, having raised only £11,000. To clinch the deal I appealed for loans from members who all, apart from one who loaned £100, made them over as gifts when we were in a position to refund. No lender wanted interest on their loan and all the loans totalled £4,000. Each donor and lender received a letter signed by James thanking them for their support.

We moved into the property in August 1976 and received a further £3,000 to cover the cost of furnishings and equipment. Incidentally, a Life Member, Peter Hill, did a 200 mile sponsored walk, again supported with the backing of James and Clarissa. This raised £1,400 of the amount.

A plaque was placed at James Mason House to mark a special day – November 11th 1976 – when James and Clarissa paid another visit, this time to officially open the offices.

We asked James and Clarissa to honour us following the opening of James Mason House by becoming joint presidents to which they agreed. As stated earlier, James and Clarissa have been personal friends of mine for many years. This friendship has been consolidated by the several visits made to James Mason House. These visits have been enjoyed and the staff and I have looked upon them as family gatherings.

We shared with James the pride when he received the Rudolph Valentino award, a solid gold statuette in honour of the contribution James had made to films. The award was received by James accompanied by Clarissa at Lecce, Italy where Rudolph Valentino was born.

In August 1980 Clarissa, who was supported by James, started a fund called the Heidi Fund for Animals in Distress with a cheque for £300. This was to help owners of pets who could not afford to pay vet bills in cases of accidents. Since then we have helped many, and so perhaps enabled a lonely lady to keep her cat or a lonely man his dog.

In the Autumn of 1981 James sent me the first copy of his book *Before I Forget* which I really treasure. In 1983 both James and Clarissa presided at our Coming of Age celebrations (eighteen years) when the patrons, trustees and the staff at James Mason House were guests to a birthday lunch. This was followed by hundreds of members coming from all parts for an afternoon of entertainment.

What more can I say? It was James's encouragement and leadership that has made Animals' Vigilante the organisation it is today, and in Clarissa we see an equal stalwart – like James – not afraid to speak and act for our dumb friends.

James made one more attempt to go back to the live theatre. He had found a play which he not only admired but which seemed to be a perfect vehicle for Clarissa and himself to do together. It was a three-hander called *The Faith Healer* and was quite a challenge for them both. James knew that Clarissa would give a great performance in the part of the Woman and felt that he could handle the part of the Healer himself. They found the necessary backing in America to get the venture going. But they were beset by problems, after a very short run the curtain came down on James's last performance in the theatre. But there was plenty of other work. Much as he loved thir home in Switzerland James could get bored if there was no film to think about, and there was no shortage of offers. One job in particular gave him great enjoyment and, even better, the chance to work in his beloved Yorkshire again. The film was *The Water Babies* and his part Mr Grimes the evil chimney sweep. The cast included the comedian Bernard Cribbens and the location was full of fun and not without incident – indeed, the local press made much of the comic moments when members of the cast were thrown by the somewhat unco-operative donkeys used in the filming.

This was in 1976 and James was 67, but falling off donkeys and playing character parts in unbecoming costumes just added to the zest for living which was so apparent about him these days. The producer of this part of the film (it was part live action and part animation) was Ben Arbeid and he recalls with great affection the contribution James made to the film, and the pleasure of his company while they were working on it. When the mud and make-up had been removed in the evenings they would dine together at a local restaurant where, while they were visiting Ben, his wife Heather and young daughter Kate joined them. James discovered that Kate was mad about football and her one ambition was to be the first female football team manager in history – especially if it could be Leeds United where her hero, Peter Lorimer, played. James's own favourite team was Leeds United and he was delighted to find another supporter in this little girl and they maintained their mutual interest for years afterwards with a periodic exchange of post-cards discussing the fortunes of their team.

Yorkshire was still James's spiritual home and if he could possibly have returned to live there he would have done so. But the tax laws which would apply to him after so many years absence prohibited any chance of returning to spend the last years of his life where his roots were laid.

So still he visited, going back to see his brothers and to work there whenever he could. He bought more of Peter Brook's pictures to hang on his walls in Switzerland and remind himself of the familiar landscape of home, and he liked them so much he bought many others to give away as presents to his friends.

James took a special delight in commissioning work from friends and artists that he admired, and he devised a wonderful surprise for Clarissa's forty-fifth birthday present in 1976. In January that year he had visited London to record some poetry at a studio in Soho's Dean Street and in the window of some offices opposite he had spied a wooden rocking horse of such beauty that the owner had displayed it for the pleasure of passers-by. He fell in love with it and went straight in to find out who had made this fabulous carving, for it wasn't just a wooden horse – it was a sculpture with a unique life and beauty of its own. But James saw in his idea of a gift for Clarissa more than just the poetry and beauty of a superb piece of carving; there was an extra significance in the image of the horse – for it was a horse running as Lady Cleves that had made their marriage possible.

As soon as James returned to Vevey he wrote to Ken Bright, the artist who had made the horse, saying "I would like nothing better than to be the possessor of one just like it". His first enquiry gave away nothing about his intention that it should be for Clarissa, or why, but as Ken Bright entered into a long correspondence with him it became clear that he was party to a romantic conspiracy. The horse was to be unique, for Ken never made two alike – each one was dictated by the grain and contours of the piece of wood he used – but they both had in mind an ancient Chinese jade carving of a tiny horse's head which James knew in the Victoria and Albert museum. The sculptor was intrigued that he should be familiar with the piece because it was so small – to know it at all you have to know your way around the museum very well – but they both recognised the superb delicacy, the quality and life of the piece, and they were agreed on the spirit of the work to be commissioned. Beyond that James left its execution to the artist.

Clarissa's birthday was on the 17th September and, in order that the horse should be delivered safely and on time without any possible leakage of the secret beforehand, Ken and his wife Mary decided to take it to Vevey themselves. The finished horse was very big, large enough to seat an adult comfortably, and it was mounted on two huge and gracefully curved rockers. The flowing mane and tail were carved in wood and the whole thing was extremely heavy. So the Bright's packed Michael (as Clarissa was to christen him) carefully in a transit van and set off for Switzerland.

The journey was fraught with hazards. The horse rocked into the side of the van when they went over a hump in the road and one of the ears fractured so it had to be mended en route in France; then the weather deteriorated so that the driving conditions were terrible; when they got to the border the guards decided that the croquet set, which James had asked them to bring with them, was actually an arms cache and they demanded that the horse should be unpacked and weighed in case there were more weapons concealed in its belly; they were caught in a terrific rain storm which made the next part of the drive through the mountains quite terrible; they got trapped between the gates of a level crossing and were only saved from the oncoming train by the swift action of the crossing keeper; and finally they spent the night guarding the horse by sleeping beside it in the van and woke in the morning to find the back wheels about 2 feet away from a sheer drop down the mountainside. It was all very dramatic, and seemed to imbue the horse with some extra emotion and "vibration", although Clarissa was later to say that it was something to do with the spirit she is convinced inhabits it.

They finally arrived at the house to find James waiting for them, bursting with apprehension and excitement. He had managed to despatch Clarissa into the town on some excuse but she would soon be back. Nonetheless, he knew the Brights had been travelling non-stop and would be very tired so he asked if they would like to rest before they unpacked the horse. Anxious to have it in place before she returned they thanked him and, to his relief, insisted that they set to work at once. Carefully removing the layers of protective padding they revealed his gift to an enchanted James. He was overjoyed with it and followed them into the house as they carried it into the upstairs living room and placed it in front of the great picture window with the view of the lake and the mountains – where at once it looked as though it had always belonged. It could not be seen from the road below so they went gratefully to their rest, knowing that it would indeed be the great and romantic surprise James had so carefully planned. They had hardly settled themselves when they heard the front door open upstairs, footsteps . . . silence . . . and then a wonderful squeal – a shriek of sheer delight "Oh, James! . . . Oh, James!!!".

Ken Bright and his wife Mary remained their friends thereafter. Peter Brook and his family, Ben Arbeid and his family, they added to their number all the time but still the old friends remained dear and important.

In 1978 James made a cameo appearance in a story of Jews fleeing Nazi Europe, only to find no refuge – *The Voyage of the Damned*. It was a film full of guest appearances by famous stars who turned up in the course of the story, and James's part would take no more than half a day to complete. His own schedule scarcely allowed that because he was booked to work for just the Saturday morning and was leaving England by plane in the afternoon. It would be tight, and they would have to get it right before he left at lunch time. Another part in the film was played by Victor Spinetti. Victor remembered something that occurred between the sequences they did that morning which he found unexpectedly endearing. While they were chatting together waiting for the next set-up to be completed Victor mentioned that the image he carried of James in his head was the moment when he struck Ann Todd over the hands in *The Seventh Veil* and that, when he had seen the film as a youngster, he had gone straight home to practice the piece of music she was playing at the time. "Can you still play it?" asked James. Victor said he could. "Right, there's a piano over there – let's go and do the scene and I'll lay the ghost for you". So while the technicians were re-arranging the cameras they went across to the piano and Victor sat down as Ann Todd to play the music and James towered over him, brandishing an imaginary stick and declaiming "If you won't play for me Francesca, you won't play for anyone else – ever again". Of course the camera crew stopped, the director stopped and everyone turned to watch. He didn't give them a reprise, but he was clearly having fun. He was relaxed and gently uninhibited in a way that no-one who had known him in the wilderness years would have recognised.

In 1979 James celebrated his seventieth birthday. He and Clarissa had known each other for ten years – ten years of the kind of happiness which, until that time, he had never expected to experience. Their life together had given him the time and space to grow and expand and to find within himself qualities which had been suppressed for so much of his previous life. He still carried his sketch book around with him as he always had done, but his sketches were gentle, skilful records of the things that pleased and intrigued him rather than the constant stream of drawings that he produced for the amusement of his friends or to satisfy his own almost obsessive need to explore people through his talent for caricature. He didn't reach constantly for the small book in his breast pocket to record the passing moment or place for, as Clarissa said, "Every moment we spent together was wonderful, and no single time or place was more marvellous than the others while we had each other."

Their life had settled into a pattern that suited them both. Enough work away from home to provide the travel they both still enjoyed and the means to see the friends they valued, but plenty of time in between to watch their garden flourish and enjoy the peace of their home and their quiet and loving life together.

The house is built on a hillside – on two levels – overlooking the lake. Almost hidden from the road below, which winds up around the side of the garden. A narrow access, just wide enough for a car, opens onto a paved area in front of the house. On the left is the small terraced vegetable garden behind which the orchard slopes upwards on the hillside, protected by its screening of trees which mark the outer boundary. On the right is the house itself, a low, white building with blue shutters and doors – apparently only one storey. Inside, light and bright, the main rooms look out, away from the entrance hall, to the mountains beyond the lake. Stairs lead down from the hall to the lower (ground floor) level where James's original flat gives on to the garden, with the same wonderful view of mountains and lake. There is a small sitting room, known as the garden room, with a glass door which opens out into the garden. In general the space is used economically and the main rooms are compact and practical. But the living room is broad and long with great windows all along one side through which you can gaze at the sublime view across the lake to the mountains.

The house is filled with light and sunshine, and everywhere there are photographs and pictures on the walls – pictures they loved, not investments. It is homely and comfortable, a happy and serene place in which to enjoy the business of everyday living. The breathtaking view dominates everything when the weather is good and adds an extra dimension to the house. But the comfort of the furniture, the bright cushions, the books and ornaments and the papers waiting for attention on the desk all combine to create a room to relax in and enjoy, whatever the weather.

Outside, there is a flower-filled garden of marvellous imagination and beauty. Like the house it is informal and unpretentious, and it blooms as a garden only can when it is tended with love and wisdom. There are no straight lines in this garden. The flower beds are curved and there is no uniformity of shape or design. There are hidden corners with seats or greenhouses, a summerhouse, a hammock and a wicker chair curtained by trees and shrubs. The paved area between the house and garden is a riot of colour and life with pots, urns, boxes and tubs overflowing with geraniums, petunias, and fuchsias. Roses, wisteria, jasmin and honeysuckle climb the walls. A wild orange tree grows in a tub on the paved area by the door of the garden room where a large white table and some chairs wait to be occupied for tea in the sunshine, and warm perfume wafts across in the sweet soft summer air, intensifying as the sun goes down.

The two stone lions from Croft House lie on either side of the house watching the mountains beyond, one in the sun at the left and the other in the shade of the cherry tree at the right of the house that was "planted" by Churchy the jackdaw. The lawn in front of them is soft and green, sown with sweet penny-royal. To the left of the house the ground rises at the side, sheltered by trees, where a white wrought-iron table and two chairs are placed in the shade of two firs – called "The Chelsea Corner" after the style of the furniture. At the extreme right of the front garden, as you look out over the lake, grows the tallest tree in Vevey, a huge fir tree, over 100 feet high and measuring more than 14 metres around the trunk. The wall which marks the boundary of the front garden, below which the ground falls away to the road beneath, is covered in various fruiting shrubs, including raspberries and kiwi fruit and more honeysuckle. There are potting sheds and a large, rich compost heap near to the great fir tree, and in front of them and before the boundary wall are the flower beds. These beds extend, in un-regimented groups, right round the front of the garden from one side of the house to the other. At either side trees and shrubs grow tall to give privacy from passers-by, and there is a walnut tree encircled by a white wrought-iron seat, on the right-hand-side at the front, which James planted when he was still alone. Roses are planted in the larger beds in front of the house; each bush is different from its neighbour. But there are many other flowers – delphiniums, stocks, pinks, daisies, dahlias, sweet peas (of which Clarissa picked over 9,000 last year and the record is more than 10,000 in a season) lily of the valley and cosmos (which were the simple flowers James liked). In the Spring the garden is filled with jonquils, crocuses, tulips, bluebells, violets and lilacs. There are all kinds of herbs, common and rare, including lemon verbena which makes a marvellously refreshing infusion. The clematis climb amongst the trees and over arbours, (there are about 150 different kinds in the garden) and there are sunflowers, buddleias, viburnums, philadelphus, agapanthus, impatiens, and many more. There are water lilies on the pond under the hedge, and a Christmas rose further along. More honeysuckle and clematis entwine the fruit bushes which make up this hedge and in front of the vegetable garden (which is quite small but cleverly arranged on different levels on a brick-built terrace and which produces fresh salads, herbs, leaf and root vegetables in abundance) sits their old car. They couldn't bear to see it go to the knacker's yard when it finally wore out so it was left there in happy retirement, in its old parking place, to be COVERED in clematis! Near to the car is a greenhouse beside which grows a very special clematis. Called the Mary Rose it is one of five cuttings taken from a plant nearly 400 (or more?) years old which was found, still growing and almost as big as a tree, at an old house in Devon. Prince Charles and the Queen Mother also received cuttings from this unique clematis, whose flowers are tiny, deep purple, thickly petalled clusters. Above the clean, fertile and well-tended vegetable garden, the orchard follows the upward slope of the hill. It is quite steep. Tall fir trees fringe its boundary and there are blossom trees growing amongst them. The grassy slopes are planted with a wonderfully rich variety of fruit trees, apples, pears, cherries, plums, greengages, yellowgages, loganberries, mulberries – even a medlar tree. Silver birches grow here and there, and there are rosebeds planted with "Clarissa" and the "James Mason Rose". There are blackberry and blackcurrent bushes, and more roses and clematis climb amongst the trees. Half-way up, between a James Greave apple tree and a fir tree there is a bench where James would sit and touch the fresh-growing fruit and relish the idea that it was his to pick and eat. He adored the garden and took equal delight in everything that grew in it. He and Clarissa would both sit here in the evening and watch the skies. From the lower, front, garden, where there are fewer trees and so more sky to see, they would star-watch in the dark . . . and hunt for glow-worms.

The delight they found in the garden was equally shared. Together they would walk around it, touching the trees to encourage their growth, discovering new blooms and young blossom, the first fruits and new shoots. There are bird-tables here and there, all different, and bird-baths on the lawn, and each day they would scatter food and watch for their favourite birds to come down and feed. There are nesting boxes under the eaves the length of the house, and the sound of birdsong is loud all day. A flock of ring-necked doves have made their home nearby and their gentle coo-ing mingles with the sounds and scents of the garden. James and Clarissa made a habit of greeting the wild things which lived in their garden, the birds and butterflies, trees and flowers, sun, moon, stars – even the rocks which marked their daily 4½ mile jog had names. On summer nights, when the glow-worms began to appear, they would keep a count of the number they found as they walked in the dark amongst the trees and sweet-smelling night flowers.

In the evenings the sun sets across the lake to the right of the garden and the water and mountains glow pink, throwing the peaks and crevasses into sharp relief for even in summer the snow stays on the very high slopes away to the left reflecting the sun.

Quite early in their marriage Clarissa had joined the Royal National Rose Society based near St Albans. She had recently, as a result of her support and involvement with that organisation, been made an Honorary Patron. She was well known by rose-growers, for she and James had often ordered their roses from England, and in fact, Peter Harkness had named one of his new blooms, "The Clarissa Rose" in recognition of her expertise and enthusiasm. In 1980 the Society decided to approach James, as a great supporter of his wife's interest in their work, to open their Annual Show, which was to be held at their headquarters in St Albans, Hertfordshire. They thoroughly enjoyed the occasion and James was delighted when Peter Beales, another famous rose-grower whose customer he had been for some years, asked his permission to name one of his new roses after him. The James Mason rose is a dark red summer-flowering hybrid Gallica, with a rich yellow centre. It flowers only for a short period in the summer, but Peter Beales felt that it was right for James's personality and he was very proud that James was present to receive one when it was first exhibited at the Chelsea Flower Show.

James's personality was as well known as his appearance. The years of his unpopularity and apparent arrogance were long forgotten, and most people associated him now with his Englishness and the gentlemanly behaviour which had always been so much a part of him. One of the reasons for this was that, however dubious the films he appeared, in he always gave of his best, and his indefinably unique quality of personal integrity would lift his characters up and beyond the banality of the film.

In 1978 the managers of the new Ritz Casino Club were about to open their new premises in the Ritz Hotel. They wanted to mark their inauguration with an occasion that would live up to the image of their name, and they wanted to find someone who would represent style and elegance of the surroundings and a name and reputation which was "as big as the Ritz". James fitted the bill and was delighted to accept the invitation to launch it.

DAVID GRAY

Once we knew that the famous James Mason was willing to launch our venture we decided to create something special and unique as an opening ceremony. Moet and Chandon, the Champagne people, offered to perform something hitherto, to our knowledge, never seen before in England. A cascade of champagne involving a construction of 300 glasses into a pyramid with a single goblet at the very peak – built in such a way so as to have every glass filled as you pour Champagne into the top glass and let it cascade down. It is a fine art and takes a while to do – also only an expert can perform the first necessity which is to cleanly strike off the top of the bottle with a sword in the old tradition of the Napoleonic days, when the soldiers on horseback collected Champagne or whatever and struck the neck of the bottles off with their Sabres. A quick way of reaching the contents!

For our ceremony the Baron Henri de Montesque wearing the full dress uniform of a Chevalier performed the trick with speed and elan and as he did so James called out "Three cheers for the Ritz." The international press gave us very good coverage the next day, it was a truly spectacular opening night. All the staff called him "Sir James". I think the title of "Knight of the Ritz Casino" tickled him, he was a very humorous man."

James was now something of a father figure in the film industry. His professional achievements over more than forty years, his wide-ranging endeavours, and the consistently high quality of his performances had given him a position of authority amongst his colleagues, and because of his indisputable star status he carried an aura of glamour with him, even as he approached old age. It was in this capacity that he was approached by Kevin Brownlow to narrate a forthcoming television series on the history of the cinema, called *Hollywood*.

KEVIN BROWNLOW

My first meeting with James Mason came about in an unusual way –
as a great film enthusiast I had found in a junk shop in Baker Street,
four very old silent films and I had great fun running them on my
equally old projector. One of the movies starred Douglas Fairbanks
Senior, and in the cast list I saw the name of Albert Parker. On the off
chance that he (by now in the early sixties, a famous agent) would be
interested in viewing the film, I contacted him. He asked me to go to
his office that very day to show it to him, and, soon after, to bring it
again to show some friends at a dinner party elsewhere. To my
delight, James Mason was present.

I not only ran the four films I had found but also, with a certain
amount of trepidation, a section of film that I had begun to make
myself with Andrew Mollo, called *It Happened Here.*

Shortly after the dinner party I was astonished to receive a letter
from James encouraging me to make a career for myself in the film
industry. I was amazed that such a big and famous star should have
taken the trouble to write to me personally and later on I found
James had a very genuine and positive interest in seeing that young
and independent film makers were encouraged and this extract from
his letter shows his spontaneous friendliness.

> "I was much impressed by what I saw of your film. The camerawork,
> angles, cutting and the handling of your actors were of high profes-
> sional standard, spiced now and then with unpredictable touches
> which gave individuality. I was held too by the storytelling and left
> with a strong desire to know how it was all going to turn out. I look
> forward to seeing the completed opus. See you again, I hope, before
> long. Meanwhile, good luck!"
>
> Yours, James Mason.

Then, in 1979, I was looking for the right person to narrate my
series on the early years of cinema history for Thames Television. My
production manager, Liz Sutherland, suggested we ask James Mason
because, as she said, "I have always loved his voice."

At the time I felt we had no hope of getting him to do our series
Hollywood, because probably he would not be available and anyway
he was really too big a star to be interested. But I was wrong.

He would, and he did, do it, and proved to be the most rewarding
person possible to work with – there was never any question of "star

status" with him, he took direction professionally and without fuss or question, often delivering his own version of what was wanted which considerably enhanced what had been originally required.

He was so charming and approachable, that you forgot he was a film star, and lunch times were a joy – he would talk so naturally (not "hold court" as Orson Welles and others tended to do). Even at the age of seventy he had an everlasting touch of youthfulness which left one unaware of his age. My deepest regret, in view of his sudden death, is that we never tape recorded our conversation for posterity so as to tap the rich source of knowledge and experience that James had of the film industry.

James had thoroughly enjoyed his involvement with this documentary series and when, a year or so later, he was approached by Ken Evans and Roy Pickard to narrate a similar series, *The Golden Age of Hollywood*, for radio he was delighted to agree. Roy Pickard remembered how thrilled they were to find how approachable he was, because they had assumed that he wouldn't really be very interested in the medium of radio – or the very low fees that they were forced to offer him. But James had loved the work he had done for radio in New York when he first arrived in America and he had no reservations about accepting the job. This is how Roy Pickard recalls him.

ROY PICKARD

When we returned from Hollywood with fifty interviews under our belt, we were dismayed by the fact we had no suitable presenter for the programmes.

With some trepidation and apprehension I suggested we invite James Mason to do the job, and having sent him the first five scripts we were delighted when he responded saying that he liked the project and accepting the offer. As we could not exceed standard BBC fees it was certainly not the money that swayed his decision! From the time we started the project to the time we completed James was the perfect gentleman – if he wished to alter the script in any way he would not only ask but give his reasons for wishing to do so – always polite, always thoughtful.

We were covering the years from 1927 to 1981 and he was enormously interested in our history of Hollywood, although he was surprisingly bitter about the old Hollywood he had known.

Sidney Lumet, who had been a TV director from the early days of live television, was a great favourite of James's because his method of working was to rehearse, taking several days reading and learning lines, before the actual shooting took place. This was a way of preparation which appealed to James, serious and no time-wasting in front of the cameras. He did not like the improvisation which some directors required to give "reality" to a performance.

We had allowed one stipulation that James said was essential when agreeing to our project, and that was that he would record all that he could in London but should he have to work elsewhere we would have to fit in with him, and continue our series wherever he went. The first two sessions were completed, but then it was – "Sorry chaps – see you in New York."

As we were limited there to using the BBC New York studios for three hours only, 6 to 9 pm, this presented considerable problems for us, but after a few sessions James had to return to London for the premiere of *Evil Under the Sun* so we got a few more recordings in the bag there before he returned to Switzerland with us in hot pursuit!

There we had a great time, and Clarissa made us so welcome and took immense pains to see that we had everything we needed. They seemed absolutely devoted to each other, so happy and content with their lives and their home, a haven in which he could relax and revive his appetite for work, which was prodigious.

We spent hours discussing films and I learned that *Odd Man Out* was his favourite, not only because of Carol Reed but because it broke the labels that had been tagged on him as "The Man you love to Hate" or "Mr Brutal" – many films had given him both pleasure and satisfaction, but working with Carol Reed surpassed all others.

Lolita and *A Star is Born* were films which gave him a sense of achievement, but somehow I had the impression that James regretted having gone to Hollywood when he did. "I took the decision without sufficient thought, it was too soon. I should have remained in Europe. The fact is too few parts really stretched me."

One surprise for us was that James could be a big fluffer of lines. If he could read a script through without any mistakes, all was well, but if he should fluff once or twice he found it difficult to stop. Being very methodical, pronunciation of names places and so on had to be absolutely accurate, so it was no wonder he could get caught up if sentences were too long or the phrasing poor. None the less he would pass nothing less than perfect, that was the measure of the man – and his capacity for work amazed us.

When we began his recordings we had a photograph taken of the whole team and James, the star, revealed an endearing hint of vanity when he tied his favourite pink scarf round his neck before it was done so as to disguise the signs of age. He was a perfectionist and a great artist.

As Roy Pickard noticed during the recording of the narration, James would tire quite easily. He paced himself carefully, and Ken Evans made sure that the sessions were limited to only a couple of hours with a long break in between, but even so sometimes the voice would begin to suffer and the iron control slip to allow small fluffs. James still looked tremendously good, and was astonishingly youthful and energetic for his seventy-one years. He kept faithfully to the pro-gramme of healthy eating and exercise that Clarissa had worked out for him and she was careful to see that he didn't overtax himself. But at last his strength began to fail and in 1983 he went into hospital to have a pacemaker fitted. It was very successful and he was once again his old self and so confident of his improved health that he decided to go back to work. Almost immediately, he was approached to appear in an adaptation of Graham Greene's novel *Dr Fischer of Geneva*. Producer Richard Broke recalls it.

RICHARD BROKE
James clearly wanted to play Dr. Fischer very much, and I wondered why he was so anxious to do it.

On the surface the character is a monster – but is he? The whole debate in the book is "Is he the Devil or is he God?". Is he profoundly evil or is he the opposite? He is an enigma and, in his own way, so was James. Fischer was determined not to be liked and there was something of this in James too, until he got to know and trust you. He liked to like people, but he wasn't terribly keen on being liked. He sometimes did things that tested people's liking of him and I think now, although I didn't realise it at the time, that there was a consciousness in him that there wasn't very long to go. I think he saw in Fischer, this strange sort of apocalyptic figure, a kind of metaphor for himself.

Graham Greene refers in his book, every now and then, to Dr. Fischer's smile – which he says is the most dangerous thing about him. When Fischer smiles it is a harbinger of something really terrifying and when I was writing the script I didn't know what to do about it. Knowing that James was to play the part and that he felt so strongly about it I decided not to mention it in the script at all or to give any stage directions about this smile. I knew I was writing for one of the greatest film actors in the world and it was not for me or the director to tell him when Fischer would smile – James would know. I felt I was writing for an actor who knew much more about the character of Fischer than I did.

Both James and Graham Greene wanted Clarissa to play Mrs. Montgomery, as I did, and James was as much interested in her part in the film as his own. He clearly saw in it an opportunity for her to make her mark with the European audience, and he was overjoyed to have her working in her own right alongside him.

They were tremendously pleased that we would be making some of the film so close to their own home. We shot about ten days in England first and then we went to Switzerland where we filmed the great Bonfire Party in the garden of an extraordinary and huge chateau beside a lake. It was very odd, being in this dramatic location with a number of extremely distinguished people, most of whom were rather old. The weather was hostile and we had James, who was 74, we had Cyril Cusack who was about the same age (they had worked together on *Late Extra*, James's first film, in 1936), we had Graham Greene who was 80, although he wasn't there all the time, and there were plenty of others. Barry Humphries, who was playing Dean, the drunken actor, was thrilled to be there because he knew Clarissa from years back in Australia. James and she were tickled pink that Barry was in the film – they were very amused by him and so was Graham Greene, who couldn't believe that Dame Edna Everage was there with them on location. One of the joys of the filming was the mutual respect and liking which existed amongst the people who were working together. Alan Bates, who is an extremely funny man, adored James and Clarissa and his presence added to the fun.

I remember it was so cold on the first night's filming. Clarissa had to hold up a glass of martini from which she had to sip during the take. She slowly turned the glass upside down and nothing happened, the martini and the cherry stayed put because it had frozen solid in her hand. The cast were all swathed up in thermals to try and beat the cold.

Clarissa and James were highly critical of our catering arrangements, in which they were absolutely justified. The food was very inadequate and Clarissa said "This won't do – we can't have this. These people (and she meant everyone on the location) aren't being properly fed."

This story is about the Masons as a married couple, not the movie star and his wife. They felt highly paternalistic towards the crew and the rest of the actors, and they felt they were not being properly sustained in this disastrously cold location. So on the second night they turned up at the chateau with enormous quantities of hot food for everyone. They hauled it out of the car and, wrapped up against the cold James marched into the house carrying huge flasks full of soup saying "Here's food! Clarissa says everyone has got to eat." Then she marched in after him carrying covered containers and Theresa followed her with yet more, and after that it was hot meals every night – and every night it was something different – boeuf bourgignon, chicken chasseur . . . and on top of all that there were the cakes.

If the Masons as a couple had a weakness it was for cakes – Barry Humphries used to say that they lived in Vevey in order to be near the patisserie. They knew every patisserie in Geneva, Lausanne and Vevey, but particularly Vevey where they were absolute afficionados. Each night they brought us a mountain of cakes which they had gone to choose themselves for us. Some of his favourite ones were green I remember, Clarissa used to point at them and she would say "Have one of those green ones before James does because otherwise he'll eat them all." But James would sneak off for another one or two while she was getting changed and couldn't see him, and he would say to us "Go on, have one of those, they're good", and he'd make sure everyone had had enough. Clarissa wasn't too keen that he should have very many, because of his regime, but he loved them. The crew were absolutely entranced by the whole thing.

I remember one moment, though, when I saw the darker side of James. We were having lunch on location in an English stately home when the lady caretaker who kept an autograph book for the signatures of all the famous people who ever came there came up to our table to ask for his signature. He made no attempt to conceal his irritation but Clarissa dealt with it beautifully and the lady departed happily with her autograph.

A moment or two later Clarissa left the table to go and get ready for the next scene and James looked at me and said "Clarissa's very good at all that sort of thing you know. I'm not. I'm a bit of a [four letter word]. That's why I'm playing Doctor Fischer of Geneva and that's why I'm quite good at it." And he smiled.

He was an extraordinary mixture of determination and insecurity. You would think that film stars like him would have the pick of roles, but of course that's not so – they have to fight hard for the parts they want. He had just made *The Verdict*, and he told me that he had been considered by Sidney Lumet for the more sympathetic role of the man who hires Newman to work on the case, but James felt he could play the part he eventually did – the nasty lawyer who opposes Newman – and he went all out to persuade Lumet that he could do it. It was fascinating, first of all that he wanted to tell us about this and secondly that it happened that way at all to a star of James Mason's magnitude. He rang up Lumet almost every day and he used to read scenes over the phone to him to persuade him that he could do it.

You'd think he would neither want nor need to bother like this at his age and it was strange that he should want to tell me, whom he didn't really know that well, this story – he didn't mind me knowing that he'd had to struggle to get that part. James didn't care about an image – I don't think he even thought he had one. It wasn't a part of him, and it wasn't important to him. On the set Barry Humphries was regarded by the Masons as a sort of court jester and he could say anything he wanted. He wasn't there as Edna Everage, in which guise he could do that anyway, he was there as himself and he would say the most outrageous things to the Masons which they adored – they thought he was terribly funny. He used to refer to James as "the living legend" and he would always put on a very strong Australian accent when he talked like this. Clarissa would give James his supper first and then serve Barry who would walk to the table where James was already dining and say, "Oh, look at the living legend tucking in to his dins" – "It's a nice meal tonight, isn't it, Legend?" and James adored it.

When we came to the filming itself, it was an extraordinary pleasure to watch a man with all that experience. He could condense and intensify a performance for the camera in a way few others can. In rehearsals the others would almost exhaust themselves sometimes because what they were trying to do was to find out what they were going to do in the scene. But what was so marvellous about James Mason was that he knew exactly what he was going to do in the scene. This was particularly apparent in the great scene, Fischer's final scene between him, Alan Bates and Cyril Cusack, when he confronts this man whose life Dr Fischer has entirely ruined many years earlier – a most extraordinary scene between three wonderful actors.

I did notice, though, how carefully he conserved his energy. He would walk very carefully down from the chateau to where the scene was set in the garden and you could see that he knew he was now an old man. He would never use any energy unnecessarily so that when he was needed for a take he could give it everything.

We ran into difficulty with the final scene. James had to leave the next morning to take up his role in *The Shooting Party* and we were pressed for time. We needed snow on the ground for this sequence and the visual effects people had a problem with the artificial snow required to add to what had fallen naturally. It would be possible to cover the ground and some of the branches of the surrounding trees but not to provide the falling snow that we wanted so badly. It was 10 degrees below zero and it was a very long night for we were going on until dawn to make sure we finished before James had to go, tiring and unpleasant for all of us, let alone a man in his seventies. We went into the chateau at midnight for a meal break, cold and despondent. Suddenly the first assistant director appeared in the room and said excitedly "You'll never believe what's happening – it's snowing!" I think six grown men almost burst into tears – it was a miracle. It's there in the film, it's real snow – even on the branches of the trees – and it fell on the coats and shoulders of the actors as though all the elements were conspiring to make the final scene work.

We weren't really aware of his physical frailty at the time. James seemed so sturdy, and you have to remember that Clarissa was there. She was totally in charge of James – there was no point my worrying about James because she was his guardian angel and she wouldn't have let James do anything that he shouldn't have done. She was deeply protective of him but he also was of her. He was always coming up to me and saying "Make sure Clarissa's got her coat on."

And he was deeply interested in her performance, wanting to know if each scene had gone well for her. He was so thrilled that she was in the film with him – and she was very good – she was perfectly cast. When James and Clarissa were not needed in the day-time sequences they would go together down to the little terrace by the lake from where there was a marvellous view across the water, and they would stand there for ages to watch the birds that lived there. Sometimes I joined them and I discovered that they shared a passionate love for these creatures and had an encyclopaedic knowledge of them and their habits. They knew every variety and could identify each bird, what stage in it's breeding cycle it was at, what it would eat, where it would nest. If one flew overhead James would look up, identify it and tell you all about it, even explaining why its wings were a particular shape or how it differed from its mate, why it behaved in the way it did and why it would choose to live and breed on this lake rather than any other. He talked about them as though they were people. He was a great expert and a great teacher – one learnt so much from listening to him. It was an aspect of the man I would never have guessed at, and this extra dimension of his character added to the enormous liking and admiration I had for him.

It is odd to think that while James was enjoying his off-duty moments on *Dr. Fischer* communing with wild birds he was committing himself to another film which dealt with the wholesale slaughter of game birds. But there were good reasons for this apparent contradiction.

The Shooting Party was a star-studded production of an adaptation of Isabel Colgate's novel about a country house weekend wild-game shoot in 1913. The assembled group of elegant upper-class men and women dine, gossip, shoot and indulge in discreet adultery, unaware that their sheltered world will soon be shattered forever by the coming war, and the slaughter of the birds presages the slaughter that will take place in Europe the following year. On the very first day's filming the leading actor, Paul Schofield, was injured in an accident. His broken leg meant that he could not possibly continue with the carefully planned schedule and each day lost was a financial disaster for the production. James was the immediate choice of the director, Alan Bridges, to take the role over. He knew that

James was already working on *Dr. Fischer* but nonetheless, because he had met him on several occasions and was convinced that he would be wonderful as Sir Randolph Nettleby – he contacted him. James read the script and realised how crucial it was that the right person should be found to play this pivotal and charismatic character and how urgent it was for everyone concerned that it should be settled at once. He felt that the film was an important one and decided, whatever the difficulties, that he would do it.

The logistical problems this caused for both Richard Broke and Alan Bridges were enormous. James would be working for them both at the same time and they had somehow to juggle their schedules to share him between them. It was not too hard while they were all working in England, but almost impossible once the *Fischer* location moved to Switzerland. These kinds of headaches added to the workload of the producer and director, but the physical strain on James of doing both jobs at once was tremendous. However, he felt he was fit enough, he thought it was a marvellous part for him and he wanted to help out a group of colleagues who were in serious trouble, so he plunged into a punishing schedule and began work on what was to be his last and, many think, his finest performance.

It didn't take Alan Bridges long to realise that James was not as well as he wanted people to believe. He would sometimes go very pale – almost "grey about the gills" – but if Alan asked him if he was alright he would say very firmly "I'm fine", and shrug it off. His determination to fulfill his commitment to both films demanded an extraordinary effort from him. In order to be where he was required for *The Shooting Party* on the day following his last night's work on *Dr Fischer* he finished his final scene in the garden of the chateau in the falling snow at 2.00 a.m., drove with Clarissa to an hotel in Geneva where he slept for three hours before catching the early flight to London. At Heathrow airport a helicopter was waiting to fly him from London to the location in Bedfordshire, and he reported for work just as the cameras were ready to turn over at 10.00 a.m. It would have been tough for a man in the prime of life – but for a man of 74 it was amazing.

Although Alan Bridges didn't have any sense that James might have thought his time was running out, he said that he was struck by the mystical quality of his performance. It was patrician, in the best sense of the word, and James endowed his interpretation of the head of this aristocratic family with his own special qualities. He created a portrait of a man representative of a unique class, born to lead and administer his estate, with a deep concern and responsibility for the people around him. But a man somehow removed from these people, who stood apart and observed them and their activities with a rare combination of wisdom, intelligence, dignity, and compassion for mankind. There was one speech in particular which he delivered with great pathos and sensitivity and which seemed to reflect his own philosophy of anti-violence and pacifism: "These are hard times. No-one cares about the country any more. Sometimes when my thoughts about the future are particularly gloomy I find myself feeling more and more lighthearted. I suppose I have always rather fancied the idea of taking to the hills when the Barbarian hordes over-run us. I think I should enjoy it".

During the filming one small incident occurred which Alan Bridges felt illustrated James's qualities as a gentle mediator. They were rehearsing a scene and one of the other actors involved objected to a simple suggestion from the director, implying that he knew better what would work. Before tempers were lost James quietly intervened, saying to the actor "Keep calm, he's trying to help us – all of us" – playing the peacemaker and father-figure in real life as well as in the story.

The only reservation James had had about doing this film was over the shooting of the birds. Their slaughter was a metaphor – they were symbols of the men who were going to be killed in the coming war in Europe, but James was tremendously concerned about the fate of these creatures and he made his doubts very clear. So Alan Bridges told him the truth – that the birds would indeed have to be shot but they were all game-birds, bred to be killed, and if they didn't shoot them someone else would do so anyway. None of the actors would have live ammunition and there would be expert shots stationed out of sight of the cameras to make sure that the birds were properly targeted and would suffer as little as possible, and in view of the message that the film would carry and which embodied his own belief in the awful senselessness of war, James accepted this. Whatever his determination to do this film as well as *Dr Fischer* may have cost him physically, he gave no indication of any fraility. With real courage he disguised any stress or fatigue he may have felt and brushed aside any suggestion that he should take things more easily.

The Shooting Party re-united James with his old friend John Gielgud. They had known each other for half a century, for it was more than fifty years since they had met in London and Gielgud had directed the young James in "Queen of Scots", and it was with great pleasure that James and Clarissa accepted their invitation to Sir John's 80th birthday party on 14 April 1984. It was a wonderful occasion and James found a host of people there with whom he had worked and now shared many memories. Robert and Carmen Flemyng were there. Carmen had witnessed his wedding to Pamela in 1941 but after he went to Hollywood they had more or less lost touch. Now they made plans to meet again soon, and there were many more old friends to enjoy and arrange future meetings with.

Claire Bloom was also a fellow-guest. She had last seen James in the previous year when she stayed in Switzerland with Oona Chaplin after her mother had died. James had known her mother and so when he and Clarissa came to dinner at Oona Chaplin's house it was a link with the past in more ways than one and a real pleasure to see each other again. But now Claire perceived a change in James which gave her much anxiety for him. She recognised something about him she had seen in her mother before her death, and although he was plainly enjoying himself his skin-colour was strangely pale and transparent, like alabaster. She said to her companion "James is ill – I think he has come to see people and say good-bye".

A few weeks later, on 9th May, James celebrated his own 75th birthday. While they had been in London finishing work on *The Shooting Party* Clarissa had been hatching her own secret plans. She wanted to do something that would give him as much joy as she had received from him on her 45th birthday with her fabulous horse, and she had decided that a party was the answer. She asked their friend David Gray, the manager of the Ritz Casino, if he would involve himself in her conspiracy for it seemed to her that this would be the very place to have this special celebration. She contrived all kinds of excuses to slip away from James while he was working so that she could organise the guest list and arrange the details with David Gray, and by a miracle James remained in complete ignorance of her plans. An amazing feat, as he liked her to be at his side for as much of the day as possible. He was delighted when Clarissa suggested to him that they should mark his birthday with a quiet dinner together at the Ritz Casino and in the early evening prepared himself for a pleasant meal out with his wife.

Clarissa had kept her secret well and James's surprise was total when he arrived at the restaurant to find, not a table for two, but a room filled with about a hundred of his friends and relations gathered to wish him what must have been one of the very happiest birthdays of his life. His brothers, sister-in-law, niece and nephew were there, old and valued friends like Sir John Gielgud, Elspeth Cochrane, Kaye Webb and Katie Searle, Paul Grunder from the Dorchester Hotel, Spike Milligan, Susan George and Frank Finlay, and colleagues who had become friends in the later years, Alan Bridges, Richard Broke, Ben Arbeid, and Alan Bates, and scores of others who had come from far and wide (some even crossing the Atlantic to be there) to show James the affection and esteem in which he was held. If he noticed that both Portland and Morgan were conspicuous by their absence, although of course Clarissa had invited them and hoped they would be there, James said nothing and did not allow it to spoil the joy of the moment. Once he had got over the initial amazement he plunged into the party, greeting friends and accepting their gifts and good wishes. As David Gray had done so much to help Clarissa organise the evening she asked him to make a short speech to mark the occasion, and as he did so James seemed to be overcome with emotion and needed a few moments to compose himself before making his reply. But when he spoke, as David Gray said "His words were exactly what we all expected – simple, grateful and charmingly modest". If tears were shed they were tears of happiness, and James's birthday party was everything that he and Clarissa could possibly have wished.

The party over, James and Clarissa returned to Vevey for the summer to enjoy a rest and relax in their beloved garden. But Clarissa now had to hide from James the premonitions of tragedy which had begun to haunt her.

James came from a long-lived family – both his parents had survived into their nineties – and she had guarded his health so carefully that she had every reason to expect that there would be many more happy years ahead for them to share. But during the filming of *Dr. Fischer* something had happened which she could not put out of her mind and which had shocked her profoundly at the time. Her grandmother had possessed second sight and Clarissa herself had the same gift but she had always found it disturbing and from the age of 17 had tried to suppress it. For some while before work started on *Dr. Fischer* Clarissa had been uneasy and when they came to film the sequences in the cemetery she had a frightening experience. They had been dressed and made up in their house and James had left first as she was not needed until a little while later. A car was sent back to collect her when they were ready for her, and she set off to the location alone with the driver. She had never been to the cemetery before and as she was driven through its gates she felt herself gripped by a terrible fear and she thought "I'm going to be bringing James here soon – he's going to die". She was convinced the car was going to turn to the left and the fear became a physical pain. She was wrong, it changed direction and she was driven to the right. As she approached the area where the filming was in progress she saw James standing – but he was standing beside an empty grave and the sight of it terrified her.

It was only when she returned, six months later, that she realised that the turning to the left inside the gates led to the Crematorium.

Surely nothing could really be wrong? James seemed so well and happy? Clarissa tried to banish her fears and when they returned to England to concentrate on *The Shooting Party* James seemed to be in such good form that she managed to put all her worries out of her mind. Towards the end of May they went home to Vevey and once again she found herself plagued with fears for him, although still he appeared to be in good health and good spirits. The weather was lovely and he spent much of the day in the garden or in the bright drawing room upstairs where the picture window that runs the length of the wall looks across the lake to the mountains beyond. He was relaxed and cheerful, content with the blessings of his quiet and sunny home. But during the day on July 26th Clarissa realised that something was wrong and by early evening she knew he was ill. She called the doctor, an ambulance was summoned and James was taken to the local hospital. He had had a heart attack and although the doctors told her not to despair Clarissa knew that she had lost him. At 6.00 a.m. on 27 July 1984 at the age of 75 James Mason died.

His memorial service was held on Thursday 1st November at 12 noon in the Actors Church, St. Paul's, in London's Covent Garden. The church was crowded with friends and relatives, the famous and the unknown side by side. The hymns were familiar and comforting ("The King of Love my Shepherd is", "All things Bright and Beautiful" and "For All the Saints Who from their Labours Rest") and James's nephew Christopher Mason read Psalm 121 "I will lift up mine eyes unto the hills from whence cometh my help".

James had adored the Goon Shows and his friend Spike Milligan read Ogden Nash's poem *Isabel, Isabel*. There was a flute solo (Mozart's Concerto No. 2 in D, 2nd Movement, *andante*) played by Judith Hall, and Jane Manning sang the song from *The Fantasticks* which James and Clarissa both loved "Try to Remember". It was a festival of the kind of things that James had enjoyed. His friend Vivian Cox read some lines from *The Prophet* by Kahlil Gibran and Sir John Gielgud gave an eloquent and moving address. But for the assembled congregation emotion was hard to contain when James's own recorded voice filled the church with Robert Browning's poem *Home Thoughts from Abroad* and *Prospice*, and later the reading from 1 Corinthians 13 which ends "and now abideth faith, hope and love, these three; but the greatest of these is love."

A lone piper entered the church, processed up and down the aisles amongst the mourners and as he left the lament faded away leaving a moment's quiet in which to consider the words that Clarissa had spoken in her own address "Never say in grief that James is gone but always say in thankfulness that he was".

Every summer since, the Christmas rose in the garden at Vevey has bloomed on July 27th, the anniversary of James's death.

EPILOGUE

THE story does not end there. Only time can tell the next chapter in the saga of James Mason and his family. For my part, the last time I saw him in 1981 – ten years after his marriage to Clarissa, in all the years that I had known him I had never seen a man so transformed, reborn, his joy in living restored, his confidence buoyant. In a nutshell James was supremely happy, and on this note I close my memories and leave the final words to others on one of England's brightest and greatest stars!

The last years of sheer blissful happiness that he spent with his second wife were to change his whole perspective. At last his home, his hobbies, his work, were to be shared with someone whose love far transcended everything that had gone before. Travel, animal welfare, love of roses, poetry, friends, became part of a rich tapestry, bringing his life all the rewards that he so richly deserved, and in his last film, *The Shooting Party*, he was to receive the unreserved praise and acclaim hitherto denied him.

Thankfully his life was spared long enough to allow him to savour such a whole-hearted success, and I, who must admit to having seen only a small proportion of his films, believe that this last performance was the most moving and perfect piece of acting he had ever achieved. If I have to say that James was not my favourite actor, I can say categorically that he was my favourite relative, and the superlatives heaped on his head for that last performance gave me enormous pleasure.

Finally, if I seem to accept his death with equanimity, it is because I believe that he passed into the gentle loving hands of God, having suffered no long, painful or crippling illness, and the end that we must all know came to him swiftly and silently, as a friend.

Those who attended the Service of Thanksgiving at St Paul's Church, Covent Garden, will have heard the recorded voice of James speaking the words of his favourite poet Robert Browning, but for those who were unable to attend, I leave the words as requiem for a dear and gentle soul.

Fear death? – to feel the frog in my throat
    The mist in my face,
When the snows begin, and the blasts denote
    I am nearing the place,
The power of the night, the press of the storm,
    The post of the foe;
Where he stands, the Arch Fear in a visible form,
    Yet the strong man must go:
For the journey is done and the summit attained,
    And the barriers fall,
Though a battle's to fight ere the guerdon be gained,
    The reward of it all.
I was ever a fighter, so – one fight more,
    The best and the last!
I would hate that death bandaged my eyes, and forbore,
    And bade me creep past.
No! Let me taste the whole of it, fare like my peers
    The heroes of old,
Bear the brunt, in a minute pay glad life's arrears
    Of pain, darkness and cold,
For sudden the worst turns the best to the brave,
    The black minute's at end,
And the elements' rage, the field-voices that rave,
    Shall dwindle, shall blend,
Shall change, shall become first a peace, then a joy,
    Then a light, then thy breast,
O thou soul of my soul! I shall clasp thee again,
    And with God be the rest!

AFTERWORD

I WOULD like to close this book with some appreciations of James given by those who worked with him, and who can testify so eloquently to his unique character.

BARRY NORMAN

James Mason was one of those actors who was always good – no matter how bad the material. He would often raise the level of the scenes he played above the rest of an ordinary film and he could give "class" to an undistinguished film – a rare and valuable quality in an actor. As in a game of cricket, he could be "brought into bat and stop the rot". He was extraordinarily versatile and could play all manner of roles with equal conviction.

In his early successful films he became famous as a romantic villain and he had an edgy sex-appeal which the female audience found irresistible. He was wasted in Hollywood where the very quality that made him such a success was overlooked. He remained staunchly British and that limited his opportunities in America.

Odd Man Out was the best film he ever made. *The Wicked Lady* was intended as a vehicle for Margaret Lockwood but it is James that is remembered – he brought so much more to the role than was written and gave it depth and class. Humbert Humbert in *Lolita* was a far more difficult role than he made it seem and he gave the character an intellectual dimension and pathos. Although *A Star Is Born* was Judy Garland's film, James was not overshadowed by her. He was not as great a star as she was, but he was a greater actor, and you remember him in it in a way that none of the other actors who play the part of Norman Maine in the various re-makes achieved. In *The Shooting Party* he bowed out with a performance as full of grace, skill and charm as any he has ever given. It was a deeply thoughtful performance from the star who rose steadily and never faded. You could witness his thought processes, see the doubt and anguish in his mind reflected in his face, feel him thinking the words before he said them so that they belonged to him alone. He brought the character out with total conviction and walked away with the film without trying. He was surrounded by a wonderful cast of fine actors but he outshone them all in a role that could serve as his epitaph.

DILYS POWELL

James Mason made an astonishing contribution to the British cinema in the early part of his career in films which are now regarded as classics. He did something for the melodrama which nobody else has done – he turned a villain into a dramatic and memorable character – and he did it at a time when women were just beginning to make their place and presence felt in the cinema. He brought something real and alive and interesting to characters which were brutal and unpleasant. His savage performances in films which were about the assertion of women contrived to lift his characters beyond their stereotypes, making them remarkable.

It is interesting that he could play equally well the villain and the victim, for in *Lolita*, Humbert Humbert was the victim of his own passion, and in *A Star is Born* Norman Maine was the victim of his wife's success.

He did very little real comedy and not enough Shakespeare. As Brutus in *Julius Caesar* he spoke his lines quite marvellously, as though they belonged to him, combining authority and regret with dignity and pathos.

In the later stages of his career I would look forward to seeing a film just because he was in it. He was really a character actor and perhaps that's why I don't think of him as playing heroes, but I admire his astonishing range and I do think of him as one of our most remarkable film actors. He was always interesting, and he could transmit emotion from the screen to the audience from within himself. He was an actor who brought to the characters he played, whether they were villainous, pathetic, disagreeable or admirable, the sense of a real human being.

James's appeal still lingers. In his hey-day he was a bit of a heart-throb and in his younger roles he still has terrific appeal for the modern generation. He was, and remained, very attractive.

His last performance, in *The Shooting Party*, is perhaps the most subtle thing he ever did. It is a statement about "class" and he conveyed perfectly the serious attitude of devotion to his duties and responsibilities reflected in the character of the English gentleman he played. It is an astonishing piece of work. He was, in fact a real actor.

SIR ALEC GUINNESS

"Ay, but to die, and go we know not where . . ." That line, and the whole magical speech which follows, spoken by James Mason in Guthrie's production of "Measure for Measure" in 1934, is one of my most treasured theatrical memories. Mason's stillness, the beautiful and disturbing quality of his voice and physical presence, premeated everything he played. Even his definitive performance as 'Yasha' in *The Cherry Orchard* – vain, arrogant, shallow and subtly vulgar – couldn't escape some of his very personal quality. Later, when he became a big film star, the quality was still there, of course and I have always regretted that he never gave us a Hamlet, Iago or Othello.

In the thirties he and I often used the same, small, inexpensive restaurant in Frith Street, Soho. One lunch time I found him alone there, drawing on the back of a menu. "What are you doing?" I asked. He turned the menu so I could see and there, quite beautifully drawn, were two or three Siamese cats. "I only draw cats" he said. But he was an artist and I didn't quite believe him. I hope he kept the menus – or that the restaurant had them framed.

SIR JOHN GIELGUD

I first saw James Mason on the stage at the Old Vic Theatre in the early thirties and soon afterwards I directed him in my production of *Queen of Scots*. In those days James was very quiet and solitary. He smoked a pipe at rehearsals and was reputed to live alone in a flat in Covent Garden.

I met him again, years later, in 1952, when we were both in the film of *Julius Caesar*, which was directed by Joseph Mankiewicz. By this time James was quite a big star in Hollywood but he was extremely kind and helpful to me. He encouraged my fairly inexperienced efforts at film acting and was very generous in working on the scenes in which we played together. I was lost in admiration of his accomplished technique, especially in close-ups, when he could express thoughts and moods with little facial change. We became real friends after that, and appeared in several more films together.

He was a great humanist, a charming companion, quiet but with a dry wit, and intensely dedicated and professional – not at all put out by delays and frustrations and never unkind in his relationships with other people. I shall always miss him as a most cherished colleague and a dear man.

GRAHAM GREENE

James Mason, who had that innate sadness in his eyes – was the perfect man to portray Dr. Fischer.

GEORGE CUKOR

If James Mason is in front of the cameras – just leave them rolling. He never makes a mistake!

CLAIRE BLOOM

If there was ever "a parfit gentle knight" it was James. He was one of the best actors England has ever produced in films, and his poetry readings were simply superb. His voice was a great instrument, never properly used on the screen, and visually I always remember his wonderful profile. But when you place James in Yorkshire somehow the voice, the personality and the physical presence make sense. Working with James on The Man Between was one of the high spots of my career. He and Trevor Howard were the best of English film actors. There is nobody that touches them as far as I'm concerned – not a one.

JACK CARDIFF

I would class James amongst the best of technical actors – like Trevor Howard. These actors would be more adventurous than most and give something more than was required. They would attack a role from a different angle to what might be expected – not settle for just what was in the script. In a supporting role James always stole the film. He was a fine actor and he had a marvellous voice and he was always in complete control of himself.

KAYE WEBB

I believe James will become a cult figure – he was unique. I think that people will remain aware of him as a real presence in his films for years and years to come. He was one of the greatest stars to have come out of this island country.

INDEX

PHOTOGRAPHIC ACKNOWLEDGEMENTS

Rex Mason: 1; 2; 3; 4; 5; 6.
British Broadcasting Corporation: 33, 34.
National Film Archive, London: 7; 8; 9; 10; 11; 12; 13; 16; 17; 18; 21; 22; 23; 26; 27; 28; 29.
The Kobal Collection: 14.
Walt Disney: 20.
Clarissa Mason: 30; 31; 32.